HOW TO START EXPAND & SELL A BUSINESS

HOW TO START
EXPAND & SELL
A BUSINESS

THE COMPLETE GUIDEBOOK
FOR ENTREPRENEURS

by **JAMES C. COMISKEY**

with GARY CONNER, Esq.

VENTURE PERSPECTIVES PRESS
SAN JOSE, CALIFORNIA

Publisher's Note

Disclaimer: This book is designed to provide general information on the subjects covered. It is sold with the understanding that the author and publisher are not engaged in rendering legal, accounting or other professional advice or service. If legal or other expert assistance is required, consult a competent professional in that area. The author or publisher also shall not have liability or responsibility to any person or entity with respect to loss or damage caused or allegedly caused by the information contained in this book.

This book is available in quantity discounts to promote companies or services. For information write Venture Perspectives Press, 4300 Stevens Creek Blvd., Suite 120, San Jose, CA 95129.

Copyright © 1985 by James C. Comiskey
First Printing 1985
Second Printing 1986
Third Printing 1986 Revised
Fourth Printing 1987 Revised
All Rights Reserved

Library of Congress Cataloging-in-Publication Data
Comiskey, James C., 1938 -
    How to Start, Expand & Sell a Business.
    Bibliography: p.
    Includes index
    1. New business enterprises
    2. Business enterprises—Purchasing
    3. Business enterprises, Sale of
    4. Entrepreneur
I. Title.
II. Title: How to start, expand, and sell a business
    HD62.5C64   1985   658.4'2   85-15814
    ISBN 0-932309-39-9

Published by Venture Perspectives Press
4300 Stevens Creek Blvd., Suite 120
San Jose, CA 95129
(408) 247-1325
ISBN 0-932309-39-9

Dedication:
To all those willing to try.

Contents

Acknowledgements

I sincerely wish to thank all of these fine people who contributed to the development of this book:

Bill Abraham, Mindy Bingham, Nancy Bergman, Claudia Browne, Bill Chalmers, Rick Charles, Gary Conner, J. Anita Coit, Don Dible, Sally Ditto, Bob Egan, Bill Elliott, Mike Ewoldt, Michelle Feinberg, Terry Feinberg, Sam Felish, Pete Graveley, Ken Grant, Lew Horne, Bob Johnson, Stella Johnson, Ron Lighty, Don McMahon, Jon McMahon, Abby Mintz, Steve Muhlhauser, David Newman, Mike Owings, Bob Palmer, Betty Pauley, Jim Peasley, Dan Poynter, David Quilici, Emmet Ramey, LeRoy Stark, John Sullivan, Nancy Weber, Dave White, Louise Winters, Leon Wortman.

Typing: Renee Winter, Tri-Pro, San Jose
Typesetting: BookPrep, Gilroy, CA
Cover Design: Electric Art Studios, Mountain View, CA
Paste Up: Aristographics
Book Printing: Delta Lithograph Co., Valencia, CA
Editing: Alice Kemp, Dorothy Wortman
Proofreading: Hannah Comiskey, Pat Peasley, and Andrea Thomas
Statistics: Susan Comiskey

Introduction
Before You Start

This is a book about making money . . . let's have no doubt about that! However, it's not about getting rich quick or easy, or being lazy. It's about hard work and about using your personal and financial resources to open and successfully operate a business. If that works well, then how to expand that business, and finally how to successfully sell it, and cash in on your investment and all your hard work. How long will that take? Certainly not overnight—so much for getting rich quick!

Before beginning, I have a confession to make. I'm not a writer, I'm really an entrepreneur. Oh, I've written a few sales and operation manuals, but never anything as challenging as a book. For twelve years I owned and operated a chain of retail stores. Feeling burnt out, I decided to get out of retail and try something else. I sold the stores and after agonizing over the idea for a year, I started writing this book. It took 11 months to complete. It was the hardest, most intimidating, loneliest work I ever undertook. Yet, at the same time, it was very gratifying. I sincerely felt I had something valuable to contribute to fellow entrepreneurs.

Before starting the project, I set up four objectives. It is important that you know these, because, in effect, you will judge the book on whether I have delivered on these goals.

1. It must be a realistic, authentic and comprehensive book on starting, expanding and selling a business.

2. It must be an easy-to-read, factual, no-nonsense, entrepreneurial roadmap for readers to follow.

3. It must be a well organized series of examples, checklists and worksheets in order to involve the reader, so he or she gets maximum benefit from the material.

4. Finally, it must encourage people to recognize that successfully starting, expanding or selling a business is not easy, yet very attainable. If careful preparation is done, then one can achieve significant financial security and unique personal satisfaction.

Those four goals became my constant guide. I was forced to rewrite many areas because I felt that I somehow hadn't quite fulfilled one or more of these objectives.

In addition to my own experience, I interviewed over 25 other business owners, consultants, attorneys, accountants, brokers and bankers. I also read twenty plus books on the subject of small business. The research continued throughout the writing. I went back several times to add additional pertinent information to what was already written. However, the *core* of this book comes from my personal experience. With only three exceptions, every book on the subject of small business management was written by a professor, consultant, or professional writer. I was in the entrepreneurial trench for twelve years. I started a business with a small investment, parlayed it into a successful chain, and eventually sold it, becoming financially independent in the process. I believe that's what makes this book *uniquely valuable.*

You will receive a lot of specific advice in the following chapters. Naturally you may want to know what credentials I have that give me the right to speak with such authority, and that's only fair. Let me briefly tell you about myself. After graduating from college with a marketing degree, I joined a consumer products company as a salesman in San Francisco. Although that work was not financially rewarding, it did give me the selling fundamentals that would eventually be a part of my entrepreneurial success. Two years later I was promoted to a marketing job in New York. That gave me a glimpse of the ivory tower and the corporate political arena, neither of which did I particularly enjoy. I did, however, enjoy the work and I learned a great deal. Part of that learning experience came from a mentor and friend to whom I shall always be indebted, and part came as a result of having considerable responsibility thrust upon me. My final job was as director of new product development, and I was still under thirty years of age.

It was the political intrigue plus a burning entrepreneurial drive that finally made me consider starting my own business. My first step was the purchase of a secretarial school franchise. That served two purposes. First it got me back home to California, and second, it made me real "street-wise". The franchise was illconceived, poorly planned and hastily implemented, but it had a nice full-color brochure. I naively bought the brochure and ended up in a law suit. Fortunately, I got out with all of my investment only to be propelled into another franchise—retail pet stores. Yes, you read right, pet stores! My only experience, up to that point with pets, was as a kid. I had a small dog who in fact didn't like me very much and used to bite my feet. However, this franchise's full-color brochure was backed up with sixty operating stores, and some impressive bottom-line profit potential. I had gone from marketing consumer products, to marketing typing and shorthand, to marketing puppies—all in less than a year. But, I found it was all basic marketing. The products changed but not the concepts.

During the next three years, I acquired a partner, dropped the franchise, expanded to six stores with combined sales of $2.5 million and had the entrepreneurial ride of my life. You will read about parts of it as you turn the pages. I felt that this experience was just too *valuable* not to share.

Basically I wrote this book in three parts. The first part involves the options and strategies necessary to start a successful business. The second part talks about how to grow and expand that business. The last part provides a plan for selling your operation; something that each entrepreneur thinks about at least occasionally, from the moment they start their business.

Although the parts are distinctly different, there is considerable overlap of valuable information. For example, if you are already in business and thinking about expansion, the early chapters on site selection and lease negotiations will be very helpful. Similarly, if you are starting from scratch, there is a detailed plan for building a operation in the expansion section. Even if you are now planning to sell your business, the chance of starting another is better than 50/50. So, reading the first section may provide the necessary input to launch you on your next venture. Lastly, the final chapter on "How to bail out and land soft" should be read by everybody perhaps often. During the time I had my businesses, there were frequent occasions, I could have implemented the survival strategy outlined in this chapter.

Throughout the book, you will read a number of examples that relate to retail or service situations. You may be interested in opening a wholesale, manufacturing or construction firm. Don't worry, the concepts are actually very similar. Whether you're planning to open a deli or a computer distributorship, you will have to go through the same prebusiness steps if you want to improve your chance of success.

Perhaps you're planning to sell a large business and the example in Chapter 15 on valuing a business relates to a relatively small business. The formula used has application to virtually any size business. Consequently, as you read through this book, don't be too concerned about the type or size of the business, but more importantly, recognize the *parallels* in the concepts.

Writing this book was like taking a trip to a distant place. I had been there before, but this time it was much more *intense*. I discovered more than I ever imagined. The process was both exhilarating and frustrating. When I finished a section or chapter I felt that I had achieved a major milestone, only to be plunged right back into researching, organizing, and writing the next part. That was a very humbling experience. At times I felt I had completely lost the ability to put a meaningful sentence together (you may actually find a few). On other occasions I would write for ten hours straight and lose all awareness of time.

Although this book was far more difficult and took longer to write than I had initially anticipated, it was well worth it. It was both a learning experience, and a significant personal achievement. I sincerely hope you find some wisdom and perspective within these pages. More importantly, I hope it's helpful to you in reaching your entrepreneurial goals. I wish you every *success* with your future.

P.S. Eventually I will sit down and revise this book. I would welcome any suggestions, anecdotes and experiences. If you just want to write about your impression of what's been written, I would appreciate that too. As I was writing I really felt a sense of connection with you, the reader, even though we've never met. I tried to write directly to you as if we were discussing the subject face-to-face. Let me know whether I've helped. Thanks!

PART ONE

STARTING A BUSINESS

Chapter 1
Becoming an Entrepreneur

The thought of starting your own business can be very *frightening*. It's a major financial commitment for an unknown payoff—some may feel more comfortable taking their money to Las Vegas. Why do so many people gamble everything on their ability to successfully run a business? Because the drive and desire is stronger than the self-doubt and potential for failure. Indeed, the entrepreneurial dream is alive and well, stronger today than it ever was before.

In 1970 there were 5.7 million self-employed people. Today there are over 12 million, not counting those involved in agriculture. Over 700,000 new corporations are started annually. In addition, an estimated 2.4 million sole-proprietorships and partnerships are also begun. Granted, some may never get past the stationery and business card stage. But there is a thriving determination to become independent. We are presently experiencing an entrepreneurial boom!

These independent small businesses represent a wide variety of enterprises in retail, wholesale, manufacturing, construction, service, etc. They also appear to show where the action is. Over 60% of the workforce is now employed by small businesses. Of the 20 million new jobs that were created in the past ten years, approximately 70% were in small and medium-sized firms, with the remainder going to government and non-profit organizations. How many new jobs were created by the largest 1,000 corporations? None! They actually are losing employment. *The entrepreneurial spirit is back.*

The Major Questions

Someone once said a good newspaper article answers the questions who, what, why, when, how and where in the first paragraph. I've always remembered that. However, since this is a book, I have the first chapter to answer those critical questions.

Who. Who are these new entrepreneurs? Inevitably, when talking to a group of strangers at a party, the subject of work comes up. Quite proudly I state that I have been self-employed for the past fourteen years. You can see envy in their eyes. Some say that they've always wanted to, but . . . Others say that they would like to, but . . . Still others say they will, when . . . It reminds me of what someone once said about people in general, "Folks are divided up into three groups, some spend their lives doing things, others spend their lives having things done to them, and the rest watch". Entrepreneurs are the *doers* of the world!

Entrepreneurs are also visionaries. The friends and relatives who say "You must be crazy to start your own business," are confusing insanity with vision. On the other hand, it may help if you are a little crazy.

For the most part, today's entrepreneurs are ordinary, sane people from all walks of life—school teachers to factory workers. Some are highly educated, others have very little formal training. Education doesn't seem to either help or hinder. What these people have in common is the dream of becoming *independent*—the desire to get away from the dead-end treadmill of working for others.

Formerly it was a man's world, today that's not the case. The number of businesses owned by women have skyrocketed to almost three million from 1.9 million in 1977, a gain of 37%. By comparison, during the same period, new firms opened by men only grew 10%. In some states—for example, Hawaii, California and Maryland—women now own one-third of all the small businesses. Congratulations, ladies!

What. What do they start, and what's it like? Entrepreneurs start everything from taco stands to high-tech semiconductor firms. No one can say that independent businesspersons lack imagination.

More important, though, what is it like to be an entrepreneur in America today? It's both rewarding and scary. There's a very competitive world outside and the struggle is fierce. Starting your own business can be dangerous. You can lose a lot of money, and gain a bruised ego in the process. However, when you succeed, it can be both financially and psychologically gratifying. Being an entrepreneur today is almost patriotic. It's like being part of the Olympic team. You don't have to win big, it's important just to be there. You separate yourself from the rest by your willingness to try. That makes you a part of a very select club.

When. When do they become entrepreneurs? When they get tired of the corporate hassles, or get fired, or get enough courage. It also helps to have enough money and enough experience. The last two factors contribute to the over-35 syndrome. Most people have to wait that long until they have enough resources and enough wisdom to start their own business.

How. How do they do it? It starts with a fantasy, progresses through several stages, and finally emerges a reality. Some people plot their escape to business ownership as they would if they were trying to get away from a prisoner-of-war camp. They save, learn, explore, examine, research, and finally jump. Others close their eyes and plunge right in. Which works best? Starting a business is complex. It pays to do some planning if you want to improve your chances of success.

Why. Why do they do it? Most people do it because they believe they can make more money and have some control over their own destinies. They are frustrated with non-rewarding careers, boring work, and the lack of control over their lives. The entrepreneurial individual visualizes owning a business as a way of putting meaning and purpose back into his or her existence and at the same time making a fortune. It may not be totally realistic; yet one's perception of reality is, in fact, that person's reality.

Where. Where do they start? People start businesses in small towns and large cities, in shopping centers and warehouses. The most important element of the where factor is whether it will work. The age-old cliche—"Location, location, location"—still prevails as one of the most important criteria of a successful business. Those who can carefully read population shifts and other market dynamics can be assured of prosperity. Those who do not can count on some frustrations.

The System Has Failed Us

In many ways we are being forced into entrepreneurialism. The traditional systems just aren't working any longer. The promises of a rewarding future, upward mobility, and stimulating work are becoming hollow. Large businesses can no longer guarantee happiness if you "play the game". The payoffs today are plant layoffs, stagnating careers, and corporate politics. Virtually every industry is being battered by foreign competition, propelled into automation, and forced to reduce staffs. So much for safe and secure careers!

Sparked by this disillusionment, ambitious people are creating their own upward mobility by becoming entrepreneurs. Almost all of the individuals that I spoke with told the same story. They started their businesses out of frustration. The system could no longer fulfill their expectations of personal success and financial security, thus they saw few alternatives. They knew that if they worked as hard in their own ventures as they did in someone else's, they were bound to be successful. Their goals of meaningful work, personal satisfaction, and control over their destinies could only be achieved in their own businesses. The failing system has been the catalyst for giving entrepreneurship its greatest boost.

The Profile of An Entrepreneur

Entrepreneurs are not supermen or wonderwomen. They are, for the most part, ordinary people. Of course, it helps if you are in good health, can get along well with people, have a high level of self-confidence, are willing to take risks, and can make good decisions.

However, it is extremely difficult to draw an accurate profile of the successful entrepreneur. It takes a number of personal assets and characteristics to measure up to the tasks of running a business. Frankly, some people shouldn't be self-employed. A friend of mine is a prime example. You could never meet a nicer guy—talented, dynamic, and an excellent manager. He had worked for a medium-sized firm for about three years and ultimately became their general manager. Since it was a family-owned business, he had moved as high as he was going to. With some reluctance, he decided to open a similar operation, he was well-financed and had a good plan. However, after six months of operation, he closed his doors. He admitted the pressure was too intense, and the responsibility of handling the entire management role too overwhelming. Perhaps the recession had some bearing on the decision, but in reality, he wasn't entrepreneurial. He made an excellent general manager, but a poor owner.

How do you know in advance whether you have what it takes? That's a difficult question, and perhaps it can't be answered. Nevertheless, you should try to evaluate your personal profile in order to determine if you should actually take the fateful step.

Reading this book will provide an opportunity for you to evaluate your entrepreneurial instincts. If you feel comfortable with the contents, then you probably have the self-employment characteristics. However, if you feel uncomfortable and become pressured by the checklists, examples, plans, etc., then carefully re-consider the decision to start your own business.

Another way to evaluate your entrepreneurial stamina is to review the checkist in Figure 1-1. There's no score or grading to these questions. The list simply contains a number of entrepreneurial characteristics that help people evaluate whether they will be comfortable owning their own businesses. No one is totally comfortable owning a struggling small business, but some people are more adept at handling it.

Don't be intimidated by this checklist. Very few aspiring entrepreneurs could honestly and without hesitation, check off the first box in each section. Looking back in retrospect to when I began, I probably couldn't. I was naive. I saw my business as an adventure, and it was certainly that, and more. After six months to a year, you lose your innocence and become battle-hardened and far more realistic. However, one note of caution: if you find that the first box in each section makes you hesitate, give some more deep and self-analytical thought to the concept of starting your own business. There are those who are cut out for it and those who are not.

Ten Rules of the Road

Like every endeavor, there are certain classic rules by which to succeed. Whether you are starting a retail store, a service or a manufacturing venture, these rules will prevail. They are simple to state, somewhat more difficult to implement. Nevertheless, successful entrepreneurs throughout the country follow, to some degree, each of them.

1. Quickly become knowledgable about your business.
2. Have adequate capital to do the job right.
3. Location, Location, Location.
4. Know how to buy low and sell high.
5. Control your money very tightly.
6. Keep a positive attitude.
7. Know how to hire, train, and motivate people.
8. Know how to promote merchandise and sell.
9. Keep accurate records.
10. Plan ahead.

If you focus on these ten rules, you will considerably increase your chance of success. This book will explore each of them and hopefully will help you prepare for your challenging entrepreneurial journey.

Rewards and Benefits

There are several rewards and benefits when you launch your own business. Many people think that money will be the most rewarding aspect. However, most entrepreneurs derive greater satisfaction from achieving a level of *success*. Money is simply a way of keeping score—a way of determining whether your team is winning. The emotional payoff from your business has to be substantial in order to reward you for your time and energy it took to create it.

Independence is also considered one of the major benefits. The ability to put your creative ideas to work, without someone second-guessing you, is indeed satisfying. A real entrepreneur feels better at running his or her own small business than running somebody else's big business.

Then there's *pride* of ownership: that's a powerful reward in itself. The ability to say "That business over there is mine!", has a way of genuinely enhancing one's self-esteem. Our society tends to rank entrepreneurs high on the social value scale.

For some there is no other greater motivational benefit than the fulfillment of a *dream*. These individuals won't give up until they have their own businesses. Each is totally consumed with the thought that his or her concept will work. Each one knows how it's going to operate before the first nail is driven. Seeing a dream become reality is the ultimate reward.

A Message to Your Spouse

This section is actually directed to your spouse, and it is hoped that she or he will read it. Since perhaps as many as one-third of the readers of this book are women, I've attempted to relate this section to the husband or wife of the entrepreneur.

Being married to an entrepreneur is difficult, particularly if you do not share the same instincts. It may be hard to understand what motivates your spouse to start his or her own business. How can they give up job security and take on what appears unacceptable risks? What do they get in return? Long hours and hard work, with no guarantees! It borders on the irrational.

Nevertheless, the entrepreneurial urge is strong. It's difficult to talk someone out of it, even if you wanted to. The motivations are complex and unique from person to person. Some seek life-long dreams and fulfillment of their visions. Others simply want freedom. Many see it as a way to make more money, while others just want to get away from a trapped feeling in a corporate world which has not lived up to its promises and expectations. Most corporate escapees are disillusioned and dissatisfied. The corporate myth of stability and upward mobility is just that—a myth. There's no security. The job satisfaction may have been lost long ago.

FIGURE 1-1
ENTREPRENEURIAL CHECKLIST

Select the answer which best describes, or comes closest to your feelings.

Willingness to risk capital:

☐ 1. As long as I feel that there is a good chance of success, I'll go for it without hesitation.

☐ 2. I'm willing to invest some capital, but I always want to leave a sizeable cushion, just in case.

☐ 3. I have never really felt comfortable risking money or time on things I'm not absolutely sure of.

Independence:

☐ 1. Most of all, I want to be my own boss; it's my major goal.

☐ 2. I don't mind working for other people, but I'd rather be on my own.

☐ 3. Being on my own really scares me. I'd rather have the security of being an employee, and let someone else worry about the problems.

Flexibility:

☐ 1. I adapt to change quickly and decisively.

☐ 2. I move, but it takes time and careful consideration.

☐ 3. I would rather see things stay the same; I get uptight when change occurs.

Self-Confidence:

☐ 1. I am very confident in myself and know that I can handle most situations.

☐ 2. I am confident most of the time, particularly when I know the ground rules.

☐ 3. I'm not in control of my destiny; other people really control my future.

Attitude toward people:

☐ 1. I am naturally drawn to people; I like them, and they like me.

☐ 2. I find most people enjoyable, and most people are attracted to me.

☐ 3. I like things more than people and don't have many friends.

Knowledge of the particular business:

☐ 1. I know the business that I've been thinking about well and will enjoy it.

☐ 2. I'm reasonably confident, I can learn the business, and it appears that I will enjoy it.

☐ 3. I am not familiar with this type of business, nor do I know whether I will enjoy it.

Ability to start from scratch:

☐ 1. I enjoy the challenge of building something from scratch on my own; I'm a self-starter.

☐ 2. If given basic guidelines, I can do a good job.

☐ 3. I really prefer to have the entire job laid out, then I'll do it well.

Commitment:

☐ 1. I have a high drive and commitment, and won't stop until the project is done.

☐ 2. I seem to have a higher level of perseverance when things are going well.

☐ 3. I start many projects, but rarely find time to finish them.

Common Sense:

☐ 1. I consider myself realistic, and "street wise" when it comes to business.

☐ 2. Most business situations make sense, but there are areas where I feel out of step.

☐ 3. I am inexperienced and impractical in business matters.

Willingness to accept failure:

☐ 1. "Nothing ventured, nothing gained" is my motto.

☐ 2. I want to succeed, but if I fail, I will accept it.

☐ 3. I want to avoid failure, and won't take a risk if it doesn't look like a sure thing.

Health:

☐ 1. I have excellent health and feel good, both physically and mentally.

☐ 2. I get sick on occasion, but it doesn't last long.

☐ 3. I have problems with my health; illness always seems to get in my way.

Work habits:

☐ 1. I plan before I start and then work my plan; I'm well-organized.

☐ 2. I find that I'm organized most of the time; but on occasion, I do get out of control.

☐ 3. I take things as they come, and sometimes get priorities confused.

This checklist is for self evaluation of your personal characteristics, to see if you will have a better-than-average chance of success as an entrepreneur. The material may touch on some tender personal areas; you'll have to be honest with yourself. Be careful to avoid self deception; don't brush the negatives under the rug.

Take enough time to evaluate the criteria and information, and try to relate some actual experiences from your past. Determine how you will handle things when it gets tough. Because, if you can count on anything, you can count on the fact that owning your own business operation is going to be tough.

This short personal appraisal is by no means an evaluation on whether you are qualified to be an entrepreneur. It is simply a way of focusing on your personal attributes, and it may help you decide on taking that major step. You may want to ask a few of your close friends or relatives to evaluate you, perhaps more objectively than you can do it yourself.

For your entrepreneurial spouses it's now or never. They must break out and give entrepreneurship a try before it's too late, and escape is impossible.

All of those motivations are difficult to understand when there are mortgage payments plus kids school clothes and groceries to buy. Nevertheless, if your entrepreneurial spouse doesn't try to make this change, the lost opportunity may haunt him or her forever.

If you don't fully understand what's happening, now is the time to sit down with your spouse and engage in straightforward dialogue. Be positive and encouraging, but also share your concerns. It's important that husband and wife communicate their feelings during this difficult time.

In the beginning months, you will have to demonstrate a good deal of patience. Starting a business is one of the most difficult undertakings any one can imagine. The long hours, intensity, and problems that crop up will test anyone's sense of humor. There will be time when you feel you are simply a fixture, that your spouse seems to care more about the business than about the family. Of course, that's not the case—he or she is just in a survival mode. Many of your former traditions may suffer. You will see less of your friends, because your spouse can't make it or is too tired. Then there are the money crises. There probably was never enough, but now the financial problems have intensified. If these are the penalties for owning a business, is it all worth it? Maybe yes, and maybe no. The uncertainty is based on whether the business turns the corner and becomes one of those successful little gems and whether your spouse finds happiness. You're right, there are no guarantees. But people have a better shot at "happiness" if they're doing what they want to do.

What's your role? First, be *supportive.* It's just too hard out there in the trenches, to come home to nagging. Home must be a sanctuary, full of encouragement and optimism. You must believe in your spouse, even when he or she is full of self-doubt. When your spouse says the day was good, you say "Fantastic!" When the day was bad, you respond, "Things will be better tomorrow." Your spouse feels a terrible responsibility to you and the family. Granted, it may appear that the entrepreneur is doing this for himself or herself, but in reality he or she is trying to make a better life for everyone.

You may have to take on some extra work or perhaps an active role in the business. There are many husband-and-wife teams in the entre-preneurial world. That's where the "Mom and Pop" expression came from. In any event, give your spouse the benefit of the doubt, and trust their judgment. If your family entrepreneur has blind faith, try closing your eyes, extending your hand, and following along. Keep your sense of humor, share the good with the bad, but always share. When the business does make it, there will be a team standing in the winner's circle.

Chapter 2
Picking the "Right" Business

Where Do You Begin? The first place to start is with *you!* You are one of the most important factors in selecting the "right" business. Certainly you want to select a business that will be successful and provide the income you need to support you and your family but, just as important, you will also want a business that will suit your own interests, and personal needs. Today we often hear that the rewards that one achieves from a satisfying lifestyle are as important and necessary as the financial rewards. Unfortunately, people often select businesses that they believe will make money, but they find out later that they are unhappy running the operation.

To understand this issue more clearly, you have to examine the age-old entrepreneurial rule. If you enjoy and receive satisfaction from your work, you are more likely to do a better job, be more successful, and make more money. That doesn't necessarily mean that if you enjoy horses you will be successful in the buggy whip business. Today a number of other factors must be considered. Picking a growth industry in the right location that meets your abilities and that you can run profitably are some of the key criteria. Nevertheless starting a business that you would enjoy is not a bad place to begin. As an Oriental proverb quite aptly states, "Choose a job you love and you will never have to work a day in your life."

Your Objectives

To begin this process of selecting your business opportunity, you must again take a hard look at yourself. After all, in the beginning the business will actually be you. When you first start, unless you have unlimited financial resources, most of the work will be done by you. You will probably open the place in the morning, run it during the day, and perhaps even close it at night. So, before you start the screening and selection process, give considerable and serious thought to exactly what you want from the business.

An entrepreneur's objectives (income, type of work, life-style, etc.) come in many shapes and colors. What is necessary is to determine which are important to you and then arrange them in some sort of priority. It may be helpful, as these subjects are discussed, to take a sheet of paper and make notations as to how you feel about each.

Let's start with *income*. Set specific financial objectives for your potential business. Consider what you want to make the first year and each year up through five. Putting these figures down on paper starts to add a certain reality to your overall goals. Occasionally, the difference between personal financial needs and what a business can actually deliver, will send people back to the drawing board or sometimes even back to an old career, posthaste. Unfortunately, many an entrepreneur enters a business without specifically determining what income is needed from it and quickly becomes disillusioned. He or she buys a business that has a $30,000 net profit and payments on a debt of $20,000. If it takes $25,000 to support the family, something will break—frequently the entrepreneur's spirit.

It is important that you do not set your financial expectations too high in the beginning. The first couple of years in almost every business can be very difficult; you will need patience to achieve your ultimate financial objectives.

Now, consider your objectives in terms of the *actual work*. First, look back on your previous working experience and list those jobs that gave you the greatest pleasure and satisfaction. Did these jobs involve selling, managing, planning, merchandising, buying, etc.? Now, give your imagination free rein and list the activities that, if given the choice, you would like to do in future years. Try to rank them in terms of preferences. In addition to work-related activities, consider social, hobby, and even educational involvements. You'll see a pattern emerge. This process will have a major influence on you as you select a specific business. Remember, if you enjoy your work, you probably are going to be more successful at it.

Next, consider what you want from the business on a *personal level*. For example, how do you want other people to perceive your status? Basically, there is significant status in being in business for yourself but that may not be enough. In order to illustrate this point consider the status contrast between a store that sells second-hand clothing and one that sells French antiques. Because of various factors, the recycled-clothier may be making a fortune and have a country house furnished with French antiques. On the other hand, the antique dealer may be having a difficult time paying his electric bill. The appropriate time to determine whether status is important to you is before you actually get into business.

Following is a brief list of other personal objectives. You probably can add more yourself.

1. Establish a business that can eventually be taken over by my children.

2. Run the business by working only part-time during the next couple of years.

3. Locate a business that is close to home.

4. Set up a business that my entire family can work in.

5. Establish a business that enables me to write off business trips to France (that French Antique shop).

6. Start a business that I can expand into a chain of stores.

7. Start a business where I can use my talents and experience, without having a boss.

Finally, consider what objectives as well as limitations, you have relative to your *lifestyle*. Owning a business can have a major effect, both positive and negative on your personal life. The location of your business may present you with a considerable commute problem. The amount of capital you put into your business will certainly have an effect on your family's lifestyle. If you use all your available assets (selling your house and car as some people actually do!), you will drastically alter your family's living standards. Set limitations in terms of location, hours, and investment. This will provide you with realistic parameters in your screening process.

In summary, you have now listed your income objectives, what personal and work related goals you want to achieve, and finally your lifestyle objectives and limitations. This analysis will help you examine how your entrepreneurial urge relates to other important aspects of your life. Most of us want independence, but we also need a measure of security. Life is full of priorities as well as trade-offs.

What do You Bring to the Business?

One of the problems in starting your own business is that you may have to cope with situations for which you have limited background and training. As an owner of a business, you must accept and handle the *entire* responsibility of a number of management roles that call for a wide variety of talents. In your previous jobs you were probably responsible for specific tasks and responsibilities. As an entrepreneur, you are responsible for everything! This realization should not necessarily discourage you. Take steps to learn which management skills you must strengthen or develop. Unless you are realistic about your qualifications and are prepared to learn and improve on the weaker areas, you may pay a very high price for your business venture.

Begin your skills evaluation by examining your background and qualifications. Perhaps the easiest way to do this is to create a personal resume. Later this will prove beneficial, since it is part of your business plan. Start by outlining your work experience. Cover such business activities as management, supervision, training, sales, marketing, finance, accounting, and planning. Review each of your jobs and write out how you were successful in accomplishing the various tasks. This project can prove to be quite ego-enhancing. We tend to forget just how many things we have done and how talented we really are.

Also, consider some of your other managerial attributes. Perhaps you have developed some non-related business leadership skills in Little League or PTA. What organizations have you been active in? Each of these activities involves dealing with people. The skills you developed there will pay remarkable dividends in your own business. It is also important to consider the personal traits you bring to the business — attributes like self-motivation, willingness to work hard, and good common sense.

Finally, list your educational background. Nowhere is it written that, to own and be successful in your own business, you need a college degree. There is probably a much higher percentage of non-college educated entrepreneurs than those with degrees. However, college courses have prepared people to do certain managerial tasks. They also expose students to problem-solving and proven managerial techniques. If you took any of these types of specific courses, list them.

The next area to consider is your investment contribution. At this point in time, you have probably given serious thought to the amount of money you are willing to put into the business. Your initial investment is certainly one of the more important ingredients. It will determine your business size, its location, inventory level, and perhaps how long you can survive if things don't go according to the plan. It is important, from the beginning, to establish a realistic estimate of just how much money you are willing to risk and from where it will come. Fill in the personal financial statement in Figure 2.1.

Experience

Some say it is essential that you have first-hand experience in the business you plan to enter. In other words, you should spend some time actually working in an operation similar to the one you're going to open. Certainly, a good case can be made for this position. Otherwise, you may make a lot of unnecessary mistakes that you could have avoided if you had had the experience. On the other hand, what assurances do you have that you would work for an employer who was particularly skillful or successful at running his business? You could actually accumulate some bad habits, rather than good experience.

On occasion, the business dictates that you must have some first-hand experience. For example, in a high-fashion ladies ready-to-wear, you should have specific buying expertise. If not, by the time you learned the hard way (on the job), the season would be over and you would probably be out of business. Before I started in retail, I volunteered my help on weekends in a store. Although this was a limited apprenticeship, it was helpful and did give me an indication of what to expect later. You probably will have to be the best judge in determining whether first-hand experience is necessary.

What's equally important is whether the experience is well-balanced. By this, I mean opportunity or exposure in the various management activities involved—selling, buying, personnel, finance, planning, and merchandising. After reviewing the experience you'll bring into the business and comparing it with what you will need, you may see an imbalance or some gaps. It's important that you try to acquire these skills before starting your venture. After the doors open, you'll be really busy.

You can take courses at adult education programs or local colleges. Virtually every junior college offers one or more courses in starting a business and over 250 universities now offer entrepreneurial curriculums. You can attend seminars and visit your local library and bookstore to acquire source material. Unwillingness to adequately prepare yourself for the business can become a major reason for its failure. That driving desire for independence and the thought that if you don't move now you will lose the once-in-a-lifetime chance, can prove very disastrous. Unfortunately, too many impatient and premature entrepreneurs have understood, only too late, the importance of management skills and experience.

FIGURE 2-1
PERSONAL BALANCE SHEET

ASSETS:		LIABILITIES:	
Cash in Bank	_____	Loans at Banks	_____
Stocks or Other Negotiable Securities (Market Value)	_____	Loans to Others	_____
		Real Estate Loans	_____
Notes Receivable	_____	Other Debts	_____
Value of Real Estate: (Market Value)		_____	_____
		_____	_____
Home	_____	Credit Cards &	_____
Other	_____	Retail Stores	_____
Automobiles	_____	TOTAL LIABILITIES	_____
Cash Value of Life Insurance	_____		
Personal Assets	_____		
Other	_____	TOTAL NET WORTH	_____
TOTAL ASSETS	_____	(Assets Less Liabilities)	

CAPITOL AVAILABLE
FOR BUSINESS INVESTMENT

SOURCES OF CASH:	AMOUNT:
(e.g. savings, stock, friends, relatives, equity in property, etc.)	
_____	_____
_____	_____
_____	_____
_____	_____
_____	_____
TOTAL	_____

COLLATERAL AVAILABLE
(Market Value)

Real Estate	_____
Stocks and Bonds	_____
Other	_____

Round Pegs—Round Holes

Some people are particularly well-suited to owning their own businesses. They have what it takes. It is a very difficult ability to describe but it's essentially what I call the "round peg, round hole situation". Unfortunately many people try to fit their square pegs into round holes, often for a lifetime. Somehow, you should closely examine how you fit into the potential business. Certainly this examination should be done before you make a major commitment—signing a lease or writing checks. Ask other entrepreneurs in that business what their world is like. Listen to the bad as well as the good. Try to visualize how your personality will match the day-to-day routine of the operation. You're going to make a major commitment in terms of time, energy, and money. You certainly want to fit in.

Self-Motivation

Finally, let's consider one of the most important ingredients that you will bring to a business to make it successful—*self-motivation*. This is where success begins and, on occasion, ends. Indeed, if your motivation is not strong, you will probably fail. Motivation is the brick and mortar that holds a business together.

As a person starts to think seriously about going into business, much of the thought process is in the fantasy stage. You visualize the independence, the opportunity to be creative, and the satisfaction of self-achievement. Eventually you initiate a course of action; and before you know it, you're in business. That fantasy has now become reality. You are part of a select breed of adventurous entrepreneurs. You are now writing checks—perhaps faster than you thought and larger than you had anticipated. Second thoughts start to creep into your life. Believe me, it is not very easy to start a business, and certainly not cheap. At this point, and perhaps at a number of other times in your entrepreneurial career, sheer motivation and determination will be the personal attributes that carry you through.

So if you are not really highly motivated, put your money in the bank and get a good job. In time, you can learn all of the skills of operating a business. You can learn how to manage, administer, and plan. But I'm not sure how well you can learn self-motivation. That tends to come naturally. Part of it is a high degree of self-confidence that keeps saying "I can do it!" Another part is perseverance that keeps saying, no matter how many setbacks and disappointments, "It can be done!" And a final part is the powerful desire that keeps saying, "I'm going to do it!".

Selection Process

Now that you have examined what you personally need from the business and what the business needs from you, it is time to begin the actual selection process. Perhaps you have already reached this point and have picked the type of operation you would like to own. Nevertheless, the following section will be very beneficial for you for two reasons:

1. You may reconsider your decision after finding another field more appealing. Or at least you may select a backup or secondary choice in the event your original selection doesn't materialize.

2. You will have a chance to review a number of informational sources. These may be very helpful to you in developing an in-depth knowledge about your chosen retail opportunity.

This is really the *homework* phase of your entrepreneurial search process. The better you do this research, the better your chances of ultimate success. Granted, it may be relatively easy to write a check and buy a business, assuming you have the financial wherewithall, but, that is only the price of admission. Once you are in, you have to sustain the operation through difficult times. You also have to weave yourself through an incredible maze of business-related problems. Now is the time to become prepared, when all you are spending is *time*, rather than money.

The first evaluation in the selection process is what I call the "chemistry test". In other words, exactly how do you feel about this kind of business?

It is not absolutely necessary that you feel elated when you walk through a business, similar to the one you are considering, but you should have a *comfortable* feeling. After all, if you select that type of business you are going to find yourself spending several hours a day inside its four walls. Perhaps another way of looking at it is, if you don't particularly care for young children, you probably shouldn't consider a toy store or, for that matter, children's shoes, a small people's boutique, hobby store, or even a bicycle shop.

Your objective in this selection process is simply to narrow your options. There are fifty to sixty different types of retail stores, hundreds of service type businesses, and countless numbers of manufacturing operations. Just check the index of your local yellow pages. The variety of business activities is endless. It is as bewildering as going into a floor-covering store and seeing row after row of carpets. It is very difficult to make a decision. At first you start with a color you feel most comfortable with and work your way through styles and textures. The question you want to answer here is: "What color would I like my business to be?"

For example, if you are thinking about retail, try taking a few field trips to various shopping centers, both large and small. Walk in and out of stores and try to imagine yourself owning that type of business. How does it feel? Try to keep in mind your needs, capabilities, limitations, and motivations.

The next step, once you have established a list of potential opportunities, is to attempt to isolate three or four that would best meet your personal and financial criteria. Figure 2-2 provides a helpful screening chart. This exercise may take some time but should offer valuable help in selecting the "right" business.

The objective of this chart is to rate the potential business opportunities from three to zero, depending on criteria. The totals will provide you with a

FIGURE 2-2
BUSINESS SCREENING CHART

Instructions

1. Select various types of potential businesses and list them along the top of the form.
2. Rate each with the following values.

   Value

   3. "I feel totally confident in this area and have no reservations."
   2. "I feel good and only have slight reservations."
   1. "I feel OK but there are some factors which cause me concern."
   0. "I feel uncomfortable and resistant."

3. The totals, when compared against options, will give you an indication which potential business offers the best opportunity.
4. Use a pencil for this chart, you may want to change your scores as you gain more perspective about a specific business.

Skills, Background and Lifestyle criteria.	Business Options			
1. I have the background and experience necessary to own and operate this type of business.				
2. The business meets my investment requirements. I have enough money to do it right.				
3. This business meets my income requirements. I can make enough money and also pay any debt service.				
4. I feel comfortable with this type of business. The chemistry is right.				
5. It matches my "people orientation".				
6. There is good growth in this industry.				
7. The risk factor is acceptable.				
8. My family and spouse agree that this is the type of business to enter.				
9. This business provides the status that I need.				
10. This business fits in with my lifestyle requirements (location, hours, long- and short-term goals).				
11. This business fits my selling abilities and talents.				
TOTALS				

key in your selection process. Before you start, try to firm up a precise mental picture of each possibility.

Informational Search

There are basically three major sources of information on independent businesses.

1. People presently involved in similar businesses.

2. Trade magazines and trade associations.

3. Articles and books on the field.

Before you embark upon your search for information, I'd like to caution you about a potential problem in this phase of the selection process—overkill! Some people make a career out of researching businesses. It is really not that difficult to find information about a business category. Remember, you can't make money investigating businesses, you can only make money running businesses.

Let's review each of these informational sources separately.

People in the business. You will be pleasantly surprised at how cooperative most entrepreneurs are when you ask them for information. It's satisfying to their egos. People enjoy being considered experts and will respond favorably if you explain what you are considering and how you would appreciate their input and advice.

It is understandable if you are somewhat apprehensive about calling an owner of a business and asking, "How much money are you making?" or other personal questions about their operation. Fortunately, you don't have to be that direct. Following a couple of simple guidelines will make it easier. Initially, pick a few operations that may appear to be the size and type you would like to eventually own. Telephone the owner and identify yourself. Explain that you have been exploring the opportunities of owning a similar business and are in the process of talking with a few of the owners of successful operations. To eliminate any threat of competition, emphasize that you are considering a location some distance away. Also mention that you are not interested in confidential information about the business just general background so you'll have better insight for making your own business decision.

You will find you can make appointments to see a very high percentage of the people you call. After all, they also went into business and may have great empathy for your situation. Arrange to meet in a quiet place where you do not have disturbances from customers or phones. First, explain how you have narrowed your selection. Don't provide too much information. You want them to do most of the talking and you want to *listen.* Most of them won't mind if you make notes. So be prepared to jot down their answers to questions such as:

1. How long have you been in the business? What made you select this field? (This breaks the ice by letting them talk about themselves)

2. What do you consider the major tasks of the business? What experience and background is necessary to accomplish jobs well?

3. What type of selling is required?

4. How helpful are the suppliers? How do you get their support? Who are the major ones?

5. How much capital is really necessary to start this type of business? How much reserve capital is necessary to insure success? Once operational, what are the major costs of doing business: payroll, rent, advertising, etc.?

6. When you first started the business, what were the major problems that you encountered? What are the major problems today?

7. What kind of money can one really expect to make in this kind of business? How long will it take?

8. Does advertising really work and which type works best?

9. What are the two or three major factors that you believe make a person successful in this business?

10. What sales level could I expect to achieve—first year, second year, third year?

Although many of these questions seem quite penetrating, with the right approach you'll find that most entrepreneurs will give you realistic answers. If you get good answers from a few business owners, who are honest and candid with you, the information you acquire will be *invaluable*.

You may also find that these contacts lead to a number of other interesting possibilities.

- You may accept a temporary job working for one of the businesses to gain experience and serve a valuable mini-apprenticeship.

- One of the operations may be for sale—20 to 30 percent of all businesses are for sale at any point in time.

- This initial meeting could be the start of a long-term business relationship. Having dinner or lunch with an entrepreneur who has similar interests is useful and enjoyable.

Expand your information search process by setting up meetings with suppliers and wholesalers. These individuals can provide very valuable information, particularly about the future growth of the industry. You have to be somewhat cautious though, since you are a potential customer. Explain up front that you are just considering the business and haven't made a firm commitment. Suppliers can also be helpful in providing information on what areas may be presently under-served and would therefore be good locations for the business you have in mind. They may also provide contacts to owners who want to sell their businesses.

Trade Publications and Associations. Each industry has one or more trade magazines that are published and distributed exclusively to the business owners in that industry. A partial list of these magazines has been included in the appendix. Some of these trade publications are particularly good and consistently have valuable information for those involved in the business. Write or phone their offices, explain that you are going into the business, and request a few back issues and a subscription for future issues. If they charge you a minimal price for each back issue, buy them—it's worth the investment.

Trade associations are also sources of useful information. Phone them and ask about their services. A list of trade associations is also provided in the appendix. You may be asked to join. If the fee is minor, do it. The information and services you obtain can be extremely valuable.

Library and Bookstores. Entrepreneurs typically don't have time for books. Reading, studying and planning are not activities that give quite the same satisfaction as doing. Entrepreneurs are action types. Nevertheless, when you start a business, there will be few opportunities to turn back or call "time-out" while you seek a better understanding of a particular subject. The mistakes you make because of lack of knowledge are going to cost money! Consequently, the time to learn is before you start, rather than by trial and error.

The library, bookstore and Small Business Administration booklist (see Appendix) have a wealth of information. First attempt to locate any book written specifically about your industry. Then look in your library's *Business Periodical Index* and *Wall Street Journal Index* for magazine articles on the subject. You'll be amazed at what has been written about your specific industry, no matter how unique you might think it is. Finally, ask the librarian to point out the shelf on small business management. Explain your situation. A librarian will be extremely helpful and may even do some of the research. Remember, this is your homework stage, and what better place to do homework than a library?

In Summary. Perhaps, you may be very fortunate and "fall into" a successful operation without doing any in-depth analysis. It sometimes happens. You may find a successful businessperson who wants to sell, or a business broker who presents an operation that you know nothing about— except that it makes money. You may be one of those lucky ones. All the rest of us should recognize the potential pitfalls of getting into the "wrong" business and do whatever it takes to *reduce* that possibility.

Chapter 3
Evaluating Your Potential Business

Now that you've started to narrow your options, it's time to zero in on *genuine business opportunities*. Although circumstances differ, depending upon whether you're starting a business from scratch, purchasing an existing operation, or opening a franchise, certain principles apply. Before making your final commitment, it's necessary to evaluate the overall market, the community, specific locations within it, and the competition you'll face. Then you must determine whether you can afford it.

Basically, this chapter will help you answer the question of whether the business opportunity you have tentatively selected will make money, considering a number of variables. That is, of course, the most important question to answer. You may be able to justify a business venture in a number of different ways, but if it will not make a *profit,* then there is no reason to go into it.

To determine the potential profitability of any business is by no means an easy task. As a matter of fact, it is almost impossible to do in precise terms. What we will attempt to do here is answer the overall question; "Does the business justify my initial investment of capital and time?"

Unfortunately, there are no guarantees in entrepreneurship. Nor are there any magic formulas for predicting success. The process of determining the viability of a business opportunity requires careful analysis, a lot of common sense, and good judgment.

In this chapter (and perhaps throughout the book) you'll find I focus on retailing more than service, wholesaling, or manufacturing. This is basically because of my orientation. Nevertheless, it is important to emphasize that major *similarities* exist in analyzing all business opportunities. Even if you are considering a business other than retail, you will readily see parallels and find the information extremely useful.

How Do You Start?

The analysis of business opportunities is not necessarily complicated, but it does involve some work. The steps you use to examine the various factors for justifying a business are similar to those used in approaching and solving any problem or making any decision. They are as follows:

1. Clearly state the area to be studied (for example, "Should I go into the retail shoe business?").

2. Get the facts relative to the subject.

3. Analyze and study the facts and attempt to draw meaningful conclusions.

4. List the alternatives and select the best course of action.

By using this basic approach you should be able to determine, with a certain amount of confidence, whether your business venture has a better-than-average chance of success. In the previous chapter you were able to narrow your options, based on what you need from the business and what assets and talents you bring to the business. The next step, is to narrow those options even further and perhaps arrive at an actual commitment.

Genuine Business Opportunity

Before you launch your business with a good chance that it will be successful and profitable, you must select what I call "a genuine business opportunity."This means a business that: will provide a *needed* product or service, *sold* in enough volume, will have *low* enough costs and overhead, and will generate a desired *profit.* Too often, prospective entrepreneurs see a genuine business opportunity through somewhat clouded vision. Their ambition and optimism tend to over estimate the ability of a potential business to deliver profit. A large number of businesses fail simply because they never should have been started in the first place. There was no real justification for their existence in the marketplace.

The checklist in Figure 3-1 will provide an opportunity for you to evaluate whether you have selected a genuine business opportunity. You may have to do considerable legwork before attempting to answer these questions. Still, if you can objectively state "yes" to each, you have probably found a business that justifies your investment of time and money. However, if you have many "no's,"take a second hard look at the proposed venture. You may still go forward, but at least you'll understand where your problems will be.

Analyze the Industry

Make sure that the industry you're considering has a bright *future.* You don't want to spend you money or your time on a field already saturated and with no real prospect of future growth.

For example, many industries have fewer operations than they had ten years ago. There are fewer automobile dealers, gas stations, mobile-home dealers, variety stores, candy stores, yardage shops, men's clothing stores, and appliance stores—not to mention steel plants. That doesn't mean that you couldn't be successful in any one of these businesses, but when you detect a negative trend, it's important to determine what implications it has for you.

The best way to obtain accurate information about an industry's future is by talking to knowledgable people in that business. Here again, we must rely on interviews with business owners and suppliers. Although most people are very honest in their opinions about the future health of a particular industry, on occasion you may have to interpret your potential competitor's negative appraisal as a way of keeping you out.

FIGURE 3-1
GENUINE BUSINESS OPPORTUNITY CHECKLIST

Making the Final Decision:

The following checklist outlines the criteria for a good retail or service operation. If "no" answers show up, don't rule out a particular business automatically. You might still succeed by overcoming the weaknesses with extra effort.

	Yes	No
1. **Demand Factor.** The immediate community needs another business like this one.	☐	☐
2. **Trade Area.** There is growth in the trade area — construction, retail sales, population and jobs are on the increase.	☐	☐
3. **Changes in the Trading Area.** There are no major negative shifts in population, economic downturns, change in access roads, or major competitive shopping centers anticipated in the foreseeable future.	☐	☐
4. **Population.** There are enough people in the immediate area who have need for my product and will make a trip to buy it.	☐	☐
5. **Rent.** The rent and other occupancy fees, including utilities, are in line with my budget limitations.	☐	☐
6. **Lease Arrangements.** The lease arrangements — time, use clause, deposits, etc. are reasonable.	☐	☐
7. **Lessors Cooperation.** The Lessor will cooperate with my time table and will provide a reasonable allowance for lease-hold improvements.	☐	☐
8. **Competition.** Competitors seem vulnerable, this will allow my business to prosper.	☐	☐
9. **Retailers Success.** Most retailers in the immediate area are successful and recommend the location. There is no major retail vacancy factor.	☐	☐
10. **Advertising.** There is a cost-effective media in the area that delivers results.	☐	☐
11. **Traffic.** Shoppers are attracted to the area. There is a successful major retailer (large food store, discount or department store) close by that draws considerable traffic.	☐	☐
12. **Visibility.** The business and sign can easily be seen by both auto and foot traffic.	☐	☐
13. **Accessibility.** The business is on a major thoroughfare. Cars have easy access to parking, with ample space.	☐	☐
14. **Layout.** The size, frontage, signs, window and lighting are excellent for my type of business.	☐	☐
15. **Employees.** The pool of available employees is good.	☐	☐

Picking the Right Community

Ask any expert about the most important factors that will contribute to your success, and the reply is likely to be, "Location, location, location." This overused and oversimplified statement emphasizes the most critical decision you'll make. A good location can help a marginal business, whereas a bad location could cause a good business to fail.

These factors affect your choice:

1. Where you want to live.

2. The business opportunities in a particular community—economic climate, available locations, competition.

3. Landlord negotiations.

Let's start by examining the *local community*. First choose a community that has a reasonably steady employment climate. When local industries have economic difficulties, the ripple effect is felt very severely throughout the entire small business sector. Attempt to open your business in a growing, rather than a declining market.

How can you determine the viability and health of a community? Look for most or all of these conditions:

1. Large and aggressive local retailers (department stores, grocery stores, discount houses) have opened or plan to open in the area. These retailers usually spend considerable time and money selecting locations. Following their lead can offer significant benefits.

2. Local industries are expanding rather than contracting. Although there may be unemployment, it is not chronic. People can find jobs.

3. Real estate values are rising, or at least staying constant. New housing and commercial developments are under construction.

4. There are few stores for lease in the immediate area, and the existing stores appear to be successful.

Visit the local Chamber of Commerce and local bankers. Ask them to provide you with their realistic appraisal of the community. This information can help validate your analysis whether it is positive or negative.

Can you be successful in a stagnant or declining community? Sometimes! However, it's considerably more difficult. The problem is that most areas on the downhill will continue to go in that direction. It's difficult to reverse or even stabilize that trend. When you open a business, you must consider what's going to happen in the foreseeable future. If the local economic outlook is grim, seriously consider locating in a community with a better future.

Analysis of the Local Market

The basic question to answer here is, "Can the local market absorb another similar business?" Almost any area can absorb another operation, but the new business will have to be *superior* in order to attract enough customers from the existing competition.

To help you analyze this subject, refer to Figure 3-2. There you will find, from census data, the number of people needed to support various categories of retail or service businesses. For example, throughout the country there were 11,983 people for every hardware store and 25,236 for every bookstore.

Begin your analysis by determining how many people live in the area covered by your local yellow pages. Then count the number of businesses similar to yours in the yellow-page directory. By simple division, you will have the number of people per business. Then relate that figure to the chart to determine whether your community appears over-saturated or under-developed. Notice, I used the word "appears." This analysis alone will not give you a firm appraisal of a market's potential. In order to reinforce your analysis you'll need to have straight-forward conversations with suppliers and business owners who know the opportunities in a specific market, from first-hand experience. If you are considering a business other than one on the chart, ask people in that industry how many individual similar businesses there are in the United States. Divide that number into the country's population of 235 million and you'll have the number of people per business.

Another appraisal of a local market's potential can be made by surveying the present competition. If you find certain common problems: poorly maintained operations, incompetent staff, and lack of stimulating marketing, perhaps an opportunity exists. If you can open an operation and improve significantly on these areas, you'll be able to attract their customer base. Even if there are more businesses than the population can theoretically support, there is always room for one good one! But, you must be very good!!

If *advertising* is important in your business, determine whether the community you're considering has effective, affordable advertising vehicles. Entrepreneurs who overlook this factor sometimes find out, too late, that the local advertising is too expensive and/or ineffective. Check with small businesses in the area and discuss their experience with the local media. What do they use? How effective is it? What are the costs? Since you'll initially have to reach and impact potential customers, your opening advertising will have to be affordable and effective.

Another factor to consider is the *customer profile* of an area, and how it relates to your product mix. For example, if you plan to open a toy store or hobby shop, locate it in an area with growing families. Certain retailers need a customer base that has high discretionary income (money available after necessities have been paid). For example, antique stores, high-fashion ladies' ready-to-wear, and jewelry stores, belong in this category. Gift, novelty, and souvenir shops need a tourist clientele. Ask yourself, "Who are my customers? Where do they live? Where do they presently shop?" Knowing the profile (age, spendable income, family size, etc.) of your potential customers may be the decisive contributing factor in your choice between two locations.

FIGURE 3-2
SUMMARY OF 1982 CENSUS DATA

There are approximately 1.8 million retail businesses with 1.3 million recording a payroll. (Some very small firms are owner operated and do not have employees per se.) There are also 1.2 million service businesses with payrolls and over 2 million total service operations. The balance of the approximately 12 million U.S. businesses are made up of wholesale, construction, manufacturing, transportation, finance, mining, plus over 2.5 milion agricultural enterprises.

This chart shows the number of selected businesses with payroll in the U.S. **(Column 1),** the average dollar sales by business **(Column 2),** and the number of people needed to support that kind of business **(Column 3).**

To obtain a 1982 Business Census detailed breakout of an individual industry by state or metropolitan area request the information from the U.S. Department of Commerce, Bureau of the Census.

Business	# of Business with Payroll in U.S.	Average Dollar Sales	# of People Per Establ.
Eating Establ.	257,577	$ 358,077	912
Grocery Stores	128,128	1,761,293	1,834
Gasoline Service Stations	116,154	816,331	2,023
Automotive Repair, Services	115,380	269,146	2,036
Beauty Shops	71,116	67,983	3,304
Drinking Establ.	61,188	139,922	3,840
Drug Stores	48,637	735,593	4,831
Women's Ready-to-Wear	44,084	460,729	5,330
Management Consulting & Public Relations Services	41,605	431,904	5,648
Auto and Home Supplies	40,008	510,423	5,873
Shoe Stores	36,031	314,185	6,522
Liquor Stores	34,071	503,176	6,897
Furniture Stores	29,575	581,017	7,945
Motor Vehicle Dealers New and Used	25,641	5,929,970	9,165
Lumber and Other Building Materials Dealers	24,940	1,392,930	9,422
Gift, Novelty and Souvenir	22,302	209,292	10,537
Jewelry Stores	22,240	371,478	10,566
Florists	20,907	149,485	11,240
Dry Cleaners	20,238	142,610	11,611

FIGURE 3-2 CONTINUED

Sporting Good Stores and Bicycle Shops	20,129	373,708	11,674
Hardware Stores	19,611	427,135	11,983
Radio and Television Stores	19,347	497,653	12,146
Family Clothing Stores	17,899	752,635	13,129
Retail Bakeries	17,603	206,761	13,349
Used Merchandise Stores	17,560	225,075	13,382
Men's and Boy's Clothing	17,426	441,050	13,485
Electrical Repair	16,564	245,234	14,187
General Merchandise	13,173	935,868	17,839
Meat and Fish Markets	11,029	507,748	21,307
Floor Covering Stores	10,929	453,117	21,502
Laundry and Cleaning Services	10,879	434,520	21,601
Variety Stores	10,814	727,151	21,731
Optical Goods Stores	10,551	162,685	22,272
Household Appliance Stores	10,539	539,268	22,298
Department Stores	10,035	10,670,910	23,418
Sewing, Needlework Stores	9,767	256,102	24,060
Home Furnishings Stores	9,630	307,371	24,402
Book Stores	9,312	334,526	25,236
Music Stores	9,279	413,390	25,326
Paint, Glass and Wallpaper Stores	8,929	370,617	26,318
Barber Shops	8,066	51,097	29,134
Retail Nurseries	7,862	369,928	29,890
Hobby and Toy Shops	7,680	422,673	30,598
Mail Order Houses	7,360	1,486,483	31,929
Photographic Studios	7,115	194,291	33,028
Women's Accessory and Specialty Stores	6,946	269,360	33,832
Children's Stores	5,323	256,971	44,148
Stationery Stores	4,757	315,550	49,400
Motorcycle Dealers	4,607	621,959	51,009
Pet Stores	4,495	181,090	52,280
Boat Dealers	4,122	696,223	57,011
Drapery, Curtains and Upholstery Stores	4,056	210,841	57,938
Camera Stores	3,988	472,129	58,926
Luggage and Leather Good Stores	1,884	313,376	124,734

Narrowing Down Your Choice of Location

Competition can demonstrate a number of valuable aspects of location. Are the more successful local competitors located adjacent to large supermarkets, on busy traffic thoroughfares, or in regional shopping centers? Look for common factors which you might be able to adapt to your situation.

You can also gain perspective by pinpointing the sites of major competitors on a map. This can help you locate your operation in an untapped area.

Although you want to consider the competitive factor in your analysis for a potential location, realize that competition is not necessarily bad. Locating directly across the street from a well-entrenched competitor might be asking for trouble. But on the other hand, if you feel you could get needed exposure and ultimately capture the competitors' customers, a nearby location might be a good strategic move.

Traffic

If your business is retail or service, *traffic* is critical. The basic method for evaluating traffic flow involves counting it. This is fundamental. As you narrow your location options, use a hand-held counter to determine how much traffic each location is exposed to. The results provide the input necessary for your final decision.

Traffic must be analyzed qualitatively and quantitatively. Consider the type of customers, as well as the total numbers. When comparing one site with another, you must be sure to measure similar traffic patterns. If you count traffic for one hour at a given location, you must use the same hour on the same day of the week to count traffic at the other location.

Include accessibility and visibility in your traffic analyses. These factors are particularly important for a small retailer. If you open a store that nobody can see or find, you'll start with built-in problems. We're living in an era of maximum convenience. If it's difficult to get to a store, people won't come. It's best to follow this basic rule: The site you select should have the highest traffic flow and the greatest visibility that you can *afford.*

In your search for the "right" location, you may hear someone refer to a site as a "100%" location or a "75%" location. This is a way of describing the value of a given retail site in terms of traffic. Twenty-five years ago the 100% location was probably the downtown corner of Main and Elm Street. Today that 100% location is likely to be along the main concourse of a suburban regional shopping center, halfway between Sears and Penny's and directly across from the entrance of the area's major department store. Times change! And so does the desirability and cost of retail locations. You could probably lease that downtown site for 30%-50% of what the mall space would cost.

Affordability and availability of location now enter the picture. You'll be working with trade-offs here. Basically you'll try to get as much traffic exposure as your bucks will buy. Rent will certainly be one of your major operational costs. You can rent retail space, for as little as $6.00 per square foot and all the way up to $30.00 or more per square foot annually. Normally the rent of retail space is quoted in annual figures, but some lessors express it on a monthly basis. In the enclosed shopping center you have to pay as much as $4,000 monthly for a 2,000 sq. ft. store. You will have to sell a lot of merchandise to make that kind of rent affordable.

Try to keep your rental costs under 10 percent of sales. Six to eight percent is much more advantageous. Some locations will use a percentage of sales to calculate your rental fees. In other words, your rent will either be a flat amount or percentage (normally 7-10 percent) of your monthly sales volume, whatever is greater.

Lease Negotiations

Begin your location analysis by contacting several real estate agents that specialize in commercial space. Tell your real estate agent the type of space you're interested in, the approximate size, and other factors relative to your business. A good agent does part of the legwork for you and helps negotiate terms of the lease. The agent receives a commission from the owner of the property. If you find a location on your own, use this savings in real-estate commission as a bargaining point. However, in all cases, retain an attorney to review the lease. All commercial leases are written by property owners for their protection. That's a fact of life. Don't be too unnerved by the legal language, restrictions, and commitments. Everyone who opens a business unless purchasing the property outright, signs a similar lease.

If you have faith in your business and the particular location, try to get the longest lease possible, or at least an option clause for renewal. Landlords are willing to do more, such as investing in your leasehold improvements, if the lease is long (5 or more years). As an additional benefit, the rent won't change, and you won't be threatened with an unwanted move if a short lease is not renewed.

Lease conditions are not etched in granite. Try to negotiate every possible stipulation in the contract—rent, length of lease, leasehold allowances, and use clauses. A property owner who is highly motivated to rent the space will provide a number of concessions, if you ask. The best time to negotiate particulars in a lease is prior to signing. Owners are very reluctant to provide any additional benefits afterwards.

Be cautious about going into a new shopping center with a big vacancy rate. That is called "pioneering." It may have been fine for our forefathers but it's not healthy for start-up businesses. Customers tend to shy away from half-completed retail centers. First, they perceive that there must be something wrong; and second, as the center continues to construct stores, customers end up side-stepping carpenters and plumbers.

Be sure to obtain a "site history" of the specific location. What businesses were in that space previously? Why did they leave? This analysis should be done for the entire center. Certain shopping areas have some fundamental problems, reflected by a continuous turnover of stores. It's preferable to locate in a complex that has had a history of long-term successful tenants, even though rents may cost a few extra dollars.

Analysis of Competition

It's very unusual to open a business that has no direct competition. Don't be discouraged if you find a number of competitors. This frequently indicates a healthy marketplace. Determine the following: Who are your competitors? Where are they located? What are their strengths and weaknesses?

Customers consciously or subconsciously begin to evaluate a business the moment they enter it. Negative feelings will prompt them to do business elsewhere. You must be continuously aware of this factor and keep ahead of the competition. There is no better way to get ahead than to *start ahead.* The best approach to doing that is to scrutinize your competitors very carefully. Determine which competitors seem to have successful operations and for what reasons. Figure 3-3 provides a worksheet that will help you isolate the various competitive factors for a retail business. Similar ones can be developed for virtually any type of operation. You may want to make a few photocopies of this worksheet in order to do a separate analysis for each competitive store. This checklist can be as brief or as detailed as you want to make it. You may even visit a store more than once in order to evaluate it thoroughly. Don't fill out the form while you're there . . . that could make a store management very nervous.

After completing several of these checklists you'll begin to recognize certain factors that contribute to the ability of a business to attract and retain customers. These are the *features* you will want to build into your operation. Conversely, you will see problem areas which you will want to avoid. With these competitive analyses, you begin to develop an understanding of the profile of a successful business.

During your visit you may want to introduce yourself to the owner—not as a potential competitor but as someone interested in possibly going into the business. Remember, the competition does not have to be your enemy. During the time I owned my stores I occasionally purchased and advertised jointly with "competitors". There were also countless meetings where we discussed mutual problems. The interaction with *friendly* competitors is a matter of personal preference. Owning a small business can be very lonely at times. Having an opportunity to talk with people who know and can readily identify with your concerns can be very helpful.

In addition to visiting the small businesses, visit the mass merchandisers (department stores, discount houses, etc.) if they have departments in competition with your product line. These retailers spend significant amounts of money determining the best way to merchandise their products. It may not be the direction you'll take, but it is valuable to analyze their approach.

After finishing this exercise, you will have gained considerable insight related to businesses in your area. Keep these competitive checklist forms. After you have been in operation for six months, repeat the evaluations. This time, do it in terms of how the competitors rate against your business. Even though you may have developed a friendly relationship with one or more of the owners, you certainly don't want to lose customers to them.

FIGURE 3-3
COMPETITIVE CHECKLIST — RETAIL

Store _____   Date _____

Address _____   Years in Business _____

Owner _____

Score: 3 – Excellent   2 – Good   1 – Fair   0 – Poor

Factor	Score	Remarks
Location • Shopping Center popularity		
• Nearby major retailers — (pulling power)		
• Traffic factor — (foot and auto)		
• Visibility of the store		
• Accessibility		
Store Exterior • Overall image		
• Window display		
• Signs		
Interior • Overall image		
• Cleanliness		
• Lighting		
• Layout and Traffic flow		
• Comfort feeling		
• Size		

FIGURE 3-3 CONTINUED

Factor	Score	Remarks
Merchandising • Appearance and quality		
• Width and depth		
• Special theme		
• Pricing strategy		
Sales Effort • Quality of sales staff		
• Number of Staff		
• Sales technique		
• Product knowledge		
Advertising and Promotion • Media used		
• Quantity and quality		
• In-store specials		
• Point-of-sale pieces		
Service offered • Delivery		
• Charge accounts		
• Credit cards		
• Post sale service		
TOTAL SCORE		

What appears to be the major factors for this store's success?

What areas can I improve on?

FIGURE 3-4
WORKSHEET 1
STARTUP COSTS
CAPITAL NEEDED TO LAUNCH A BUSINESS

Item	Dollar Cost	Source of Information
1. Down payment on existing business or franchise fee		Seller or franchisor.
2. Initial inventory		The wholesalers, suppliers or retail contacts will help you estimate this figure. You may get a 60–90 day dating to pay the initial inventory, but you should keep these funds in reserve, so that you don't jeopardize credit.
3. Leasehold improvements		The amount to "build out" your location or improve the existing space. Contractors or lessor will help in determining this cost.
4. Fixtures and other equipment		Fixture suppliers will help estimate this expense.
5. Deposits Rent Telephone Utilities Sales Tax Others		Check with utility companies, Chamber of Commerce and city offices to determine what is required.
6. Store and Office e.g. Stationery, Cleaning supplies, etc.		Suppliers will provide costs.
7. Licenses, permits, corporate filing fees		Check with city offices and attorney for these costs.
8. Legal, accounting, insurance costs.		Check with the appropriate individuals to estimate costs.
9. Grand opening advertising and promotion campaign		Check with media for estimate of costs and suggestions on a plan.
10. Staff (payroll)		Estimate the cost of staff prior to opening to accomplish set-up.
11. Cash contingency and other unlisted costs		Establish a cash reserve for unforeseen expenses — at least 10% of the above costs.
TOTAL		

FIGURE 3-4 CONTINUED
WORKSHEET 2
RESERVE FOR OPERATING EXPENSE

Estimate the monthly cost for each major expense. Then multiply that amount by the **factor** to determine what is needed for a capital reserve.

Expense Item	Estimated Monthly Costs	Existing Bus. or Franchise		New Business	
		Multiplier Factor	Dollars	Multiplier Factor	Dollars
Salary (staff)	7,500	2	15,000	3	22,500
Salary (owner)	2,100	1	2,100	2	4,200
Payroll taxes	766⁰⁰	1	766	2	1522
Rent	1500	1	1500	2	3000
Advertising	1,000	2	2000	3	3,000
Utilities	485	1	485	2	900
Telephone	120	1	120	2	240
Auto expense	85	1	85	2	170
Travel and Entertainment	100	1	100	2	200
Bad debt	20	1	20	2	40
Office and store supplies	165	1	165	2	330
Interest and principle on debt	2,700	2	5,400	3	8,100
Others		2		3	
TOTAL			27,750		55,000

How Much Money Will You Need?

Today it will cost you $25,000 to $50,000, or more, to open a successful bicycle shop or, for that matter, almost any other establishment. To start a business that has a reasonable chance of prospering will cost money. There is virtually no way of avoiding that start-up cost. Statistics show that businesses that are begun for $10,000 or less have a much higher rate of failure. The question then becomes, "How much?"

If you plan to open a retail operation, you will find two worksheets (Figure 3-4) that will help you determine the initial costs in opening your store. Similar worksheets can be developed for other types of businesses. It may be difficult, if not impossible to calculate these numbers now. But as you get closer to a firm commitment, you will have a better perspective of each actual cost—both opening expenses and initial operating costs. The sources for these figures can be other retailers, suppliers, and industry statistics.

If there is any area where you should attempt to use *conservative realism*, it is this one. If you underestimate your costs, you set yourself up for some rather stressful times. Insufficient capital is ranked high on the list of reasons for business failure. I am certain that if you questioned those entrepreneurs who failed because of this reason, they would all admit they grossly underestimated their costs of going into business.

If you find, after careful study, that you don't have enough capital to open the business of your dreams, don't be discouraged and quit. Many people have opened operations below their original expectations, gained the experience and a degree of success, and then relocated, or even opened up a second location.

While developing these estimates, pay particular attention to the amount needed to service any loans. Frequently an optimistic entrepreneur will accurately determine all of the costs, but neglect to consider the debt costs which must be paid out of profits.

In all fairness, many entrepreneurs open their businesses on a "shoestring." This book will even outine ways to do it. However, you must consider, as you *leverage* yourself into a business with a low initial investment, your *risk* factor becomes much greater.

Will Your Potential Business Make A Profit

Remember the key question. Will the business make money? At some point you must attempt to answer it. Unfortunately, the question is not easy to answer, either before you open or in the initial stages of operation. Determining whether a potential business will be profitable involves *estimating* a large number of unknowns—sales, gross profit, expenses, and so on. For the most part your initial estimates will be educated guesses, arrived at by questioning people already in the business. If you plan to buy an existing business or franchise, the task will be somewhat easier.

However, it is important to note, once you become an entrepreneur, you will be dealing with numbers. Welcome to business accounting. If that makes you feel uncomfortable, consider taking a crash course in small business accounting or hiring a qualified accountant or bookkeeper. There's simply no way out of becoming involved with the financial aspects of your business. You can have the most successful concept, but if you don't monitor the numbers, you may quickly be out of business.

As you read the following chapters, you will obtain a better perspective of the financial aspects of owning your own operation. In Chapter 9 you will see examples of financial statements prepared buy an entrepreneur buying an existing business. These statements include a projected profit-and-loss statement, and cash-flow forecast.

Still, the most important factors that will determine whether you ultimately make money, relate to whether you select a genuine business opportunity (*the concept*), pick the right community (*location*), are adequately financed (*capital*), and learn the business quickly (*experience*). Cover those bases and you have an excellent chance of starting a successful business.

Chapter 4
Starting From Scratch

It doesn't matter what industry or what specific business area you select, you will find people launching new operations on a daily basis. Just look around . . . you'll immediately see new stores, service businesses, and small manufacturing operations that weren't there last year. Expanding market opportunities and changing consumer trends are the driving factors that entice prospective entrepreneurs to start a business from scratch. You observe it mose vividly in the neighborhood retail shopping centers. There's a new croissant bakery, video rental outlet, computer store, and athletic shoe retailer. Magnify that by the new service businesses that are starting in office complexes; consulting practices, graphic designers, auto leasing agents . . . the list is endless.

It is estimated that over half a million *new* businesses are started annually and the figure has been growing each year. However, it is important to note the task is not getting into business—that's comparatively easy, the real objective is to *stay* in business and make it profitable.

This chapter will discuss the pros and cons of starting a business from scratch. The following two chapters will cover buying an existing business and purchasing a franchise. After evaluating these three options, you'll have a much better idea on how to start your entrepreneurial journey.

Advantages and Disadvantages

Let's begin by examining the advantages and disadvantages of starting a business from scratch.

Advantages

1. You begin with *your* concept of the business. You are not hampered by someone else's problems, image, or outmoded equipment.

2. You have the opportunity to pick your location and name, as well as to select new equipment, fixtures, and inventory.

3. You have the freedom to recruit, hire and train your own staff. You do not inherit problem employees.

4. You do not pay for someone else's good will or a franchise fee for the name and concepts.

5. You have a real sense of accomplishment and reward, seeing a vision fulfilled; it's a real challenge creating something from nothing.

Disadvantages

1. You must create all of the parts from scratch (marketing, accounting, purchasing, merchandising). This frequently involves costly trial and error.

2. You must build the business first, to a break-even point, then to a profit level from a dead start. This normally takes considerable time and costs a lot of money.

3. The process of getting started—finding a location, designing a layout, selecting fixtures and inventory—is a difficult task, particularly if you are inexperienced.

4. Obtaining product lines and establishing suppliers for a new operation is time-consuming and often frustrating.

5. Starting costs are usually "up-front" and very few lenders are willing to extend credit to new business owners.

Why Do People Do It?

All things being considered, starting a business from scratch is usually more *difficult* and contains a *higher* level of risk. When you purchase an ongoing business or invest in a franchise, you avoid a number of the initial problems and minimize the entrepreneurial risk factors. Essentially you are buying someone else's track record. You usually bypass the expensive and time-consuming process of building a business up to a profit level. Nevertheless, many aspiring entrepreneurs start their operation from scratch. Considering all the inherent risks . . . why? Well, there are a number of valid reasons.

Perhaps you have looked around attempting to find a business to buy, and they are either too expensive, too run-down, or often too little upside potential. Your options then become limited. If you can't find the "perfect" business to buy, then you're forced to start your own.

What if you found the type of business you would be interested in running and your area doesn't seem to have one. Your only choice is to start one.

You may have worked in a particular industry for a period of time and justifiably feel you could run a similar business as good as your boss. You know the opportunity exists; it's simply a matter of getting up the courage to step out on your own.

Or, you may simply be unwilling to pay for someone else's inflated perception of good will (the value in a business over and above the market value of the tangible assets). Some business owners set unrealistically high prices on their operation. Even if the business is profitable, a new owner must be able to purchase it at a realistic price in order that he or she can make a fair salary plus a return on investment. Otherwise, it may be more advantageous and less expensive to take your capital and start from scratch.

Becoming Prepared

To have a better than even chance at succeeding at a start-up, you must recognize there is work to be done . . . *homework!* You must be far better prepared to run a new business, than an on-going one. The pre-business preparation—indepth marketing analysis, location evaluation—must be done with care. Making a mistake prior to starting, by selecting a poor site or an unmarketable concept, will doom the venture before it has a chance to get off the ground.

The personal attributes of *patience* and *realism* will play a major role in the process. If an entrepreneur rushes into business without exploring all of the problems, the results will usually be disastrous.

Being able to realistically view a potential business opportunity without having one's ego get in the way will also help considerably. Reality is: it will normally take a year or two to make a profit; the problems of getting the business on track will be greater than one expects; and the costs will normally exceed projections. If these conditions are factored into the entrepreneurial process and you have the expertise and capital necessary to successfully launch the business, then starting from scratch may offer the *best* alternative.

Profile of a Startup Entrepreneur

Are the entrepreneurs who start a business from the ground up any different? I believe they are. Of course, there are those who start a business and are somewhat naive to the process. They blindly go forward and learn as they go. Some are successful; most are not. However, the profile of the entrepreneur who approaches the start-up business venture with realism appears to have certain similar characteristics.

They seem to be more *risk-oriented.* They are willing to take chances. Yet, the major factor that will contribute to their future success relates to their *judgment.* If they accurately evaluate the upside potentials against the downside risks, and proceed accordingly, the results will be favorable. Therefore, it's not just the willingness to take a chance; but it's the ability to properly assess the risk factors involved in the decision.

Experience is another characteristic that improves one's chance of being a successful start-up. Specific experience in the particular business is the most helpful. Still, having related experience can be equally valuable. In other words, if you successfully managed a retail clothing firm, you probably would be able to handle a stationery store or shoe store. If you have successfully supervised people in one type of business, the parallels will be there in virtually all types of business. Similarly, if you have successfully sold a product or service, you probably will be able to duplicate your sales expertise in your own business.

The problem arises, however, when you start a business that involves activities that you previously never experienced. That learning process can be very expensive and time-consuming.

Starting a business also requires considerable *creative imagination.* You must be able to visualize the concept and see how all the multiple parts come together. A business, no matter how small, is a very complex undertaking. Those that are successful in start-ups are able to plan almost every detail. Beforehand they seem to have a vision of how everything will work, it is only a matter of activating the process.

The start from scratch businessperson is also a *take-charge* type. A number of major decisions have to be made along the way, most involving money. You simply can't be timid about decision-making. Time is of the essence. The faster the project can be put together and up and running, the faster the money will flow in. (However, it does pay to be cautious.)

Yes, it does take a special person to start a business from scratch. Some say it's mostly luck if you are successful. I personally think the harder and smarter you work, the luckier you get. Starting a start-up definitely involves working hard and working smart.

Two Real Life Success Stories

Perhaps the best way to illustrate what it takes to start a business from scratch is to relate the experiences of two successful entrepreneurs.

John's (not his real name) story began in the mid-1970s when the cutback in the aerospace program left a number of engineers high and dry. He recognized immediately it would take time to find another managerial position in his field. While he sent out his resumes, he simultaneously started thinking about an entrepreneurial future. At a social gathering, almost in passing, someone commented . . . "What is really needed is a good dog collar and leash . . . made out of nylon, dogs have a tendency to eat the leather ones. John had some previous experience with nylon as part of the aerospace industry. He decided to take a preliminary look at the market. His first step was to evaluate the products presently being offered. He saw an opportunity existed for a better quality product.

His first dozen collars were made in his kitchen over the stove (the nylon had to be melted to form a bond). He took these "prototypes" to a local pet shop. They purchased all twelve. Back to the kitchen—more melting nylon over the stove—more sales. Before he knew it, he had two part time ladies working in his home making nylon collars and leashes, while he was out calling on and selling to an ever-expanding group of customers.

Nine years later, John is still in business. He now owns two companies with combined sales of over half a million dollars. Because of an extremely attractive cost control program, he is able to personally net 20% on sales. Not bad!

The growth and success of John's small but very profitable business highlights a number of start-from-scratch entrepreneurial principles.

1. He was patient, cautious and controlled in every aspect of his business. When you first start a business the pennies count. And when it's your own business, they always count.

2. He did his homework and created a "better product." In order to pull business away from your competitors, you have to have a better concept, product, or service; and then you must work harder just to get noticed.

3. He controlled his growth by doing everything himself before he delegated it to others. Small start-ups normally do not have the luxury of large staffs, therefore you must be willing to do every job, perhaps for quite a while.

4. He plowed everything back into the business. He actually didn't take a salary for the first year and took only a modest one for the next three years. Startups are very seldom instant money-makers and require reinvestment to reach profitability.

The next example of a successful start-from-scratch business involves the story of Pete (not his real name) and his convenience store. Pete is probably one of the most savvy small business owners I know. He's been in retail most of his adult life and owned a successful chain of four specialty stores. One of his stores was situated in a downtown shopping mall in a rather poor location. When an opening became available in a much more desirable space, Pete jumped at the chance and moved his store. Unfortunately, he wasn't able to sublease his old space. Paying rent on both locations was creating a cash flow problem.

Someone mentioned, again almost in passing, "What this mall needs is a convenience store." Pete thought about the concept, visited a number of franchise convenient stores, and finally made the decision to open "The General Store". It was an instant success! Now the shoppers, mall employees and nearby office workers were able to buy candy, soft drinks, magazines, cold remedies, snacks, cigarettes, etc. He even opened a deli and sells over a hundred sandwiches a day. He's making more bottom-line in his General Store than his larger specialty store. It's become a six hundred square foot money machine. The real accomplishment is he did it with an investment of $7,000. The fixtures were used, the suppliers financed the inventory, and the lease-hold improvements were in place.

What entrepreneurial principles does this example point out?

1. He saw an opportunity and took the risks. In the first few weeks that the store was opened hardly a day went by that someone didn't say they had thought about the concept and knew it would work. Did they try to sublease his space? No! He took the chance.

2. He had the experience . . . not in making deli sandwiches, but in running a small retail business. He simply hired the folks to do the specific jobs.

3. He didn't risk everything. Starting out with the least investment possible will not always create success. However, when you start from scratch, be extremely careful before you put your last dollar into an unproven venture.

4. He had a vision before the first fixture was put in place. He did his homework. He visited literally a dozen convenience stores, extracting the best of each and formulating a plan. Know what

you want and what will work before committing your resources.

Researching a Potential Business

Just how much can you learn about a business you're considering? A lot! However, you must be willing to do some legwork. In order to determine the validity of that premise, I undertook an actual preliminary market evaluation on my own. I decided to find out whether it was feasible to start from scratch in the retail athletic shoe business. I selected this field because of its dynamic growth in recent years. It appeared that every time you turned around another new store was opening up, catering to the "jocks of the world". Quite frankly, I didn't think that there were that many avid runners. Still, business must be good because I have yet to see one of the stores close.

Using the questionnaire in Chapter 2 (Questions to ask people in the business), I interviewed two store owners, a sales manager with a major shoe and sportswear line and a buyer for a chain of franchise stores. This took approximately ten hours. After the third interview I really wasn't learning new information, but verifying and validating what had already been said. It was both an interesting and informative experience. I cannot encourage you enough to take the same approach, no matter what business you select. The individuals I spoke with were very cooperative, open and knowledgeable. If you approach people asking for their help, you'll be amazed at the information they will provide with very little reservation.

Following is a recap of the major points—I had actually over 15 pages of notes as a result of the interviews. My major objective was to determine whether or not the retail athletic shoe field was saturated, and if not, how to get in, and what would be the costs. Here are the conclusions, not necessarily in order of importance.

1. The total athletic shoe market is approximately 3.5 billion dollars. There are almost 4,000 retail outlets positioned specifically as "athletic shoe stores". Considerable business is also done by department stores and variety stores who also feature "price-line" shoes (less expensive, non branded).

2. Stores in enclosed regional shopping centers dominate the industry and do a major part of the total business. However, to get space in a mall you must have a track record or be part of a franchise. It also appears that the saturation point has been reached in these malls, with some having three stores exclusively selling athletic shoes.

3. Fifty percent of the customers know exactly what they want, down to the brand and style; the other fifty percent want "expert help." Therefore, a store must carry the leading brands, have an adequate stock plus have trained knowledgeable personnel to sell to the undecided customers.

4. Footlocker (Kinney Shoes, a Woolworth subsidary) has 800 stores nationwide and is the leading and innovative force in the industry. In order to increase share of market or simply maintain previous sales, they have introduced Lady Footlocker catering just to women.

5. Most customers are brand conscious. The individual motivations to purchase a specific shoe run from the "purist factor" (will only run in a certain brand) to the "fad factor" (wants to be seen in only a certain style).

6. There are actually ten or more "specialty shoes" that must be carried by a full-line store. These lines relate to the various sports—track, football, soccer, basketball, tennis, etc. The combination of brands, styles, and sizes can create a sizable inventory and logistics problem.

7. To be profitable you must turn your merchandise four times per year and generate approximately $250,000 to 350,000 in sales. The markup in shoes runs 43-46% and 50% in clothing. Therefore, to generate those sales, you need at a minimum $25-35,000 plus in inventory. Payroll (including a manager) should run no more than 12% of sales and 8-10% is much more desirable.

8. The investment for a 1400 square foot mall location, including inventory will run approximately $100-120,000. Opening a strip center location will run half the investment; but a considerable amount of money would have to be allocated to promotional activities.

9. The factors that make a store successful are—location, product mix, adequate inventory (current hot styles and sizes), and a trained staff. Very little advertising is done if the store is in a high traffic location.

10. The mortality rate of stores, although not significant, is starting to become apparent. Fewer good locations are available, chains are starting to aggressively promote, and discount outlets are starting to enter the market. The shakeout is beginning.

11. There is a "catch-22" that potentially creates an unsolvable problem. You need the major brands to be successful. The suppliers are reluctant to open new accounts, particularly to small independents. This is partly to protect their established customers, and in some cases, because of inability to presently satisfy the existing market. Therefore, a new start-up will have a difficult time getting the brands in demand, and hence be uncompetitive in the marketplace. You're essentially stopped before you start . . . or at least slowed down considerably.

There is still an opportunity to enter the athletic shoe retail market, but the window is closing rapidly. To be successful, you will have to find an *untapped niche,* unless you plan to buy a franchise or an existing store. It would be virtually impossible to go into a mall location, therefore you immediately start out with a location problem. You would have to carefully evaluate areas that have not yet attracted a store, and armed with a detailed business plan, attempt to secure a buying relationship with the key suppliers. Because of the inventory needs, you probably couldn't launch a store with less than a $50,000 investment. You would also have to have a substantial reserve to handle personal expenses, and some money earmarked for opening promotion. You could also position yourself as a specialty store (joggers only), but you would be drastically limiting your market.

What this exercise graphically points out is that there are barriers in opening any kind of business. The question that one must answer—are the barriers too formidable to overcome with the resources at hand . . . *money, time,* and *talent?*

A Strategy

If after careful consideration, you feel that starting from scratch is the way to go, then it's imperative that you formulate a working strategy. Review the following points and adapt the concepts to your specific situation. These, of course, are not infallible directives, but rather guidelines to provide a safety net approach to what will be a fairly difficult undertaking.

Select a business you understand. You can buy an existing business or a franchise and be successful in spite of not having firsthand experience in that type of operation. However, it becomes considerably more difficult if you try to start one without at least some background in the particular industry. If you haven't already acquired experience, consider working in a company similar to the one you plan to open. Even volunteer your help, but do it for more than just a week. It's much cheaper learning in their business than in your own.

Limit your initial investment. Unless you have some insider information, a start-up can be very risky. Invest only that amount of money that you're willing to lose. In all cases, avoid putting your last dollar into opening cost—you'll need working capital and a personal reserve. Attempt to use credit from suppliers, dating on fixtures, and even request the landlord to give you three months free rent.

Avoid capital-intensive businesses. Some businesses require a large initial investment—manufacturing (unless a very small shop) and wholesaling (unless it's a limited distributorship) require major capital outlays. It pays to purchase an ongoing business in those categories and let the seller finance the sale. Retail and service businesses can be started with relatively fewer dollars.

Plan on an austerity program. For at least the first couple of years, very few start-up entrepreneurs can afford large cars or large salaries. It's an accomplishment to survive. Most of the excess cash flow will be put back into the business (additional inventory, improvements and promotion) to build a more solid foundation.

Study the industry. Be diligent in your effort to study the business. Talk to as many knowledgeable people as possible, and find out precisely *what it takes* to be successful. If you lack some background, take a college course or seminar on the subject. Go to the trade shows and read back issues of the trade publications; and don't forget about the library, S.B.A., and Chamber of Commerce. You can never know too much about the business in which you plan to invest your lifesavings.

Start small. If possible, start in a small way. Put your foot in the water before you plunge in. Find out whether you like it or whether it offers potential. Then put a plan together for "controlled growth". Building a small business is like building a fireplace—one brick on top of another.

Use the copy-cat approach. Don't try to reinvent the wheel. Find out which ongoing businesses are presently successful and for what reasons. Design your business, incorporating all of the good points and eliminating the bad. It's a foregone conclusion that very little new is being created lately—just variations on a theme.

Develop a plan. It's essential that you are able to express the key elements of your start-up business in a written form. It is far less expensive to learn with pen and paper than fixtures and inventory. One wise entrepreneur told me "If you can't write a relatively detailed plan of the *who, what, when, where* and *why* along with the *how* of your new business, then you don't yet know enough about starting it."

Two Major Goals

When you enter the world of independent business, you have two major goals—one positive and one negative. First, you want to make as much money as possible, and second, you don't want to lose what you already have.

Inexperienced entrepreneurs usually fail to fully understand the negative objective. It can actually be much more important than the positive one.

A pro-golfer once said, "Golf is not a game of great shots, but one of more accurate misses . . . the one who wins makes fewer mistakes." The same analogy can be made with tennis. Chris Evert's game centers on making fewer forced errors. She outlasts her opponent by consistent, accurate baseline strokes while waiting patiently for her opponent to drive the ball in the net or out of bounds.

Most successful entrepreneurs play a percentage game—rarely taking big chances or going for the quick buck. Nowhere is that concept more valid than when you start a business from scratch. If you keep your errors to a minimum, your dollars will take care of themselves. The key to winning is avoiding the mistakes.

Chapter 5
Buying an Existing Business

Buying an existing operation is perhaps the easiest and quickest ways to get into business. And, if done correctly, it can also be the safest way to become a successful entrepreneur. When you buy an existing business, you have certain advantages over starting from scratch or buying a franchise. But, like any business venture, approach it with caution. This list shows some of the advantages and disadvantages of buying an existing business.

Advantages

1. You acquire a loyal customer base and avoid the costly and time consuming effort of building sales volume.

2. A highly motivated owner may sell to you at a bargain price.

3. You eliminate expensive trial and error mistakes associated with new start-ups.

4. You purchase a proven operation—location, sales volume, merchandising, and advertising plan.

5. The owner may provide valuable assistance. You might also acquire trained personnel, along with existing lines of credit and established sources of merchandise.

6. You may benefit from a very favorable lease, signed some time ago by the present seller.

7. The seller may help finance your purchase by "carrying paper" — something a bank may be unwilling to do.

Disadvantages

1. You may pay too much because of over-eagerness or miscalculation. Or, the seller might even misrepresent certain facts.

2. The business may come with ill-will (bad reputation), rather than with good will. This handicap could be difficult and expensive to overcome.

3. The location could be marginal or in a declining area.

4. Major competition might be entering that marketplace—something of which you are unaware.

5. You may inherit obsolete equipment or fixtures, along with outdated merchandise. Essentially, you get stuck with all the existing flaws.

6. Because of the purchase arrangement, you may be faced with some trouble-making factors, such as high monthly debt payments, or a short lease.

7. In order to be successful in the existing operation, you may have to remodel or remerchandise which could cause difficulties for you.

On balance though, particularly for an individual without experience, purchasing an existing business can be the best option. The trick is to find the right one at the right price.

Buy-Sell Process

As you begin the process of buying an existing business, you will find that it has a flow or series of steps. Within each step you will be faced with analyzing information, making decisions, and above all, staying alert. Let's begin by examining the various stages of this buy-sell process.

- *Differing Motivation.* The buyer and seller begin with very different, almost opposing, motivations. This factor alone can cause difficulty in the course of the transaction.

- *Finding the business.* The buyer must find the seller, or vice versa, to begin the process.

- *Information Gathering.* To make an informed decision, the buyer needs considerable information which the seller may not be willing or able to provide.

- *Analysis.* The buyer must analyze and evaluate the data carefully in order to make an educated decision.

- *Price and Value.* The seller sets a price. The buyer must feel that it is fair and affordable.

- *Negotiations.* This stage is necessary to resolve any differences and reach agreement.

- *Sales Contract and Takeover.* Once an agreement is reached, a contract is signed and the new owner takes over.

As you can see, this is not a simple process. Many things can go wrong, and frequently do You must be prepared to undertake an involved and time-consuming task once you start thinking about buying someone else's business. Let's begin by looking at each of these steps in greater detail. They'll provide a better grasp of what preparation you need to give yourself an *edge* in the buy-sell process.

Differing Motivations

Owning a business can be very demanding and stressful. This factor alone causes many people to consider selling. Perhaps the seller's expectations have not been fulfilled—not enough profit, too many disappointments, lack of freedom. Some sellers have decided there are other things they want to do, and they need to sell their businesses to get on with their plans. They are simply looking for change. Still others cite reasons such as health, family problems, long hours, getting too old, no one to leave it to, etc. But probably the overwhelming reason is that the business is not providing enough income and/or satisfaction. Very few owners sell money-making businesses that they enjoy.

It's important, however, for a buyer to determine whether the seller's stated reason is not a *cover up* for a serious problem affecting the business, such as a local plant layoff or a major shopping center opening up nearby.

Your motivations for buying a business may include any or all of the reasons people become entrepreneurs: independence, income, greater opportunity, escape from a frustrating job, etc. However, your motivations extend beyond the "why part" and include the "how much part." In other words, when you buy a business, you want to spend the least amount of money and have the best terms possible. The seller wants the highest sum possible and on terms perhaps quite different from what you consider reasonable.

So, we begin the buy-sell process with two parties visualizing the same transaction—the sale of a business—with different motivations, objectives, and perspectives.

Finding the Business

Finding the "right" business will take time and patience. Unless you are extremely lucky, your search may last from a couple of months to a year or more. Considering the fact that more than two million business operations change hands annually, there are plenty of sellers. It is conceivable that as much as 20 to 30 percent of all businesses are available for sale on any given day. So, how are you going to find that perfect business? Your task of selecting the business to buy will be much easier if you know what kind of operation you'll feel comfortable with.

If you have narrowed the possible choices, by going through the exercise in Chapter 2, you will know what strategy to use for finding the right business. Before you start though, keep in mind the following important points: take your time and have patience; don't jump before you thoroughly investigate, know what you want; and do your homework.

Many sellers, particularly of successful businesses, never advertise their stores for sale. These businesses are frequently sold to "insiders" (already known to the seller), or to buyers approaching them directly, or to individuals who have been put in touch with the sellers by third parties (brokers, bankers, accountants, or acquaintances). A seller may take this approach for one of many reasons. He or she may not want the employees or suppliers to know about the sale until it's over or doesn't want to be bothered by a lot of unqualified buyers and "tire kickers." Perhaps the seller has been successful and just wants to get out with the least amount of hassle. The way you are going to learn about these opportunities is to make it known that you are interested in acquiring that particular type of business.

Contact wholesalers and suppliers in that field. Explain your interest, and ask them for referrals to any operation that is or might be for sale. Talk to bankers, accountants, and other people who may have an inside track to that type of business.

Another strategy that is more aggressive, and probably will give you faster results, is to contact the owners of a business directly. You may try a slightly subtle approach, asking them if they know of any operations similar to theirs that might be for sale. If the owner is even remotely interested in selling, the dialogue will begin. In any event, since all related businesses have an effective rumor mill, a few calls on owners will usually uncover several potential possibilities.

Don't neglect the "business opportunities for sale" section of your local newspaper. This is a good place to begin. You can remain anonymous with most of the owners who are advertising. A phone call with the right questions normally will provide a wealth of information. The location, price, terms, and reasons the owner is selling, are the main points. If the situation appears promising, make an appointment to talk with the owner. Don't expect to receive a folder of information on this first visit. Most often, a seller wants to size up the buyer before providing "trade secrets" of the business. Try to meet in a quiet place, perhaps for coffee or even lunch. Get off to a good start. During the first ten minutes avoid asking penetrating questions, such as "What volume did you do last year?" Those questions will put a seller on the defensive and are more appropriate at a later time. Ask how long the business has been going, whether its been an enjoyable experience, and how the seller got into it originally. That approach shows your sensitivity and will reap rewards when the negotiations become more serious.

As another way to find a business, I'd like to relate what happened to an acquaintance of mine who decided to go into the nursery business. Although his capital was limited, he had a number of years in landscaping and was very determined, as well as enthusiastic. After surveying the market, he recognized that the two or three more successful stores were out of his price category, even if they were for sale. Searching further, he found an owner who had become somewhat disillusioned with an operation that had been sliding downhill.

He approached the owner with a fair offer, but a low down payment, explaining that he would need his cash to restock the store's inventory. Recognizing that it was time to get out, the owner accepted the offer. The buyer used his cash to remerchandise and refurbish the store and then launched an impressive advertising effort to announce the new look. Within a year the volume had increased almost 60%, and the store was ranked within the top two of that market. The new owner had invested far less then if he had purchased an existing store doing that type of higher volume.

This example highlights a number of important factors involved in buying an existing store.

- Businesses with good sales volume and profit are expensive, and normally do not come on the market. When they do, they go to insiders.

- Sellers with failing businesses will seldom see value in their operations and frequently never even consider that others might be interested in buying.

- There are signals that a business may be for sale, even if the buyer doesn't place it on the market. Look for distress signs: low inventory, sloppy store, lack of promotion and advertising, ineffective sales staff. These signs show that an owner has lost interest and may be willing to sell at an advantageous price. All you have to do is ask.

Information Gathering

After making the initial contact, the buyer and seller must determine what information about the business will be exchanged. You want as much information as possible; however the seller may be reluctant to provide everything that is requested. A working agreement must be reached early between the two parties before a serious impasse or lack of good faith develops.

Here are steps you can take to enhance your credibility as a serious buyer. Be prepared to provide the following:

1. A personal financial statement showing your capacity to handle the purchase (these forms are available at stationery stores or banks). Don't tip your hand about your cash position. Minimize it, but add the amount somewhere else to represent your true net worth.

2. A personal resume of your background and experience. A seller will feel more comfortable knowing you are qualified to run the operation.

3. A signed statement that you will not divulge any information the seller provides about the business.

With this information, the seller is more likely to present the data you need to reach a decision. This also sets a positive climate and conveys to the seller that negotiations will be a give-and-take proposition.

A word of caution—do not buy a business from a seller who is unwilling to fully *disclose* all the important aspects of the business. This indicates there are problems, probably major ones. Cut off negotiations immediately with any seller who will not furnish you with the necessary information that you request.

Occasionally you may be confronted with a situation that is typical in small businesses—the lack of adequate records, or sometimes no records at all. Statistics indicate that this problem is widespread. Approximately 25% of all small businesses do not keep adequate financial records (sales and expenses going back two to three years). Forty percent of all retailers do not take inventory. Because these individuals do not have an accurate picture of their business, you might be faced with a difficult decision. Be careful. Do more homework and lower your offering price substantially on this factor alone. If the seller can't prove it, you shouldn't believe it.

The information that you need can be summarized in three categories:

1. What has happened to the business in the past?
2. What is the present condition of the business?
3. How do the past and present provide for a favorable future?

In order to evaluate these questions, consider asking for the following data:

Sales Information. Ideally you want at least three years of sales data, with as much detail as possible—by month, by category, by sales person, etc. If this information is not readily available through sales records, it may be obtained by reviewing sales tax reports and IRS statements. Without good sales data, it is difficult to evaluate patterns or trends in order to project future sales—one of your major objectives. Be sure to verify the sales data by examining two sources.

Expenses. You must know how much money is required to operate the business: rent, payroll, advertising, etc. This type of data is typically found in profit and loss statements, but it can also be compiled by analyzing checkbooks and year-end tax statements.

Cost of Goods Sold. This information will provide you with an understanding of the operation's gross profit or margin (amount remaining to pay expenses after merchandise has been purchased). If a good set of records is not available, this information can be obtained by reviewing the invoices paid to suppliers. This data, plus the figures on expenses, indicate the general health of the business. It is imperative that you attempt to get accurate figures on both of these categories. A note of caution: a seller with two or more locations may be able to enhance the gross profit picture of one by having the other locations pay some invoices. This understates cost of goods and improves net profit—inaccurately.

Profitability. Many small businesses, particularly sole-proprietors or partnerships, do not actually generate net "profits" as such. The amount of money left after expenses becomes personal income for the owners. In order to get an accurate picture of a seller's income, you must review the individual's income tax returns. Don't be dissuaded by a seller telling you "Nobody sees my tax returns but my accountant and the IRS." If he wants to sell the business, then this information must be disclosed.

History of the Company. Ask the owner to provide you with a written recap of the company from its beginning—the principals involved; major events that have affected sales trends, either up or down; advertising campaigns and their results; customer profile and marketing information; suppliers and their strengths and weaknesses; employees; legal status of the company; banking relationship; and any problems that you should be aware of. Receiving this information in writing provides you with documentation, in case any questions crop up later. If, after the sale, unexpected situations arise, you may be able to use this written record to substantiate any legal claims. It also gives you a reference point to focus on during in-depth discussions with the seller.

What You Are Buying. You want to know what assets you are buying and for what price. In the Contract-of-Sale this information will be necessary for tax and depreciation purposes. During the early stages of discussion, you want a list of assets.

Start by asking the seller for a list of all items that constitute the "assets" of the business. These will include:

- *Inventory.* All of the saleable stock quoted at cost.
- *Leasehold improvements.* Interior and exterior improvements made to a leased premises (walls, floor covering, lights, air conditioner, etc.).
- *Fixtures.* Shelving, counters, displays, etc.
- *Equipment and signs.* Cash register, adding machines, safe, desks, signs, machinery, etc.
- *Delivery vans or trucks.*
- *Real estate.* Seller may decide to retain ownership and lease it back to the buyer.
- *Accounts receivable.*
- *Supplies.*

Note: In order to gain a better perspective of buying someone's existing business, including the current tax aspects, be sure to read Chapters 13 through 18 on selling a business.

The Lease

The lease is one of the most important ingredients of a business Frequently, a seller is unaware that he or she must receive consent from the landlord to sell the business, and this may become a major problem. So find out very early in the discussions the particulars on the lease. You will want to know:

1. Is the lease transferable/assignable?
2. Does the lease have to be renegotiated? If so, on what terms?
3. What are the terms of the remaining lease?
4. Is there a renewal option?
5. Is it a percentage lease, and if so, how is it calculated?
6. Is the lease triple-net (lessee pays all costs, including taxes, insurance, and common-area maintenance)?
7. Are there any unusual "use clauses" (things you can or cannot do)?

Unless you get favorable answers to these questions, you may be exploring an unsaleable business. It is the seller's responsibility to provide these answers. However, the landlord may want to investigate you before giving final approval. The point is, do not get into extensive negotiations without clarification of the seller's lease situation.

What About Price

I think *price* is the most emotionally charged factor in the sale of a business. As the buyer and seller go through the process, each sees price from a totally different perspective. The seller thinks, "How much is the business really worth? What price should I set? What terms should I accept? How much will I have to come down?"

Initially the buyer thinks, "That's a lot of money for that business! I wonder if I can afford it? Is it worth it? What problems am I really buying? How much can I get the seller to reduce the price? Where am I going to get the extra money?"

Before negotiating price with a seller, consider some of the following points. You will see price can be a very illusive element of the sale.

- Most sellers determine the initial price *arbitrarily* and have few solid reasons to substantiate their figures.

- There is *no* scientific way to determine price.

- The price has three components: *down payment, terms, security.*

- In good times, businesses sell for *more;* during recessions, they sell for *less.* Timing is important.

- Motivation on the part of the buyer or seller (how badly the individual wants to get in or out) has profound effect on the price.

- Negotiating *advantages* go to the best informed and the best prepared.

Price may be established in a variety of ways. Some owners attempt to set value by using what are referred to as *multipliers.* These "rule of thumb" factors often simplify what appears to be a complex task. For example, some claim that a liquor store usually sells for three to four times monthly gross, plus the inventory at cost. Or, a gift store sells for from two to five times its monthly gross, plus inventory.

Certain multiplier formulas even consider after-tax profit, rather than gross sales figures. The rule of thumb, for pricing a retail store is: three to ten times annual after-tax earnings, plus the inventory at cost.

Whether you use sales or profit multipliers, the spread from the high to low is considerable. Furthermore, since many small businesses show little actual profit (for tax purposes), the profitability multiplier is virtually useless. If you are confronted with a seller using a multiplier, consider it only a ballpark estimate at best. There is no magic to multipliers!

Another often used benchmark for establishing a price, is *book value.* Book value is simply the difference between the company's assets and liabilities or, stated another way, its *net worth* (this figure shows up on the balance sheet). The problem in using this approach is that fixed assets (leasehold improvements and fixtures) are shown at their depreciated value. This may differ greatly from what the assets are actually worth (what you would pay to replace or duplicate them). Replacement costs essentially establish an asset's real value. Still, the ratio that is normally used to establish a business's value ranges between one and two times book value. To show how inconsistent this method can be, consider the example of the successful business owner in operation for seven years, who has depreciated the fixed assets down to zero. These assets may still be in good shape, therefore using a book value ratio to determine price would be out of question in this situation.

Perhaps a better way to evaluate whether a business is priced right, is to look at its *Potential Earning Power,* or P.E.P. Earning power includes profit, but it also takes into consideration the income the owner can make, plus any fringe benefits (car, medical insurance, travel, and other perks). In order to effectively evaluate a business's P.E.P., you must have *full disclosure*—an honest set of books—from the owner. Although many businesses have been known to take money under the table, be skeptical. If the seller attempts to convince you that you are going to make a fortune by not ringing up sales, he can't prove it. You may find later that it was only a ploy to persuade you to buy the business. Consider only those dollars that can be supported by deposits and cancelled checks from a bank account. If you're really interested in the operation, ask the seller who skims to run it "straight" for a couple of months, and at that point you may be willing to resume negotiations.

Once you have a grasp on the store's P.E.P., consider whether anything will change once you take over. Is there any way you can increase earnings? Be realistic. Consider what expenses will decrease, and which ones will increase. If this "adjusted" earning power is high enough to cover your income, plus expenses and any debt service, then you may have a viable business opportunity. To consider how much the business is worth and how much you should pay for it, you must go through a few more steps. First, calculate what you are presently earning and what you expect to earn in the near future. Anything above that figure that the business can generate is a key to its earning power. If that number is significant, then the business has real value and can demand a high price.

To further examine the earning-power approach, consider this analysis: As an owner of a small retail store, you will have to shoulder a variety of jobs: salesperson, buyer, merchandiser, controller, etc. If you were working for someone else, doing that same work, what would your salary be? If, for example, you consider your work worth $25,000, then you should require your prospective business to pay you that amount. Whether you actually take that much or more is not relevant at this moment.

Furthermore, a business should pay more than just a salary to the owner. After all, you have the right to receive a return on your investment (ROI). You also have taken on some sizable risks that wouldn't be part of a salaried job. Your hope is, that the investment will provide you the opportunity to improve your income, and eventually to sell the business and make a sizable profit.

A business, priced right, should enable you to get your investment back in five years. Put another way, you should expect a 20 percent or more annual return on your money, plus a fair salary. Otherwise, consider putting your capital in a nice safe T-bill and get a good job that pays well, without the inherent risks of owning a business.

In reality, you will probably use the return on investment money (anything above your salary), to pay off obligations to the seller or lenders—assuming you don't pay cash for the business. After eventually paying off the debt you will own the business free and clear and then you can sell it and retire!

To gain further perspective on the worth of the business, consider its *duplication factor*. What would it cost you to set up a similar business in a comparable location? Some experts say you should never pay much more for a business than it would cost to start from scratch. This duplication-cost factor will provide additional insight into the value of the business. Essentially, you are buying someone else's assets, rather than going out and starting from the ground up. This is another case of trade-offs. The downside is that you may be purchasing an aging business, questionable image, and antiquated stock. The upside is that you may get proven sales and profit. In this instance, you could also figure in what it would cost to build that business up to its current sales level and profitability.

Another major consideration in pricing a business is the *method of payment*. If a seller is willing to take back a note for a considerable part of the purchase price, then the value of the business to you may increase. There's an inverse relationship between down payment and price. In other words, as the down payment goes lower, the value goes higher, as illustrated in the following chart.

Down Payment	Percent of Fair Market Value
No Cash Down	150%
10%	125%
20–30%	100%
above 40%	80%
all cash	60%

For example, if the down payment is 20-30 percent of the purchase price then the price should be *fair market value*. About three out of four business sales are within that range. If a seller wants all cash, the selling price may be as low as 60% of fair market value. If you have *cash* and want to invest it in your own business, you can do some strong negotiating on price.

The same type of relationship exists with terms. The longer a seller is willing to extend payment and the lower the interest rate, then the more value is added to the business. These unwritten rules are simply based on the principle of supply and demand. As a seller reduces total price or down payment and lengthens the term of the loan, more buyers qualify and become attracted to the situation.

Although the following points are not etched in granite, they do seem to be norms of small business sales that you can negotiate from:

1. Most small businesses can be purchased with 25% down and the seller carrying the paper.

2. The interest rate charged on notes is slightly lower than current bank rates.

3. The length of these notes can vary between 5 and 7 years on a loan with straight principle/plus interest payments, or occasionally can be paid with interest only (calculated on an amortized schedule of 25 to 30 years) but with a balloon payment of the entire amount at 5 years.

4. Security for the note is usually the business, although sellers are often able to get security other than the business.

Don't be afraid to negotiate any or all of these variables. As the old saying goes: "If you can't talk price, talk terms." The main thing to be sure of is that the *cash flow* is adequate to cover the *debt service,* plus your *salary.* If you buy a business which can't accomplish that, you will find yourself in a long-term or perhaps short-term losing situation.

To summarize, essentially the right price is what a willing buyer will pay a willing seller, at a given point in time. It also relates to supply and demand. Good businesses are in demand, and the supply is limited. You can find a large number of losing businesses, and you may be able to buy them cheap. But can you turn them around fast enough to support you and your family, plus pay debt service? There's nothing wrong with buying a business that is shopworn or slightly rundown. If you know what you are doing, you can breathe life back into it. However, approach these businesses carefully. Be sure you have a proven method to revitalize the profit, plus an adequate backup position to cover any negative cash flow. Don't just do it because you think you have a "better personality." (See Chapter 15 for a thorough explanation on valuing a business.)

Negotiations

Rarely, is a business sold for the original price and terms. Negotiations, sometimes lengthy, establish a more mutually agreeable position between buyer and seller. It is important for you to try to establish from the outset a positive negotiating posture. You may not be interested in acquiring a lifetime friend, but it helps to create a favorable atmosphere so that you avoid defensive, ego positions that might derail the negotiations completely. These do's and don'ts you should keep in mind during your discussions.

Do's

Try to determine, as early as possible, how anxious the owner is to sell the business. If you understand the level of motivation and the reasons behind the decision to sell, it will help you in your negotiating position. If the seller is burnt out or must sell for personal reasons, there may be significant price concessions. On the other hand, if the seller is simply testing the water to see if somebody is willing to pay a high price for the business, you may be wasting your time.

Attempt to deal with the person actually making the decision. If you must deal with an attorney or accountant, your negotiations will be more complicated and prolonged. The same strategy applies to you. You should take a personal role in the negotiations. When you personally meet the seller, it will be the rapport you establish that frequently makes the deal come together. If you find that there is virtually no positive chemistry between you and the seller and you still feel strongly about the business, bring in a third party to assist in the process (an attorney, accountant, broker, or even a qualified friend).

Be sure to keep control over your attorney and accountant. These professionals sometimes like to make things more complicated, or they look for flaws simply to justify their position, and perhaps their fees. Certainly, your attorney and accountant are there to protect your interest and also aid you in the task of buying the business. Nevertheless, ask them upfront to facilitate the purchase, not look for ways to kill it.

Be patient. If you start to move too quickly, you tend to increase suspicion. Selling a privately owned business tends to be a rather personal experience. The owner may have a good deal of ego wrapped up in the operation. If you try to rush the process, you may find the seller resisting or even cancelling negotiations. On the other hand, unnecessary delays can cause the same result. The best way to avoid either of these complications is to set deadlines for certain things to be accomplished. If you find that the seller is consistently unable to meet reasonable timetables for providing financial information or drafts of contracts, you may have to cut off negotiations and look for another business opportunity.

While discussing the sale, pick a quiet place and let the seller do the talking. Listen for signals such as eagerness or contradictions. If a seller talks long enough, the individual tends to reveal important aspects about the business.

Don'ts

Don't make unreasonable offers. The delicacy of the negotiation process is put in jeopardy when the buyer presents a ridiculous offer. It is essential that fairness and reasonableness become the ground rules for a serious negotiation. The hard feelings that occur when people become unreasonable tend to destroy trust and create a tense atmosphere. The seller frequently becomes hard nosed and refuses to negotiate. If you really think that the price is excessive, say so. Ask the seller to *justify* the figure by giving you a detailed breakdown of the business assets, with specific values attached to each. Frequently this exercise will bring some reality into the situation, and the overall price can be negotiated more easily.

While investigating a business, don't be bashful. Spend time around the business. Talk to suppliers, and if the seller doesn't have any objections, chat with employees and even customers. You want to be well informed. There should not be any major *surprises* after you take over a business.

Don't make changes in the seller's business until it is yours. You may see a number of improvements that might increase profits, but if you provide this information two things can happen: the seller may take your advice, implement the changes, and keep the business; or more realistically, the seller may be insulted. A bruised ego can have serious repercussions in the negotiation process. The best way to deal with a seller is to be humble without appearing to be naive. Recognize the seller's expertise and experience, which may in fact be the case. Frequently, sellers are often very helpful to new buyers, staying on temporarily after the sale to assist in the transition. Making a seller feel knowledgable and important doesn't in any way reduce your status and may help create the rapport necessary to favorably conclude the sale.

No one said it would be easy buying a going business. Most businesses that you investigate will have flaws. If they didn't, they probably would not be for sale, or their prices would be astronomical. After exploring at least a few operations, you will start to develop a sense of *awareness*. You will begin to understand the subtle differences that make one business an opportunity and another a potential disaster.

Also be aware that some people make a career of looking for "just the right business" and never seem to locate it. Don't fall into the trap of having to find the perfect business. It doesn't exist. Do a careful job of evaluation. Follow the checklists. Be patient and select the one that makes the most sense. Then go to work making it an even more successful operation.

FIGURE 5-2
A STRATEGY FOR TAKING OVER AN EXISTING BUSINESS

1. Find out those areas of the business that are critical and learn them quickly.
2. If it is a successful business, make changes slowly — one move at a time.
3. Keep a relatively low profile until you know what's happening — don't let your ego as the "new owner", create conflict.
4. Pick the greatest problems and solve them first — prioritize.
5. Create a written plan and a timetable.
6. Immediately speak with employees to relieve any concern.
7. Ask for employee's feedback, but be careful not to lose control by allowing them too much control.
8. Listen to the owner — he or she has lived the business.
9. Ask the owner to stay for a short time, but on your terms, so if problems occur you can exercise your option.
10. Listen to customers — they are the ones you want to please.
11. Contact suppliers and begin to establish a favorable working relationship.
12. Don't change the name, at least initially.
13. Don't spend all your cash at once. After you know the business better, you'll be able to spend it wisely.
14. Immediately set about creating pride and enthusiasm within the business. Transfer your excitement about owning the business to the staff and they will help you make it prosper!

FIGURE 5-1
CHECKLIST
PURCHASING AN ESTABLISHED BUSINESS

This checklist provides a series of questions you should attempt to answer prior to buying an established business.

1. What trend shows up in the historical sales figures? Why?
2. How has the business done relative to the overall market?
3. After the sale will there be any problems with the established customers?
4. Are the product prices competitive?
5. Will I be able to improve cost of goods by taking additional discounts?
6. What will my fixed expenses be?
7. Can I reduce any of the operating expenses?
8. What were the previous owner's salary and personal expenses?
9. Are my profitability expectations realistic?
10. Will I be able to support myself and also pay debts?
11. What problems has the owner had, and will I have to deal with them?
12. Does the business have a good reputation and a loyal customer clientele?
13. Why is the seller actually selling?
14. Can I afford the price and terms?
15. Can the price be reduced or restructured?
16. Is the business worth the price?
17. Is the inventory saleable?
18. How much of the inventory constitutes a problem?
19. Will the seller reduce the price based on questionable inventory?
20. Is the lease assumable?
21. Is the lease long enough?
22. Will I have to make major improvements in the business? If so what will it cost?
23. What will be my cash position after taking over the business? Will it be adequate?
24. Will the suppliers work with me? On what credit terms?
25. Will I have major expenses in an opening promotion to build the business, and/or win old customers back?
26. Considering all the pluses and minuses, is the risk worth the investment?
27. What is the outcome if the business reaches its realistic potential?
28. Is that outcome satisfactory for both me and my family?
29. Do I have enough money to handle all the "worst case" situations that could come up?
30. Will I enjoy running this type of business?
31. Will the seller provide me any help and instruction in the early stages?
32. Will the employees stay?

Chapter 6
Buying a Franchise

Before starting this chapter, I should tell you that early in my entrepreneurial career, I was involved in two separate franchise operations—neither worked out well. In each case, I purchased the franchise with the intention of becoming a successful, independent businessman. Within six months I had, with some difficulty, extracted myself from the first franchise. I then purchased a second and was out within a year, vowing never again to enter the franchise world, yet here I am attempting to write objectively about the subject. Well, no one can say that I haven't had first-hand experience and a fairly good understanding of the pitfalls of franchising.

I was also very fortunate. I didn't lose money. That's unique if you have an unsuccessful relationship with a franchise operation. The major causes of my problems were overambitious franchisors, and a somewhat naive franchisee—me! The promise and expectations never materialized. Remember, this happened in 1970 and since then, government agencies have stepped in to the picture to help monitor the practices of franchisors. Nevertheless, when you consider a franchise opportunity, you must add an extra dimension to your entrepreneurial investigation process. You must not only be sure that the business itself is what you want, but you must also be certain that the franchisor and the package are right. That research takes extra time and effort, therefore be prepared.

One last comment before we begin. Let me assure you that I am not negative about franchising in general. There are some very successful franchise operations. The direction of this chapter is not to try to disillusion you. To the contrary, for certain people starting in business, a franchise offers significant advantages. I hope that you will derive from this chapter a *realistic* view of franchising, which may help you objectively evaluate the persuasive "pitch" of a franchisor.

What Is Franchising?

Essentially, franchising is a method by which you can buy a prepackaged business concept, operate it under a contract, and receive future services for a fee. Although franchising doesn't automatically guarantee financial success, it does provide a major reduction in risk. And risk reduction is probably its major appeal. Someone else (the franchisor) has removed much of the trial and error associated with small business ventures and has created a "proven concept". In addition, franchisors improve your chances of success by providing training, site selection, store design, and a plan to run and manage your operation. So, why doesn't every prospective entrepreneur jump into franchising? Well, it's usually expensive and you, as the franchisee, are not truly independent. Nevertheless, franchising appears to be booming today.

There are now over 2,000 different individual franchise operations in the U.S. These franchisors have, in total, over half a million outlets and generate 34% of all retail sales. This market share has increased from only 23% ten years ago. As you can see, franchising is making a major impact on today's business landscape, as evidenced by the large number of fast food outlets along every city's and town's main street.

Franchising actually came into existence shortly after the Civil War when the Singer Sewing Machine Co. licensed its products to independent outlets. The modern form of franchising was initiated at the turn of the century by automobile manufacturers. Gasoline service stations followed suit and a number of other distributorships and license arrangements developed. Today, you can purchase a Coca Cola distributorship or a day care center, and the contractual format will be similar. Certainly, every conceivable form of retail and service business has one or many franchises available.

Franchising has not always enjoyed such an aura of success. The industry's image was severely tarnished during the late 60's and 70's (when I was in it . . . poor timing!). At that point, franchising was unregulated. Fraudulent operators and fast-buck artists took advantage of operating in wide-open climate. In addition, a number of well-meaning franchisors created concepts that were ill-planned and poorly financed. The result was a major shakeout during 1969-1972. Hundreds of companies and their franchisees went bankrupt, putting the entire concept in jeopardy. Subsequently, a number of states have passed franchise laws, and the federal government, through the Federal Trade Commission, established comprehensive regulations covering franchise offerings and practices.

Today, as a prospective investor in a franchise, you will have a number of built-in safeguards; but it still takes considerable effort and selectivity on your part to pick the right company. As the key to success in retailing is "Location, location, location", the key to success in franchising is "Investigation, Investigation, Investigation".

Advantages and Disadvantages

The following paragraphs list some of the advantages or disadvantages of buying a franchise, compared to starting from scratch or buying an existing independent business:

Advantages

1. You reduce your risk of possible failure. Notice the word, "reduce". You do not eliminate the chance of failure. Many franchisees will attest to the fact that buying a franchise doesn't guarantee success or riches. Unfortunately, franchises do not eliminate all of the potential pitfalls that lead to business failure. They merely improve your chances of success by providing an established or "proven" business concept. Industry statistics show that the failure rate of franchises is now down to approximately 2 to 4 percent of total businesses started.

Considering that as many as 50% of small business owners cease operation within a few years, these figures demonstrate a major risk-reduction factor.

2. You receive training and a blueprint for operating your business. Many people venturing into business for the first time feel intimidated by their lack of knowledge or experience. A franchise provides a bridge. Frequently, it's a crash course involving two to three weeks, and as most experienced franchisees tell you, their real education came through "on the job experience". In fairness, the franchise does provide a formula, and you minimize costly trial and error blunders which can be very costly.

3. You identify yourself with a recognized name. Many franchises are small and lack national recognition. These operations may offer an operational concept, but the real value of franchising comes with name recognition. When McDonald's opens another location, unless you have spent the last 20 years on the dark side of the moon, you know you can get a Big Mac inside; and you probably know exactly what it's going to taste like.

Disadvantages

1. Lack of control and personal imprint. In spite of what the brochure states, you may be more like an employee than "your own boss". When you purchase a franchise, it will be the company's name over the store, their layout, their merchandising and pricing concepts, their policies, and even their products. You lose a certain amount of control, flexibility, and creativity. In franchising you operate by their book.

2. Franchising is expensive. However, some say franchising is actually less expensive than starting from scratch. The rationale goes something like this. When you buy a franchise, you get name recognition and a concept that has been proven successful. So, when you open the doors, you hit the ground running—you have instant business. There is a certain validity to that logic. On the other hand, if you want to open up a business and you basically know what you're doing, you should be able to start it much less expensively on your own.

Perhaps, though, the major financial disadvantage comes from the continuing royalty fee. The average franchise charges a royalty ranging from 2 to 6 percent of gross sales, usually paid monthly. If you have your own operation, that money would go into your pocket. Unless the services or other savings provided in merchandise purchasing can offset that fee, sharing hard-earned "profits" can prove to be a costly disadvantage.

3. The contract. The franchise contract or agreement (sometimes 30 pages long) spells out in detail how the business will operate. These agreements tend to be quite restrictive. The franchisor

reasons that the value and future success of the operation depends on consistency. That concept may have considerable merit, but as a franchisee, you may find that you are controlled in virtually everything you do. If a dispute arises, the franchisor simply points to the contract and you have a problem. In addition, the franchisor normally has the financial and legal resources to back up the contractual arrangement, putting the franchisee at a disadvantage. Most franchisees tend to accept the controls, perhaps because they see the advantages outweighing the disadvantages. If your operation is successful, you tend to accept controls more easily.

4. You suffer if they suffer. In most cases, you are connected very securely to the franchisor. If the franchise dock sinks, your ship may well sink too! If the firm has financial difficulties, and many do, you may experience similar problems, despite the fact that you're running a profitable operation. If the franchise goes out of business, it may spell disaster to your venture. When bad publicity hits the chain, you experience the fallout. To avoid this potential problem, pick franchisors that have been in business for a period of time, have established financial security, and have a good reputation.

The Franchise Package

Franchisors normally provide a number of services, both in the initial start-up phase and during the ongoing effort. Prior to buying a franchise, find out what services you will get, and to what extent. Following is a list of what's normally provided in a retail franchise. The franchisor offers:

Assistance in marketing, a marketing survey and actual site selection. Since location is so critical in retail, this service, if done right, will provide a major step towards success. However, it's important for you to conduct your own analysis. You may have a much better appreciation of the local market.

Interior and exterior design for the business, as well as a layout for fixtures and product displays. Frequently, the franchisor will be involved with the construction in order to provide you with a "turn-key" operation. Your involvement actually begins when you open the store for operation.

Negotiating for the lease. The franchisor may even hold the lease. You then become the sub-lessee of the franchisor. This, of course, puts you at a significant disadvantage. If there are any major disputes with the franchisor, the company's leverage with the lease can quickly settle the issue to your disadvantage.

Training. In most cases you will have from one to six weeks of comprehensive instruction, usually at the company's training facility. This initial training will be supplemented with ongoing assistance and advice, periodic visits from field representatives, and occasionally newsletters, updated manuals, and franchisee conferences. The franchise package will normally include operational training manuals, an accounting system, as well as a buying and inventory-control plan. These written manuals become the backbone of the franchise. They are confidential and include all of the "trade secrets" of the franchise. Some are extremely well prepared and very comprehensive. They also include the forms on which the franchisee reports his or her business activity to the home office. There are *tradeoffs* everywhere!

Financial assistance to qualified applicants. This assistance normally comes by allowing periodic payments rather than a lump sum for the initial franchise fees and other expenses. However, franchisors do have financial limitations and will turn down prospective franchisees who do not have the cash requirements.

An effective buying program. According to current law, the franchisor can only offer a voluntary buying effort. In most cases though, these buying programs are well designed and prove to be the major benefit of the franchise package.

Where Do You Start?

In order to make an informed decision, you should start your search process by writing several franchisors for their information packets. Because your interests and needs are specific, you should look for a franchise that will provide the best set of benefits for your particular situation. Begin by selecting one or more of the following directories to locate franchise opportunities.

Franchise Annual
Published by Infopress Inc.
36 Center St.
Lewiston, NY 14092

You can normally find this directory in a library, but if necessary, write to Infopress and enclose $19.95, for a copy. This directory lists 2,181 individual franchise opportunities in the U.S. and Canada, giving their addresses, persons to contact, the number of locations, capital investment, and geographical strengths.

Franchise Opportunities Handbook
Published by the Department of Commerce
Washington, DC 20402

This directory can normally be found in public libraries and all offices of the Small Business Administration. The Department of Commerce will send you one for $6.50.

The International Franchise Association
(Classified Directory of Members)
7315 Wisconsin Ave.
Washington, DC 20014

This association has approximately 350 members who have agreed to abide by a code of ethics developed to enhance confidence in the franchise system. This association also publishes a very helpful brochure "Investigate Before Investing". This publication can be obtained for $2.50 by writing to IFA.

Before you actually start writing to the various franchise companies take an important step and create an *image* for yourself. Obtain a supply of personalized stationery and envelopes; an "instant-print" store will provide 200 imprinted letterheads and envelopes (with your name, address, and phone number on off-white stock) for a nominal price. Type your inquiry letters and any follow-up letters, keeping them short and business-like. This demonstrates a professional image to the prospective franchisor and generates a positive reception.

Meeting With The Franchisor

During preliminary negotiations, you may correspond and talk over the telephone with a franchise representative. Now the time comes to meet personally. This is a critical meeting. It will give you an opportunity to obtain a first impression, and perhaps a lasting one. It's also the time the franchise representatives size you up as a potential franchisee. They will want specific information from you. If they don't ask about your financial status, your background, and previous experience, consider this a bad sign. Since representatives will be assigning a territory, store, or some other valuable interest in their franchise to you, they should be concerned with who is going to be behind the counter representing their valuable name. Be prepared to answer their questions without becoming intimidated or defensive.

However, don't lose the initiative. Be prepared to ask questions of your own. This initial meeting may last a few hours or the better part of a day. Don't leave until you have all the necessary information to begin an in-depth analysis of their franchise (copy of the contract, pro forma financial statements, disclosure form). Occasionally, the franchise representatives will meet you in your home with both husband and wife present. They want to make sure that both parties are in favor of this major commitment.

At this initial personal meeting, the franchisor is required by law (Federal Trade Commission Rule 436) to furnish you a full disclosure statement, referred to as the *Uniform Franchise Offering Circular*. In several states, the regulations are even more comprehensive than this federal law. The disclosure statement, along with the franchise contract, must be presented to you ten days before money is paid or contracts signed. Hence, you cannot be rushed into franchising. The penalties for a franchisor not complying are fines up to $10,000 per day. You can see that the past abuses were significant enough to force the government into regulating the industry to this degree.

This disclosure regulation does not prevent a franchisor from attempting to *sell* you a franchise, sometimes quite aggressively. Be prepared to listen and even view some very impressive sales material. You don't have to sign, but you do have to *investigate*.

During your discussions with franchisors, a number of subjects will be covered, both verbally and in writing. Set up a separate file for each franchisor you contact. Keep all the correspondence and material you receive, as well as any information you develop on your own in that file, including written notes of your telephone and in-person conversations. Make sure you date each entry and note the names of the people involved. If you ever have to reconstruct the chronological events of purchasing the franchise for any reason, this file will prove very valuable.

Following is a list of questions you should ask the franchisor during your initial meetings:

1. How many franchises are presently operating, and where are they located?

2. How long has the operation been in existence, and when did it sell its first franchise operation?

3. How many franchisees have failed or gone out of business and why?

4. What are the actual profits from existing operations, and how do they compare with the franchisor's pro forma or financial assumption sheet?

5. Precisely what is included in: a) initial training program; b) continuous training and field assistance, c) store design, layout, merchandising, etc.; d) site, market analysis, and feasibility studies; e) store construction?

6. Specifically to what areas will the initial franchise fees and investment be allotted?

7. How much working capital is needed beyond the original investment?

8. How much are the continuing royalties, and what are the services provided?

9. In what company-sponsored programs are franchisees required to participate?

10. What are the territorial restrictions and protections?

11. What products are offered by the franchise, and are they competitively priced?

12. What are the conditions and restrictions for renewing, selling, or terminating the franchise agreement?

13. Have any franchisees been terminated and for what reason?

14. What are the restrictions on selling "other" merchandise?

15. Will the franchisor assist in financing, and how?

16. Who are the principals in the business, and what are their backgrounds?

17. Is the franchise presently being sued, or was it ever sued by a franchisee and what was the outcome?

18. What is the present financial condition and ownership of the franchise?

19. What are the future plans for the franchise—locations, new marketing of product lines, advertising, etc.—for one year, two years, and five years?

20. How are disputes between franchisor and franchisee settled?

Danger Signals

As your investigation continues and you contact various franchisors, certain situations will tip you off to potential problems. If you find any of these, move cautiously. There are plenty of good franchise operations; don't settle for a marginal one that will give you nothing but headaches and large legal bills.

Consider heading for the nearest exit if:

- The representative is reluctant or refuses to give you a list of existing franchisees.

- They promise you a high profit opportunity with minimum effort.

- They seem more interested in your money than in the future success of the franchise.

- They insist on a deposit, or "good faith" money, up-front to "secure" a territory or location.

- They attempt to persuade you to move fast before the territory is sold to someone else.

- They try to talk you out of showing the contract to an attorney.

- If they refuse or are evasive in answering any of your questions.

Financial Projections

As part of your analysis of a franchise, you'll need a realistic *forecast* of income and expenses. Some franchise companies refer to these as pro forma statements or projections. These are really hypothetical profit-and-loss or income statements built on various sales and expense assumptions. The Federal Trade Commission and state agencies have imposed some rather strict rules on these financial forecasts. The potential earnings claimed by a franchise must have a reasonable basis to support the forecast. The material or data to substantiate the claims must be available to the prospective franchisee, if requested, and these claims must represent the type and geographical profile of the area you are considering. Make sure you request such information. The regulations even go so far as to insist that these figures be accompanied by a caution label, typically.

CAUTION: Some outlets have sold (earned) this amount. There is no assurance you will do as well. If you rely upon our figures, you must accept the risk of not doing as well.

Here is where you can really get into trouble. Naturally, the franchisor is going to present these forecasts in the most favorable light. Your task is to cut through the facade and analyze the "worst case" situations. You must know whether you can still succeed if the sales do not meet projections and expenses are higher than anticipated. How do you find this out? That becomes part of the tedious legwork of analyzing a franchise opportunity. Talk to the other franchisees, people involved in the industry, an accountant, and anyone experienced in small business management. Even when you are buying a franchise, you must do your own independent appraisal of its potential. Certainly there is no better way to shatter the illusion of your dream business, than by waking up to find that your expectations were considerably higher than the reality.

Check With The Existing Franchisees

All reputable franchisors will provide a list of franchisees. Attempt to visit as many as possible. They will be the source of extremely valuable information. Some may be very cooperative, and even open their books to you; much will depend on the rapport you initially establish. Be sure to phone first, and ask for times convenient to their schedules. When you meet, be frank and straightforward. They were once in your shoes and should identify with your concerns. Assure them that the conversation will be kept confidential and ask them upfront to be as candid as possible with their answers. You may want to use the following list of topics as a guide:

Questions to Ask a Franchisee

1. Has the franchisor been responsive and honest in dealing with you?

2. Are the figures in the company's pro forma statements realistic? If not, what areas appear to be wrong—either over or under-inflated?

3. In the initial stages of the business did the franchisor assist you with all of the programs that were promised? Where could they have been of more help?

4. Do they continue to provide assistance and training as promised?

5. Are the products competitive in price, style, and quality?

6. Are the advertising, public relations, and promotional programs working and are they cost-effective?

7. What are your two most significant complaints about the franchisor?

8. Are you making the money that you expected to make?

9. What were the major problems you encountered when you first opened the business? What are your major problems today?

10. How much money is really necessary to successfully launch this business?

11. Do you know of any franchisee who is particularly unhappy with the franchise?

12. How long have you been involved, and why did you decide to purchase this franchise?

13. Does the contract have any clauses that are particularly troublesome?

Checking Out The Company

The first step in checking out a franchise is to determine whether the company is publicly held (stock sold on one of the exchanges) or privately held (company owned by private investors). If the company is publicly held, you can obtain a great deal of information. Contact its representative or phone the home office and ask for a copy of the annual report, and 10-K report. The 10-K report will provide considerable information such as who is involved in the business, their backgrounds, whether there are any lawsuits pending, and the company's financial status. Much of this information may also be shown on the full disclosure statement. If the company is privately held, ask your banker to obtain a Dun & Bradstreet report. The bank may charge you a nominal fee, but it will be worth the expense. Contacts with the existing franchisees will be able to substantiate many of your findings. Other sources include: Better Business Bureau, the local consumer fraud departments, state agencies involved in franchise regulation, the Federal Trade Commission, and the local Chamber of Commerce.

Fees and the Franchise Contract

There are basically two things that stand in the way of making franchising a perfect way of getting into business—the *fees* involved and the *contract* you must sign. Perhaps this is the compromise factor you face when considering a franchise. Again, you have a trade-off. You're attempting to reduce your risks by obtaining a proven concept. For that security you must pay a two-fold price—franchise fees and a franchise contract. What you must determine is whether the fees are too high and the contract too restrictive.

Franchise fees come in two forms—upfront cost and the ongoing royalties. Let's consider the upfront franchise fee first. What do you get for this money? What it could include is the entire package, or what is commonly referred to as a "turn-key" operation. They hand you the front door key, you turn it, and you're in business. You have the right to use their name, their program, and their concepts; they have supplied a finished location with merchandise. Most major franchisors operate with this approach, since it insures consistency and control over their operation. The fee may also include training at the home office, as well as operational manuals. It's important to determine how much of the fee is for tangible things (merchandise, fixtures and construction), and how much for intangibles (the right to use the name and concept). As the intangible costs increase, you should be purchasing a more valuable "trademark." For example, McDonald's charges up to $100,000 just for the right to play on their team.

Evaluate whether you are getting your money's worth by determining how much it would cost to buy a similar business independently. That's the benchmark to use in analyzing the upfront franchise fee. You might also compare the costs of other companies franchising similar concepts and use these comparisons in negotiating a mutually acceptable fee. Yes! You can negotiate with many franchisors, or at least spread the costs over time without paying interest. If they want you to open in a particular area, they may be very accommodating.

The on-going royalty fees are far more important to your long-term survival. Three to six percent of gross sales may not seem much but you may be writing *away* your net profit. A small business generally does not show a large bottom-line on its profit-and-loss statement.

Don't give away your profits. That's what being in business for yourself is all about. Long hours, risks, and pressure must have some compensation. Unfortunately, many people who open their own businesses, whether franchised or not, end up working for the government, landlords, employees, creditors, and possibly franchisors. It's frustrating when you find very little money left for all your efforts. In your conversations with existing franchisees, ask them if they receive the services and support to justify the royalty fees. And also ask if there is enough left to adequately compensate them for their efforts.

Now, let's consider the franchise contract. After you have read a few, you may wonder why anyone goes into franchising. Perhaps there are some simple two-page franchise agreements, but I have never seen one. Typically, they are multi-page, multi-paragraph pieces of legal jargon written by franchisors simply for their protection. Yet, in spite of how one-sided they look, current franchise law has curtailed a good deal of that.

It's essential to have legal counsel when reviewing this agreement. Find someone familiar with franchise contracts and remember the lawyer's job is not to talk you out of the venture, but to objectively appraise the pros and cons of the agreement. The important clauses to study carefully:

- Exactly what do you get for your money? Do you have to participate financially in company sponsored programs?

- Are you required to purchase merchandise or supplies from the franchisor?

- Under what circumstances may the franchisor terminate your agreement?

- What continuing services, support, and training will you receive?

- Under what restrictions must you operate?

- Can you sell, transfer, or terminate your agreement and under what conditions?

- What happens when the franchise expires? What is the renewal or the buy-back procedure?

Remember that you can negotiate changes in a franchise agreement. These changes, prepared by your attorney, will be as binding as any paragraphs prepared for the original document. In addition, if there are any verbal representations, be sure that these are written out and signed by the franchisor. They automatically become part of your agreement.

Making Your Decision

In addition to selecting the right franchise, give considerable thought to the business itself. Chapter 2 discusses at length the type of thinking you should do to pick the right business. Franchising is no different; it's just another way of reaching your entrepreneurial objective. After signing the franchise contract be certain that you end up doing what you will enjoy doing. Go through the same probing exercises you would if you were starting the business from scratch or buying an existing business.

If you can honestly answer the questions in Figure 6-1 positively, you have probably found a good franchise opportunity.

Summary

The world of franchising has been under close scrutiny over the past few years. Most people are now aware that franchising in itself does not guarantee financial success . . . high profits require considerable effort. Franchisees are not really independent but more like partners with the franchisor, and this partnership has many difficult aspects. The franchisee must be capable of flexibility and willing to work hard within the structure. The franchisor must provide real service, not just lip service. Unless each recognizes the balance and the need for one another, the business will suffer and eventually fail. No one questions the soundness and value of the franchise concept, but, it's not necessarily the cure-all for the multitude of entrepreneurial dilemmas. Franchising does, however, represent a proven concept for an individual to get into business, and therefore it will continue to have growth potential.

FIGURE 6-1
FRANCHISE CHECKLIST

This checklist will help you determine whether you should invest in a franchise operation. Any "no's" should cause you to rethink your decision.

	Yes	No
1. Is this the type of business I will enjoy being in?	☐	☐
2. Are the fees affordable (both upfront costs and royalties)?	☐	☐
3. Do I feel comfortable with the people involved?	☐	☐
4. Do they have a successful track record, long enough to establish a positive reputation?	☐	☐
5. Do the present franchisees offer favorable reports?	☐	☐
6. Can I work within the franchising structure, accepting the rules, regulations, and supervision from the franchisor?	☐	☐
7. Do I need the franchise for support, versus going it alone?	☐	☐
8. Will I get my money's worth in terms of store setup and name identity?	☐	☐
9. Does my lawyer indicate that the contract is acceptable?	☐	☐
10. Have I done my homework? Am I looking at this opportunity realistically and objectively?	☐	☐
11. Is it a good location?	☐	☐
12. Does the forecast of income meet my personal goals, and has this forecast been verified?	☐	☐

Chapter 7
Obtaining Financing

Entrepreneurs have traditionally experienced difficulty in obtaining capital. The potential owner of a small business has few options and less time and expertise to find available financing sources. Before setting out to obtain capital, you must plan your financial requirements, determine how much money you actually need and can afford, and be prepared to spend time and energy getting results.

Terminology

Let's begin by establishing definitions for a number of terms you will be involved with while financing your business.

Equity Financing. Money placed in a business by owners or investors. It usually involves the original investment but may include additional funds put into the business at various times for further capitalization. Usually there are no requirements for repaying this investment. The more equity funds in a company, the more favorably suppliers, bankers, or investors will view the soundness of the operation. Companies with a limited investment capital are called "thinly capitalized".

Debt Financing. Money which carries an obligation for repayment and normally is interest-bearing. This "borrowed" capital can come from a variety of sources—friends, relatives, banks etc. It usually requires periodic or monthly payments. The major disadvantage, to a new or small business, is the debt service or repayment schedule. Sizeable loan payments can create a major problem with cash flow. On the other hand, debt financing has an advantage: the owners do not have to give up any of the ownership or equity in their business in exchange for the obligation.

Short-Term Loans. Business loans used primarily to take advantage of suppliers' discounts or for the purchase of increased inventory in anticipation of seasonal peaks. They are made for less than a year and are paid off by converting inventory to cash.

Accounts Receivable Financing. This allows a business to turn its receivables into cash. The bank normally will advance 60 to 80 percent of the value of qualified receivables (under 90 days) and then use the receivables as security. Essentially this method of financing provides the business with a revolving line of credit, where interest is charged on the outstanding balance.

Long-Term Loans. These extend more than a year and are normally used to finance fixtures, equipment, improvements, or additional working capital. These loans require monthly or quarterly payments and are repaid out of profits.

Secured. Business loans requiring collateral as security, which will be forfeited by the borrower if default occurs. Collateral takes many forms: accounts receivable, real estate, inventory, automobiles, or stocks and bonds.

Unsecured business loans. Normally granted only by trusting friends or relatives, or by banks to those companies with long established, profitable track records.

Boot Strap Financing. A company's uses of its own internal resources to generate funds for additional working capital or expansion. By using excess cash flow, cutting expenses, turning some assets into cash, or generating excess profit, a company obtains the necessary capital without going to a lender.

Sources of Funds

As an owner or prospective owner of a business, you can obtain money from several sources. The availability of funds will vary greatly, based on your ability to convince others of your credit worthiness. Time will also play a major part. As your business grows and shows consistent profits, new money sources will become available. If you become very successful, you may even have to turn people down. However, for the moment, let's consider where you can go to get money for a start-up or additional working capital.

1. *You* will be your best source of capital. Unless you have some money to put into the business, you will find it very difficult, if not impossible, to convince others to share the risk.

2. Family and friends become a second major source of capital for entrepreneurs.

3. You may consider partners, either silent or working. If you form a corporation, they will be called shareholders.

4. Banks and other lending establishments.

5. Small Business Administration or other government sponsored programs.

6. Suppliers, manufacturers, or wholesalers, etc.

7. Venture capitalists.

8. Leasing companies or other sales-financing companies.

Founders. Most small businesses are started by people who believe in a concept and in themselves and are willing to invest their personal funds in the business. If you're unwilling to do that, perhaps you should rethink entrepreneurship. Some say, "Why use your own money when you can use someone else's?" In the world of small business start-ups, you will have a very difficult job trying to convince others to commit their resources if you are unwilling to commit yours.

A study done by the Small Business Administration demonstrates the predominance of owner financing for small businesses. The following is a breakdown of the sources of initial capital used to fund small business start-ups.

Owner's cash	52.5%
Loans from financial institutions	15.7%
Loans from family or friends	11.6%
Previous ownership of stock or fixtures	8.1%
Supplier's credit	6.0%
Other sources	6.1%

Typically, a person thinking about going into business will have saved some money. Frequently the individual will sell an asset—a house, boat, land, or stock—or obtain a loan on life insurance, or negotiate an early payoff on a company pension plan. Wherever the funds come from, they do not have to be paid back. There is no debt service on this capital investment. These funds become the equity you hold in the business. Hopefully, this multiplies over time, and when you sell the business, you can buy a yacht and sail around the world.

Borrowing From Friends and Relatives. Many new ventures are started with funds from friends or relatives. Frequently they are the only ones who can be persuaded to invest in your dream. But, before asking for money, you must make a difficult decision: Should you ask for a simple interest-bearing loan or will the money establish an equity or ownership position?

In either case, major problems occur when you are unable to *repay* the funds. People have a tendency to become emotional about their money, and it's important for you to consider this while developing your strategy. First, select investors who can lose the money without becoming financially ruined. Second, provide a written copy of your plan to show that you've done your homework. Last, take the time to do it legally. Document the loans or agreements so that everybody knows precisely what the rules of the game are.

Bank Financing. Perhaps the best way to understand bank lending is to understand bankers. A bank lending officer is normally a nice person, with a mortgage, 2.5 kids, and the responsibility to make money, not lose money, for the bank. They are well aware of the mortality rate of small businesses and recognize that if they make start-up loans and the entrepreneur defaults, they have major problems—perhaps costing them their jobs. Consequently, it's easier for them to say "no". A lending officer will never be faulted for turning down a high-risk loan to an entrepreneur. How can you get past this predisposition of bankers? It is not easy, and it takes time and a lot of personal persuasion.

To begin with, very few banks will even consider lending money to a start-up business. If they do, they will tie some major restrictions to the loan. Banks prefer lending to established operations where they can review financial records that show the ability to repay the funds. If they can be persuaded to lend you money on a new business, they will want security—a second deed of trust on your house or perhaps a co-signer with financial clout. Actually, most banks don't like small businesses, in spite of all the advertising and public relations to the contrary. They feel that small businesses cost them too much for the benefits received.

Nevertheless, if you feel you have a possibility at a bank, give it a try . . . the worst they can say is no, and you are prepared for that. Here are some factors that will improve your chances considerably.

1. Put 50 percent or more of the needed capital into the business. Some banks will automatically turn down loan requests from owners who have less than 50 percent equity. Be prepared to secure the loan with personal or other business assets. Banks normally require a *second source* of repayment. In other words, if your business fails, the bank can look to your other pledged assets for repayment.

2. Be able to answer all of the following questions in writing:
    *   Why do you need the money?
    *   Precisely how will it be spent?
    *   How much do you need?
    *   When do you need it and for how long?
    *   How will you repay it?

3. Have a detailed business plan. (See Chapter 9).

4. They may ask for conditions to be attached to the loan: restriction on salary, no other borrowing, periodic reporting, compensating balances (non-interest bearing checking account balances). And, you must be willing to sign personally, not as an officer of your corporation.

One individual I spoke with used a slightly devious yet very legal approach to fund his start-up venture. He anticipated he'd have trouble getting financing from his bank if he told them his plans. So, while he still was employed with a steady, verifiable income, he borrowed $30,000 on a home equity loan. He also obtained an unsecured line of credit and increased his major credit card limits. Yes, he was taking a chance. But, he believed in his business and was willing to take the risks to see his entrepreneurial dream come to reality. With the loan proceeds and personal financial cushion, he opened his business.

Remember, most lenders will not loan you money if you can't show income capable of making the monthly payments, in spite of the fact you're providing collateral. Furthermore, department stores, oil companies, and other credit card sources will refuse credit if you state you're newly self-employed. Consequently, get all that taken care of before launching your business. If you do fill out credit applications while owning a business, don't go on an ego trip. It's better to simply state you're the sales manager than to say you're the owner.

Finance Companies. Although finance companies are not considered a major source of funds for small businesses, a number of them will lend money when the conditions are right. Usually the points (front-end handling charges) and the interest rates will be higher than at commercial banks; but if funds are needed, these firms may provide the answer.

Venture Capitalists. Much has been written recently about venture-capital funding, particularly in the high-tech area. Unfortunately, venture capitalists demand a high rate of return for their investment. Normally, a typical small business doesn't provide the capital appreciation that most of these firms need. Nevertheless, a number of individuals and small venture firms have money and may want to invest in your business for a percentage of the equity.

Finding these people presents a challenge, but the results can be worth the effort. These are sophisticated investors who will insist on a well-documented business plan. Remember, they are sharing the risk with you and want to participate as *partners* rather than as lenders. You must be comfortable with the relationship and the terms of any formal agreement. What may start out as a silent-partner role can turn into a rather noisy one if things don't go as planned. Make sure you acquire good legal counsel in drafting any written contracts.

Suppliers. A good working relationship with your suppliers will provide valuable financing by means of extended credit terms. Depending on the industry, trade credit can extend from thirty days to six months. The best way to secure this type of financing is by developing an honest, loyal working relationship with your suppliers. Many of these firms recognize how vital you are in the movement of goods out of their warehouses and will frequently provide financial assistance to "valuable customers," regardless of size. Being small sometimes is a major benefit, since suppliers have less at risk. Cultivate your suppliers. You may need their help sometime in the future. (I would not have been able to expand my business if it weren't for a cooperative supplier who extended very liberal terms.)

Sales Finance Companies. Once you are in business, and if you have high-ticket items (jewelry, furniture, appliances), you may want to develop a relationship with a sales-finance company. These firms will purchase your installment contracts. When a finance company buys your "paper," you will have instant use of cash without the responsibility of handling accounts receivable and their related collection problems. These arrangements have a number of variations and costs. For example, some finance firms will purchase your paper at a discount and without recourse. In other words, the face value of the total contract is discounted by perhaps 5 percent, and the finance company assumes the responsibility of collecting.

Small Business Administration. The Small Business Administration financial assistance programs have gone through some turmoil over the years. In 1977, because of some rather poor management controls, the SBA was severely impacted by bad loans, resulting in five hundred million dollars in losses. During the following years, the agency had virtually no direct lending capacity and only participated in bank guaranteed loans. Most recently though, as a result of much improved top management, the SBA is again starting to play a more active role in small business lending. They still largely participate only as a guarantor of commercial bank loans.

The problem with SBA guarantees is the banks. Many banks see SBA paperwork as too time-consuming and unprofitable. If a bank won't lend you money on your credit worthiness, it is reluctant to work through the S B A channel. Some banks even have a policy of not considering SBA-guaranteed loans. Additionally, the SBA has guidelines that make it very difficult for start-ups to get initial financing.

Despite these negative factors, it still does pay to stop by an SBA office. They are located in virtually every major city. Talk with their lending officers and determine the possibilities. They will be able to give you some valuable direction. In 1983, the SBA guaranteed over 15,000 small business loans. There is no reason why you could not be one of them. If you decide to submit the loan request, there will be a number of detailed forms to fill out. Although the SBA states that approval or denial will be forthcoming in five days, plan on more time since the loan also has to be processed by the lending institution.

Seller Financing. If you are buying an existing business, your chances of having the seller "carry back" a loan are excellent. As many as 80 percent of all small business sales are seller financed, typically with 20 to 30 percent cash down and terms more favorable than what the bank would charge. So, if it is impossible to get a bank to lend you money, you may find a motivated small business owner, who would like to extend credit to you if you buy the business. Chapters 15 and 17 cover financing the purchase of an existing business in detail.

Leasing Companies. Leasing companies will often provide funds for virtually everything in a business (with the exception of lease-hold improvements and inventory) if you are a credit-worthy risk. Autos and trucks are prime examples of lease situations. A leasing company may also finance your fixtures, cash registers, signs, and other equipment. For a start-up business with limited cash available, this may provide the leverage necessary to make your venture viable.

Cost of Funds

Banks and other lending institutions obtain money from various sources and must pay interest on those funds. Over the past few years, that interest has fluctuated considerably. Additionally, the rate has been high and probably will continue to be high in the foreseeable future. The days of 5 percent interest are gone forever. In its place is an array of CD's, Money Market Accounts, and interest-bearing checking accounts. What this means to the entrepreneur in search of cheap money is—sorry!

The banks make money on the "spread" (the difference between the interest rate they give to depositors and the interest rate they charge you, the borrower). When the cost of their money was 5 percent, they could easily lend it out at 10 percent, and make a profit. Now their cost is 8 to 9 percent or more, and they must charge accordingly. One additional factor has been the volatility of interest rates. In efforts to cover themselves, banks have set up variable or floating interest rates. In other words, as their costs rise, so does the interest on your loan.

Today, small business borrowing, both short and long-term, is tied to the prime rate (what the banks charge their most credit-worthy customers). Since you are not General Motors, you may have to pay a slight premium—one to four percentage points above prime. That means that your interest rates will fluctuate with the moving prime rate. Unfortunately, during the 1981-82 credit crunch, a number of small businesses watched their rates rise from 12% to 22%. Servicing a loan, whose payments can rise so substantially causes serious cash-flow problems. If you had borrowed $100,000 at 12 percent and the interest floated to 22 percent, your interest costs alone would have jumped from $12,000 to $22,000 annually. The whole point is: there is no inexpensive money for an entrepreneur at a lending institution. That should not deter you from using borrowed funds to start or expand your business. However, it should encourage your awareness of the need for accurate and realistic financial planning.

Structuring a Bank Loan

With the proper approach, you can save yourself considerable money by negotiating the multiple conditions of a bank loan in your favor. Do your homework, be prepared with your rationale, and *don't* be abrasive. Remember, a banker can always say no. However, the good news is there's another banker a block away. Following are the conditions in a loan agreement that you can negotiate.

1. *Interest Rates.* Attempt to negotiate a variable rate not to exceed 2.5 or 3 percent above prime. If you are going to secure the note, this figure might even be lower. Also ask for a ceiling (highest rate the interest could go) offering a floor (the lowest possible interest rate) to fix the costs within a range.

2. *Term.* Request a term (length of the loan) providing monthly payments that you can afford. You may also be able to obtain a delay on the start of payments or a balloon payment at the end of the loan.

3. *Pre-Payment.* Avoid a contract with a pre-payment penalty. If interest rates drop significantly, you may want to re-finance the package. Or, if you sell the business, you should be able to pay off the loan without penalty.

4. *Financial Statements.* Limit the frequency and complexity of the financial statements you must provide. It is reasonable for a bank to ask for periodic documentation, but occasionally this demand becomes "overkill" and simply costs you money.

5. *Loan Covenants.* There are several restrictive clauses (e.g. no additional buying, limit on an owner's salary, etc.), that can be written into a loan contract. Attempt to limit these, particularly ones that will restrict your future growth.

6. *Default.* Be certain that there is a time provided to remedy a default. Ask for a 30 day period; otherwise most commercial notes are "on demand" if default occurs.

7. *Collateral.* Try to establish a favorable financial history, and you will eventually be able to obtain unsecured loans. Prior to that time, try to limit your personal exposure by using business assets as collateral. If personal assets (house, stocks, or bonds) must be pledged as security for a loan, attempt to limit the amount and time. Ask that the security be released if you have a two-year favorable payment record.

Strategy

Whether you need $10,000 or $100,000, if you do not have the money available personally, you need a *strategy* to obtain it. This section will provide a step-by-step plan to obtain financing. The key word here is: *anticipate.* Lay groundwork well in advance. Bankers or other lenders usually reject last-minute requests almost automatically. Keep this point in mind when approaching friends and relatives also. They'll feel much more comfortable if you have a plan well thought out in advance.

Begin by evaluating your personal expenses. Once you've made the commitment to open your own business, you must be willing to accept some lean months, perhaps even a year or so. Very few businesses get off to a flying start. In the beginning, you must also be willing to plow back profits into additional working capital, building inventory, or increasing advertising and promotion. Your living expenses may have to be financed from your personal savings.

Some experts suggest that you have six months to a year of living expenses as a cushion before you go into business. This may seem conservative, but the rationale is sound. If you count on a struggling young business to finance its growth along with your lifestyle, you may be expecting too much. Things can unravel very quickly if cash flow doesn't provide enough to cover both business and home expenses. As the pressure builds, the customers, staff, and suppliers will feel the tension, and you'll be faced with the possibility of becoming one of Dun and Bradstreet's failure statistics. So, be certain you build into your plan a cash reserve for personal expenses.

Next, determine, as accurately as possible, how much money you will need and on what you plan to spend it. Use the form in Chapter 3 to develop these figures. The greater detail you can provide as you forecast expenses, the less opportunity for Murphy's Law: "Whatever can possibly go wrong will go wrong, at precisely the wrong time." No matter how well you anticipate, the costs will probably be a little higher, the time a little longer, and the problems a little greater.

The development of a business plan is your next step. Business plans can take time, and they are generally outdated almost the moment they are finished. Nevertheless, people lending money seem to be very impressed by them. They feel that a business plan is evidence that the entrepreneur did his/her homework. The projections in the plan also give bankers the opportunity to look back at some later point in time to determine if the business is on target. A typical business plan is covered in detail in Chapter 9.

The Small Business Administration will also give you help with developing a business plan. Their SCORE (Service Corps of Retired Executives) group of retired business executives are enthusiastic and have assisted a number of entrepreneurs in starting their venture. You may even want to contact the business school of the nearest university and hire a graduate student to help you develop the plan.

Next, start establishing your banking contacts. Business relationships are built over a period of time. Banking relationships are no exception. Begin by contacting the managers of some local banks. Explain that you are thinking about starting your own business. And ask what criteria they consider in a lending relationship. You will quickly determine whether the bank has a rigid policy on new business start-ups or if they are at least open to discussion. Initially, commercial banks will be the most conservative. Don't be too discouraged.

Contact the closest Small Business Administration office and get to know the people involved in lending. Ask them what sources they recommend; they usually provide a list of three. Then, if you are still unsure of where the money is going to come from, start making a list of friends and relatives who have shown some genuine interest in you and who have money to risk. Review the other sources of financing in this chapter and make preliminary inquiries. If you are persistent and start well ahead of time, the money will be there.

On the other hand, it's always good to have a backup position. If you can't obtain the needed financing, perhaps you should reduce your expectations. Look for a less expensive operation. In other words, if you can't get a McDonald's, how about a Wendy's? You may actually make the same amount of net profit with a smaller investment.

Or you might want to consider putting your plan on "Hold" until you can acquire the necessary capital. Frequently, a person rushes into a business because of necessity (loss of a job), or belief that it's the only real opportunity in the world (someone else is going to get that location), or the psychological need to make a change (it's my last chance; I'm getting too old). Unfortunately, all of those reasons are emotionally oriented and can result in serious problems. There are always other opportunities at other times, in other places.

Chapter 8
Structuring the Business

In this chapter you'll become acquainted with the various ways to operate your business—sole proprietor, partnership, or corporation. There are advantages to each and much will depend on your situation. You will also be introduced to the importance of good financial records. You'll learn what local licenses you need and to what government regulation you must conform. However, there are some professionals you can turn to for assistance, and they also will be in this chapter.

What Legal Form of Business Should you Select?

Before starting a business, you'll need to select a legal structure under which to operate. This major decision will effect your taxes and your personal liability. Fortunately, you have only *three* options to choose from: sole proprietorship, a partnership, or a corporation. Small business owners usually start out as sole proprietors or in partnerships.

In 1985-86, sole proprietorships accounted for 76 percent of all businesses in the U.S., and 78 percent were partnerships. Sixteen percent were corporations, yet they produced 88 percent of all the revenues. This demonstrates that big businesses tend to be incorporated. Nevertheless, you need to consider the pros and cons of each option. Later in the chapter, I'll discuss partnerships and corporations in greater detail and show how to choose the ideal partner.

Sole-Proprietorship is the simplest and least expensive form of business to start. In most areas, a business license and a certificate to conduct business under a fictitious name are all that is required. The major disadvantage is that you personally assume all the liabilities of the firm. If the business is unsuccessful, creditors can sue you personally to recover business debts. Basically you are the business. The income generated by the business becomes your personal income. Your income tax will be based on the profit of the operation.

Partnerships are similar to sole-proprietorships, from the liability and taxation standpoints. In partnership, two or more people share the ownership of the business, the risks, and the profits. Each partner has an *unlimited liability*. Any claim against one partner, in the course of doing business, is a claim against all partners and against their personal assets . . . Ouch! Additionally, if you die as an owner of a sole-proprietorship or partnership, legally, the operation must "wrap up business" and cease to exist. However, an attorney can show you how a carefully drawn up partnership agreement can circumvent this problem. There is a variation of a partnership called a *Limited Partnership*. Using this type of business form a person can invest money in an operation, have liability to the amount invested, and have the tax benefits of the partnership. The limited partner, however, cannot participate in management.

Corporations are legal entities. If properly structured and maintained, they offer a number of benefits. First and foremost, a corporation limits your personal liability. If you sign contracts as an employee of the corporation and if for some reason the business is unable to pay, creditors can only be compensated to the limits of the corporate assets. They will not be able to proceed against you. A corporation theoretically eliminates any personal liability; but, in fact, many creditors recognize their vulnerability here and will ask owners to sign personally, thereby eliminating any corporate protection. If you, as an officer and stockholder of a corporation, should die, the business can continue. Still, there are some negatives to a corporate structure. Sometimes it costs more to start a corporation than a partnership or sole proprietorship, and the government paperwork is slightly more extensive.

There are a number of important differences in taxation between sole proprietorships, partnerships, and corporations. Some important tax implications created by the Tax Reform Act of 1986 may cause you to think carefully about the corporate form or to consider using an S-Corporation (taxed much like a partnership, but offering corporate protection from personal liability). Before deciding on a business form, it pays to consult an attorney or accountant who can provide a clear explanation based on your particular needs.

The Human Side of a Partnership

How many times have you heard, "Partnerships are like marriages?" Yet, partnerships are not made in heaven. To the contrary, they are very earthly. They are usually the product of two or more people trying to make their fortunes in the business world. There are numerous examples of ordinary people pooling their talents and creating extraordinary long-lasting profitable partnerships. Sometimes their successes are unparalleled. There are also cases, and many of them, of partners and ex-partners who are disillusioned, burnt-out, frustrated, and cynical about the entire institution of partnerships. Perhaps, in fact, they are a lot like marriages.

The term "partnership" simply means the sharing of ownership of a business enterprise. For our purposes in this discussion, we will consider *closely-held* corporations in the same perspective. As you will see later in this chapter, there are many legal differences. However, the human dynamics remain very similar.

If you have never been in a partnership, then it is rather hard to understand precisely how difficult it can be. The chances of finding one or more people who share the same expectations, will work equally hard for the same objectives and will see all things eye-to-eye, is a difficult proposition. Most partnerships experience conflict from time to time. The question becomes a case of *intensity*. When things are bad, you can feel your energy drain away. You become unproductive, oftentimes even counter-productive. Conflict interrupts meaningful tasks, like running the business and making profit. You may wonder how I can speak with such authority. Well, I've been there!

My experiences with a partnership graphically illustrate the problems inherent in "partnering". During the early hectic years we were too busy to be concerned about minor differences. The expansion from one store to six in less than three years gave us all we could do to keep the ship afloat. But, when the stormy seas calmed, we proceeded to start our own personal World War III. It took a year to dissolve the partnership (we were actually a 50/50 stock-held corporation). There were lawyers and legal bills, and we almost ruined the business as we tried to extricate ourselves from a very bitter situation. Like a marriage, a partnership starts out with great hope and expectation, and some times ends up in highly charged emotional anger. Then why do people ever go into a partnership? Perhaps the main reason is that it seems like the best thing to do at the time. But then times change!

When people begin to visualize the possibility of a business venture, there are many valid reasons to consider a partnership. Frequently you are not financially or psychologically prepared to go it alone. You need help, and a partner may provide that extra capital and encouragement to get the operation off the ground. You may also find that the business is too complex, and you need a partner to handle a part of the venture where you lack experience. A partnership can also provide what is called "synergy". Basically, it means a combination of talents and efforts, creating a result greater than the sum of the individual parts. This phenomenon has been seen most vividly in the high tech area. Small groups of people will get together in some one's garage, and before you know it, they're going public with a company name that's hard to pronounce and more difficult to spell . . . but they have a winning product.

Mostly though, people get together and form partnerships to *make money*. It usually begins with someone you know. You start to talk about how much money could be made in a particular business. You both agree. Then there's the moment when someone says, "Well, let's do it." And away you go.

Now that I have totally disillusioned you on partnerships, let me say this. I would do it again! I firmly believe that with the right person or persons you can get more done than if you work on your own, if two factors are present. 1) you are the type of person who can be a partner, 2) you are very selective in your choice of partner(s).

Some people cannot partner well. They are too independent. They don't like to share responsibilities, and they would prefer to do everything themselves. For that type, a partnership can be a disaster. So, before you even think about partners, assess yourself. Can you co-own, co-manage, and co-operate? The level of success of a partnership is directly proportionate to the degree to which each partner cooperates. It's a *team effort,* and you have to be a team player. You can't be insecure or feel competitive toward a partner. Your partner may actually do many things better than you; that's what a partnership is all about. If you are the type who is more interested in personal success and achievement than you are in the firm's success, then you may find a partnership rather uncomfortable. It's the working together for the common goal that makes a partnership really successful.

Choosing the Right Partner

In order to put some definition to this subject, I have developed a checklist of eight principles. Above all, be very cautious about partnerships. They seem to be so easy to get into and so difficult to get out of. In choosing the right partner:

1. Make sure the *chemistry* is right. Do you get along with the person? Can you discuss the business and generate new ideas and plans? Is there mutual trust? Do you work well together synergisticly, and the end result is greater than the sum of the individual contributions?

2. Share the same *common goals*. As part of the exploration process, each of the partners should, in writing, express his or her individual view of the objectives of the firm. Then compare these to establish a common set of goals. Each partner should agree on these objectives. Never start out with different ideas of where the business is going or how it is going to operate.

3. Clearly establish *responsibilities*. A partnership works best when each person has specific jobs and does them. It becomes a problem when two or more people try to do the same tasks. Set up mutually agreed upon job responsibilities, and let each do the assigned jobs without unnecessary interference.

4. Everybody should agree on *expenditures*. It may even be a good idea to have double-signatures on checks, although it's somewhat inconvenient. But often a person will get very touchy about how you spend "my money".

5. Agree on how much *income* will be taken out of the business and when. Frequently partners have different personal financial needs. One partner may want to put everything back into the business; the other may have to buy groceries. Establish the income agreement before you start.

6. *Communicate* frequently. Make it a point to sit down once or twice a week to discuss the business. Be open during these discussions. You don't have to play "Monday Morning Quarterback" but if something is bothering you, get it out. It's the unsaid things that create the deepest conflicts.

7. Find a partner who has the same level of *motivation*. Nothing can be more frustrating to a hard-working partner than a golf-playing partner. Look for someone who shares your devotion to the work as well as the hours and the intensity.

8. Put the partnership agreement in *writing*. The courts are full of people litigating verbal agreements. People have very selective memories when partnership trouble starts.

Your Written Partnership Agreement

Your written agreement should include the following provisions:

- Company name, address, and description of the business as well as how long the partnership is to last, if there is a limitation

- Names of the owners, their respective shares of ownership, their equity contributions (either in money or other assets), and what happens if additional capital is needed later

- Descriptions of responsibilities and commitments of each owner

- Salaries and other income to be paid to each owner

- Method of selling interest in partnership or withdrawing (buy-sell provision)

- Restrictions on transferring ownership as well as forced withdrawal of a partner

- Methods of valuing the business or insurance provision in the event that transfer occurs by death or disability.

- A fail-safe provision indicating how the business should be liquidated in the event that a buy-out cannot occur

- Provision for amending or updating the agreement

- Provision for handling disputes

- Signatures of all parties, including spouses

In addition to the possibility that irreconcilable conflicts could arise, there are other reasons why one or more partners (or shareholders, if you start a corporation) may elect to transfer their ownership. Besides the possibility of death or permanent disability, one partner may want to "get out" and do something else. Unless you have some sort of written agreement among the co-owners, the situation can get sticky. The remaining owners may be very reluctant to pay the "departing" member a fair price. A dispute then arises, often resulting in a court battle where the only ones making money are the lawyers. Therefore, before you start a partnership or closely-held corporation, create a Buy-Sell agreement that covers all the contingencies.

A well drafted Buy-Sell agreement should establish a technique to value the business and a method of transfer for all five possibilities: 1) death, 2) disability, 3) voluntary withdrawal, 4) involuntary withdrawal, and 5) retirement. Select an attorney with experience in this type of agreement.

Since death and disability are two of the most common causes for ownership transfer, it is imperative to purchase insurance to fund these possibilities. Typically, money from the business is used to pay the premiums. It provides that the heirs, in the event of death, or the owners, in the event of disability, would collect an amount equal to their percentages of the business. If that money had to be provided out of operating funds or profits, it could crunch most small businesses. With insurance you avoid long battles over how much money is due, over what period of time, and at what interest rate. Since there are some technical and legal aspects of this type of insurance, it is important to seek the advice of a good insurance agent.

Should you Incorporate?

Personally, tax considerations aside, I believe that incorporating your business is a smart thing to do. Certainly, it's the safest. Sole proprietors and partners have unlimited liability in terms of the debts of the business and any legal judgments against it. Additionally, the business assets are liable for any personal judgments against the owners. As far as the law is concerned, there is now separation between a sole proprietorship or partnership and the owner(s); they are, in fact, one.

Here's an example of how that can impact you. Let's say you've been operating successfully for a period of time and have accumulated a large personal net worth. An employee making a delivery in the company van causes a serious accident. After months of legal hassle, there is a $1.5 million judgment. Your auto insurance only covers you to $500,000. There goes your net worth. I've seen it happen! A very successful bakery, in business for years, fell victim to a legal judgment that wiped out the personal assets of the partners, as well as the business. Part of that could have been avoided with adequate insurance coverage. But if the business had been incorporated, losses would have been limited to the value of the business, even if it was under-insured.

There are over one million partnerships doing business in the U.S. today. The unlimited liability problem that exists with sole-proprietors is multiplied in a partnership. If the minor child of your partner is involved in an accident while driving the company car, your personal assets and shares of the business are jeopardized.

If a partner dies or withdraws from the business for any reason without a binding buy-sell agreement, the partnership, and hence the business, may have to dissolve. If the remaining partners continue to operate the firm without specific authority outlined in a buy-sell agreement, they must continue to share the profits with the ex-partner or the estate; but the remaining partners must accept all the losses on their own.

It is important to note, in all fairness to this debate, sole proprietorships are far less complicated than corporations, and partnerships are generally more flexible. Furthermore, a good insurance policy will protect you against many, if not all, business liabilities.

Other Aspects of Incorporation

There are some fringe benefits you may enjoy as a stockholder-employee of a corporation that would not be available if you were a sole proprietor or partner. For example, group life, medical, and dental insurance premiums are tax deductible for key employees of a corporation, while sole proprietors and partners must pay these out of after tax dollars. However, other fringe benefits such as *business-related* auto, travel, and entertainment are deductible in all business forms.

There are some interesting corporate tax implications that result from the Tax Reform Act of 1986. Some of these are positive, while others are negative. First, let's consider the new corporate tax structure and compare it to the pre-1986 percentages.

Federal Corporate Income Tax Table as of 1986

Income	Percent in Taxes
$50,000 or less	15%
$50,000 to $75,000	25%
$75,000 to $100,000	34%

(profits over $100,000 are surcharged 5% until the average tax becomes 34%)

Federal Corporate Income Tax Table before 1986

Income	Percent in Taxes
under $25,000	15%
$25,000 to $50,000	18%
$50,000 to $75,000	30%
$75,000 to $100,000	40%
Over $100,000	46%

As you can see, the 1986 tax law has a positive effect on both large and small firms from the standpoint of maximum tax liability. However, several items, such as accelerated depreciation and investment tax credits, have been eliminated.

The issue becomes more complicated with double taxation aspects. For example, if you use the sole proprietorship, partnership, or S-Corporation form of business, you declare the business income or loss personally. As a corporation, you can leave profits in the business after you deduct your salary as an employee. You then pay corporate tax on these profits. If at a later point in time you take these earnings out in the form of dividends or when you sell the business, you are taxed again on a personal basis—double taxation! To avoid this, most small-business owners using the corporate form pay themselves a salary or bonus and often leave little retained earnings in the operation.

Still, there are some benefits in leaving profits in a corporation. This is particularly true if you plan to expand or invest these retained earnings.

Let's assume that you are in the 28 percent personal tax bracket (maximum federal tax rate, starting in 1988). And you left $50,000 retained earnings in your corporation each year for three years. Your cumulative corporate tax would be $22,500 ($50,000 x 15% x 3 years). If you took that money out in salary or bonuses, your personal tax impact would be $42,000 ($50,000 x 28% x 3 years). By leaving the money in the business, you have a net gain of $19,500 in cash. That extra capital will do a lot more than the fewer after tax personal dollars if you plan to expand your business.

Probably the greatest disadvantage of incorporation is when you sell the business. Prior to 1986, if you were incorporated, you could elect certain strategies to avoid double taxation when you sold your operation. That is no longer possible. Any gain will be taxed at both the corporate level and your individual level. For example, let's assume that you initially invested $50,000 in the corporation. It prospers, and ten years later, you sell it for $300,000 at the corporate level. The corporation will pay a federal tax of $102,000 leaving $198,000 to be distributed to you as the shareholder. You will have a personal gain of $148,000 ($198,000 less the original $50,000 investment). The federal tax on that gain will be $41,400, for a total tax bill of $143,440. If you held the business as a sole proprietor, partnership, or S-Corporation, the federal taxes would have been only $70,000 ($250,000 x 28% maximum personal rate). Less than half! This is why the S-Corporation has become so attractive as a form of doing business.

A skilled CPA or tax attorney can help you do the planning necessary to minimize your tax consequence. The key message here is planning. It's impossible to restructure your business after the fact. So it's prudent to spend time planning the best approach with the help of a professional.

Basic Rules

If you do form a corporation, be sure you follow some basic rules. Do not commingle your personal funds with corporate funds. Keep separate corporate records and bank accounts. All your letterheads, business cards, yellow-pages advertising, receipts, media advertising, etc. should indicate your corporate status by including "Inc." or "Corp." in the business name. Additionally, any time you sign your name as a corporate officer, you must indicate your status. For example, you are John Jones, President, XYZ Corporation. If these simple procedures are not followed, creditors may set aside your corporate protection. This in known as "piercing the corporate veil," and it makes you personally liable.

As previously mentioned, you may want to seriously consider establishing as an S-Corporation (formerly called the Sub-S-Corporation). This business entity combines the protective features of the corporation with the tax advantages of the sole proprietorship and partnership by allowing all profits and losses to pass through to the stockholders. No double taxation—the corporate tax is eliminated. One significant advantage of the S-Corporation occurs when the business is operating at a loss. The operating losses can flow directly to the shareholders to the extent of their investment. This may offset personal income from other sources. Some states do not recognize S-Corporations; therefore, it may add accounting complexities to your operation. Yet because of the federal tax advantages, it still may be advantageous. Since the details of acquiring S-Corporate status are complex, ask your attorney or accountant for an explanation of the benefits of this option.

Seeking Legal Help

Before you sign any contracts (leases, Buy-Sell agreements, partnerships, or corporate documents), consult an attorney. The cost of forming a simple small business corporation can vary from $250 to $1,000, plus filing fees, but it's worth it.

Ask friends and acquaintances to recommend a lawyer, preferably one who is familiar with the type of business you're starting so that you can benefit from the firm's expertise. Before making a commitment for legal services, discuss prices.

Financial Records

Typically, entrepreneurs find that keeping records is a tedious and occasionally painful job. But, it is an essential task. You must monitor sales, purchases, gross profit, net profit, and expenses in order to satisfy the Internal Revenue Service and to maintain your perspective. Financial records tell you where you are, where you've been, and where you're going in terms of dollars and cents.

The following seven points underscore the rationale for keeping good records:

1. A good set of books provides you with 20/20 vision that covers yesterday, today, and tomorrow. Otherwise, you're operating in the dark.

2. If you ever intend to expand your operation, financial controls will be essential. Begin early and establish an effective proof system.

3. A good financial control system gives you quick feedback, allowing you to make corrections and adjustments before it's too late. Your judgment will be only as good as your information.

4. You must keep good records for the IRS and other state and federal agencies.

5. If a check was improperly coded, trying to recall what it was for, a year or more later, is next to impossible.

6. Good records are like a football scoreboard. They provide gratification if you're ahead and increase your motivation if you're behind.

7. Good records enable you to pinpoint departments that need more attention. You also learn how well a promotion, advertising campaign, or sales-training effort worked.

You have several choices in "doing the books". I recommend handling the work yourself in the initial stages of your business. Your other options include hiring a part-time bookkeeper or an accounting service. Many experienced homemakers and college accounting students are eager to work a few hours per week doing the books for a small business.

Bookkeeping is not terribly complicated. Initially, it's necessary for you to gain a basic working knowledge of simple accounting principles and procedures. An accountant can set up the books, journals, and basic recap forms, or you can purchase a pre-packaged bookkeeping system from an office-supply firm. "One-write" systems, where you record cash receipts on the same page as cash disbursements, are particularly advantageous for small firms. *General Business Systems* and *Safeguard* have excellent "one-write" pre-printed checks and record-keeping journals. Check your yellow pages for their representatives, and review several systems to determine which best fits your specific needs. Some trade associations and larger suppliers may provide formats for bookkeeping specific to your industry. Whatever method you select, put the system into effect early in the game, preferably before you open. Changing accounting systems in midstream is frustrating and time-consuming.

You only need two basic records—cash receipts (money coming in) and cash disbursements (money going out). It's what you do with these records that determines how well you understand the critical financial implication of your business—*the flow of cash.*

Cash is the lifeblood of your operation. Controlling it is essential. You can work creatively, succeed with your merchandising, sales, and advertising programs, and still go out of business, because you fail to monitor and control cash.

All necessary financial records can be generated internally without an accountant or CPA. A hand-held calculator and a good set of basic accounting books are the only "tools" you need. To keep everything under control, every business person should have the following records, as a minimum:

1. Daily cash report.

2. Monthly profit and loss statement.

3. Comparison reports showing current data against last year's figures and/or your budget.

4. An expense ledger, usually a checkbook with totals by category.

5. Employee payroll records.

6. Tax returns and reports to state and federal agencies.

During my retailing days I found two forms particularly helpful—a daily cash recap report and a monthly profit-and-loss statement. There are, of course, many other areas you should monitor, and it's rather easy to create simple forms. You don't want to over-analyze, but certainly figures can provide all-important clues to problem areas. They can also reveal *opportunities.*

Daily Cash Report. This report reconciles the day's cash receipts with the amount rung up on the register and received by mail. All cash registers will provide an opening and closing balance but some won't allow these totals to be adjusted. After each day's business the receipts can be counted, recorded, and then deposited in the bank. This recap sheet gives you a permanent record of what happened that day and can be attached to the cash register tape and other written receipts. Enter these figures in your cash receipts journal, showing any overages or shortages.

Profit-and-Loss Statements. This financial recap shows the general health of your business by monthly periods. For the first few months it will only provide a superficial appraisal of your operation. As time goes on, and you compare sales and expenses over a longer period, you begin to generate valuable information. It's helpful to record quarterly totals for comparison purposes. In this way, many of the monthly highs and lows are smoothed out, providing a more accurate picture of what's happening. Looking at the percentages of gross profits and expenses against net sales, is perhaps the easiest way to spot trouble. When expenses get out of line, this shows up graphically. For example, if last year for the second quarter, payroll was running 16 percent of sales, and this year it is running 21% of sales, you know you are probably eating up 5 percent net profit with too many people on staff. Or, an alternative explanation is that your sales have been dwindling.

Many experienced entrepreneurs claim that *cash-flow* management is one of the most difficult aspects of running a small business. Without a good set of books, it's difficult to determine precisely where you stand financially from day to day. It may not be vital to know the exact position of your accounts payable versus cash available, but if you are operating as most small business owners do, with a limited cash position, it pays to have a good handle on the subject.

Forecasting cash needs is a valuable technique. Basically, this helps you predict the amount of cash the firm will need in order to meet its expenses over a specific time period. Retailers who have seasonal business peaks find such forecasting essential. An example of a cash-flow forecast can be found in Chapter 9. Initially, you will probably have to use a crystal ball to determine what figures you should plug into the cash-flow forecasts, but, as time goes on, you'll find your projections more sophisticated and more accurate. The more skillful you are in predicting the future cash flow of your business, the more confident you become, and the better you'll sleep at night.

Licenses and Regulations

Whether you start from scratch, buy a franchise, or take over an existing business, you'll normally have to acquire certain licenses, register with appropriate local agencies, and then stop by to see Uncle Sam. That's the cost of doing business!

In order to generate revenue most cities, towns, and local incorporated areas issue business licenses. The rate and permit requirements differ from area to area. But generally, they're not expensive or overly restrictive. Most local governments have prepared lists of agencies and permits necessary to open a business. Contact the local government clerk's office for information and the necessary forms.

Additionally, most areas require a filing of a "statement of fictitious business name". This simple procedure provides a degree of protection to the public since most businesses do not operate under the names of their owners. For example, if your business is called the "Village Men's Store", your statement provides a public record so that local residents can find out who owns the business.

In areas where sales tax is collected, a business must apply for a permit normally called a resale license. This license is generally free, but frequently you are required to provide a deposit, or post a bond, for an amount up to 60 days' tax liability. In other words, since you will be collecting sales tax, but not forwarding for a period of time, the government needs security. If you estimate your sales at $20,000 per month and a 60 day security deposit is required, that will cost you $2,400 in an area where the sales-tax is 6%. Insurance companies will provide bonds for reasonable premiums. However, it's wise to be very conservative about your sales estimates when filing your sales tax permit form. This avoids an excessive outlay of money.

Government Laws and Regulations

Labor Laws. Most states have strict labor and industrial safety laws with severe penalties for non-compliance. What the state doesn't cover the federal government does. Contact your local government as well as federal labor offices for copies of the regulations.

Employee Payroll Returns and Reports. First, let's look at Uncle Sam's regulations. Generally, the tax law requires all businesses with one or more employees to withhold federal income tax and social security taxes from the wages paid. First, you must obtain an Employer's Identification Number. That's easy. But the federal forms and quarterly reports can immerse you in paperwork. Obtain your number at your local Internal Revenue Service office, and ask for a copy of Circular E, Employer's Tax Guide, which explains the various tax requirements in detail.

In some states you will need a separate state employer identification number. And most states have their own requirements and forms for reporting and paying your employees' income taxes, disability isurance, etc. You get used to it after awhile, but in the beginning you may believe that being an entrepreneur is merely a way of perpetuating the government bureaucracy. I always hired a competent bookkeeper with proven experience in government forms and regulations. Then I was free to run the business.

Professional Support

Throughout your business career, you'll need professional support in several areas: banking, accounting, legal matters, and insurance. Picking the right professionals to work with will lighten your managerial load.

Your Banker. All bankers are not alike. It's important to select a banker who understands your business and relates to your needs. The right banker can be your ally when you first begin the business and as you expand.

In addition to setting up a checking account, your banker can assist you in establishing MasterCard and Visa programs. Most banks are competitive with their credit-card fees; but be sure to negotiate before signing on the dotted line. Some banks offer accounting services for a nominal fee. These include check-writing and payroll preparation.

Sometime in the future you may need money for expansion or for short-term inventory requirements. Begin a public relations effort with your local bank's lending officer long before you reach that point. Establish a favorable rapport by inviting the banker to lunch, discussing business in general, and mentioning your future plans. Bank loans are based on credit worthiness, but they are also made by people. You probably won't obtain a loan if you're in financial trouble, but if you show a good track record and have developed an ongoing relationship with the banker, you can normally get what you need.

Bankers can also be helpful in recommending accountants, attorneys, and insurance agents. They usually have their fingers on the pulse of the community and are willing to provide a wealth of local market information free of charge.

Your Accountant. If you establish a working relationship with a skillful accountant or CPA, you'll see results in your bottom-line net profit. In addition to setting you up with an appropriate financial control system, an accountant will provide guidance on cash-flow forecasting, credit and collection, budgets, and financial planning.

Most small entrepreneurs simply use their accountants at tax time, and this is a waste of good talent. Although the owner of a cash-strapped business doesn't welcome a large accounting bill, an expert accountant can be a valuable "silent partner." He knows what works and what doesn't. That expertise can be especially helpful when starting out, particularly if you are intimidated by profit-and-loss statements and government tax forms.

Select an accountant with specific experience in small business operations. Ask a few local store owners for recommendations, and make appointments with one or two CPA's to discuss your needs with them. Make sure to discuss their fee structures. You don't want any surprises later on. If the chemistry is right, you can proceed from there.

Your Attorney. A lawyer is in many ways similar to an accountant, and depending on the circumstances, may provide some valuable assistance at particularly critical times. You definitely want to discuss with an attorney any contracts you plan to sign. Your lawyer will also provide input under what legal form of business to operate. But, a good attorney is most important when trouble "hits the fan". The crisis takes on a different perspective when you are sitting in your attorney's office, and he or she says, "Don't worry, it's under control." Don't wait until the problem arrives, and then look in the yellow-pages to find that calming voice. Again, try to pick your lawyer by means of a referral. Sit down and talk before making a commitment, and ask about fees.

Your Insurance Agent. You should certainly develop a rapport with a good insurance agent. Purchasing insurance for your business reduces your risk and provides peace of mind. Owning a business opens you up to a significant amount of additional liability: people slipping on your floor, a fire wiping out your inventory as well as your ability to earn a living, an employee getting injured on the job. All such disasters can be covered with a premium that's relatively small compared to the potential loss. Some business insurance, like workman's compensation, is actually mandatory. In addition, most leases spell out how much casualty insurance tenants must carry, and proof must be submitted. It will probably take a couple of hours to consider all your insurance options. And your decision will more than likely be based on the confidence you have in your insurance agent.

Your Small Business Consultant. As the owner of a new business, you may also want to seek professional help from a business consultant. This person may provide some valuable assistance to you. I don't say that simply because I am one, but because it is true. Unfortunately, very few new entrepreneurs use business consultants, partly because they don't know these experts exist. After you finish reading these chapters on starting a business, I'm sure you recognize the complexity and seemingly endless number of factors and decisions that must be considered. A consultant can help you through this entrepreneurial minefield. The fees run from expensive to free. SBA's (SCORE) group provides considerable help free of charge. If you feel uncomfortable with the prospect of using your hard-earned capital to start your own business, even with the help of this "highly comprehensive book," then consider discussing the project with a small business consultant familiar with your type of operation. They are found in the yellow-pages under Management Consultants or Business Consultants.

Chapter 9
Bringing it Together With a Business Plan

Owning your own business isn't easy. There are no magic formulas that can guarantee success. However, there are some fundamentals that give the entrepreneur an improved chance for success. One of these fundamentals is good *planning*. Planning in itself will not make a business prosper. But it forces you to think through the complex set of factors leading to success. I personally believe planning gives you a better-than-even chance of survival and success.

The business plan, as outlined in this chapter, essentially serves two vital purposes for a prospective entrepreneur. First, it provides a written guideline outlining the objectives and methods which will help make the business successful. Second, it becomes a useful tool for obtaining financing.

Virtually every well-run medium sized or large business today operates under a business plan. There is no reason why small business owners can't utilize the same techniques and achieve the same positive results. These larger businesses plan because it provides them with concrete benefits. Following is a list of seven major results of good business planning:

1. It organizes objectives.

2. It develops strategies for accomplishing the objectives.

3. It sets priorities.

4. It develops schedules and timetables.

5. It clarifies activities and delegates responsibilities.

6. It anticipates problems and creates solutions.

7. It sets financial guidelines and goals.

Larger firms share another characteristic that allows them to operate more effectively—specialized management. Essentially they have people performing specialized functions: marketing, sales, financial, manufacturing, etc. They have this luxury because of their size, you don't. Being small gives you the responsibility, but unfortunately it doesn't provide you with all the experts to accomplish the various tasks. That's what makes running a small business a bit hair-raising sometimes . . . you must wear many managerial hats. When a large business is faced with a problem, management calls a meeting. The specialists define the problem, analyze the various alternative solutions, and select a course of action. As a small business owner, you must operate as the merchandising specialist in the morning, the financial specialist in the afternoon, and the sales specialist throughout the day. Now, that is a real challenge.

When you speak with an entrepreneur who has had serious problems running a small business, you frequently find there was no plan, written or otherwise. Without a plan, it becomes much more difficult to organize, control, and coordinate the multiple functions of one's business. Without a plan, you don't know where you're going or how you're going to get there. You don't have a road map and you're driving by the seat of your pants in the tangle of Los Angeles freeways. You can be one of the most dedicated, hard working, committed, small business owners in the world; but without some sort of a plan, you are a ship without either rudder or navigational chart, and your chances of running aground are very real.

Advantages of Planning

Planning helps an entrepreneur set goals and objectives. By writing down these goals, they become commitments—powerful stimulants that may help supply the energy and perseverance you will need when things get tough; they will from time to time. A good business plan breaks down the total process into simple steps that are attainable and manageable.

A business plan is incredibly useful in the pre-business learning stages. It will help you gather and analyze information. It becomes a reference file as you accumulate the knowledge you need to make your business successful. Planning also puts a sense of realism into the process of going into business. It's a way of looking over the horizon to anticipate what you must cope with and understand. It may take a couple of weeks or a couple of months to create a comprehensive business plan. But, during that time you are learning on paper which is much less expensive than learning by trial and error.

Business Plans Raise Money

Very few entrepreneurs, who decide to start or expand their businesses, can manage without at least some outside capital. If you cannot convince friends or relatives (unsophisticated lenders), then you must turn to the more sophisticated sources of capital such as banks, the Small Business Administration, suppliers, and venture capitalists. Without exception, these individuals will insist on a business plan that describes and justifies the new or expanding operation.

If it is necessary for you to submit a formal business plan, do a good job, but not so slick that it looks as if a plan packager created it. It's more important that your plan have substance (well documented financial data and a well conceived concept), than just form (a pretty package).

When I was expanding my business, I went to the bank three times for financing. The first time it was an adventure. In order to get the loan, I had to put up virtually everything I owned as collateral. Incidentally, it was a SBA-guaranteed loan. I didn't have a formal business plan on that occasion. The next two times I arrived with a well-prepared plan in hand. I was able to get funded in both cases with unsecured notes. I'm convinced the business plans were one of the major factors that made the difference.

Some Entrepreneurs Find Planning Difficult

Planning is actually a difficult task for many small business owners.

The thought of starting a business can be very intoxicating for the typical entrepreneur. Most want to jump in with a sort of abandonment and "make it happen." They are action types who don't have the time to sit down and put details on paper. These are, unfortunately, the same people who ask six months later, after locking their doors for the last time, "What happened?"

You may even have another problem with planning. You never did it before. The idea intimidates you. You have no idea where to start or what should be put into it. Don't worry, it's not that big a task, even though the outline that follows may seem to contain at least a hundred things to do.

How Do You Start

The actual process of planning is *cumulative*. In other words, you probably won't isolate yourself in a room and emerge a week later with a written plan. Rather, it will be a collection of many observations and inputs that finally tie together for the total plan. Whether you ever "package it" in a formal way will depend on your need to obtain financing. Even if you don't formalize it, your plan will serve as a workbook for you to accumulate valuable know-how for a successful business operation.

In order to put practical realism on the task of planning, consider this method. Take a three ring binder and separate it into ten separate sections, using index tabs to label each category, as are outlined in Figure 9-1. In this binder, you can start accumulating bits and pieces of your plan. Don't be concerned by the number of points in the checklist. It may initially seem overwhelming. You wonder, "Do I have to do all those things to successfully run a small business?" Probably yes, at some time or another. Some parts will be necessary before you open your doors, other sections can be added later as your business evolves.

For example, you may want to refixturize a store you plan to buy. Commit to writing precisely what you plan to do, from what company you will buy the fixtures, the delivery and set-up dates, and the costs involved. Once you commit that information to paper and file it appropriately under "The Operation", you can get on with the other problems and decisions you have to make. If you don't plan and write out these details, you try to remember too many things, soon finding that parts will not come together. Frustration sets in, and you become very unproductive. Remember, you probably won't have any specialists to whom to delegate the tasks. An entrepreneur is the one who does it all alone . . . that is, until he/she can *afford* help.

Putting it All Together

The best way for you to visualize how "going into business" comes together is to review the example that follows. You'll find out how Bill Edwards, a typical prospective entrepreneur, finds, negotiates and finally purchases his own business. Although this example depicts a retail store, the same scenario is played out daily with manufacturing, wholesale, and service firms. While this situation involves the purchase of an on-going business, you may be interested in starting from scratch or buying a franchise. The steps may change but essentially the process is the same.

FIGURE 9-1
BUSINESS PLAN OUTLINE

The following provides a comprehensive checklist for small business management. Whether you are starting or expanding a business, consider using these points as a reference for establishing a working plan for each area.

1. Business Concept
- ☐ The business I am really in.
- ☐ My customers.
- ☐ My marketing area.
- ☐ The future of my market.
- ☐ Methods for making my business succeed in this competitive world.
- ☐ My talents that help cause business success.
- ☐ My resource limitations (capital, time and talent).
- ☐ My non-financial goals and objectives for the first year, second year, third year (e.g.: growth, expansion, remodeling, new merchandising lines).

2. The Operation
- ☐ Location: advantages and disadvantages.
- ☐ Size: advantages and disadvantages.
- ☐ Leasehold improvements.
- ☐ The layout, (an actual plan of the interior) fixtures, window signs.
- ☐ Business image and personality to be projected and method.
- ☐ Lighting and color combinations.
- ☐ Hours.

3. Financial Plan
- ☐ Start-up requirements.
- ☐ Source of start-up capital.
- ☐ Repayment plan.
- ☐ Pro formas, profit-and-loss statements, and balance sheets.
- ☐ Cash-flow statements.
- ☐ Bank-relations plan.
- ☐ Sales and profit objectives for first year, second year, and third year.

4. The products
- ☐ Lines to be carried (and reasons for selection).
- ☐ List of suppliers and terms.
- ☐ Opening inventory cost and timing.
- ☐ Pricing policy and controls.
- ☐ Markdown and discount policy.
- ☐ Inventory control system.
- ☐ Special buys and promotional goods.
- ☐ Seasonal programs with timetables and buying trips.
- ☐ Plan for building inventory.
- ☐ Turnover objectives.

FIGURE 9-1 CONTINUED

5. Promotional plan
- ☐ Calendar of special promotions.
- ☐ Advertising plan, including media and budget.
- ☐ Window displays.
- ☐ Interior displays and promotion.
- ☐ Co-op advertising plan.

6. Personnel plan
- ☐ Timetable for hiring staff.
- ☐ Recruitment and hiring criteria.
- ☐ Orientation and training plan.
- ☐ Salary and incentive pay structure.
- ☐ Benefits program.
- ☐ Evaluation criteria.
- ☐ Motivational program.

7. Administrative plan
- ☐ Accounting system.
- ☐ Sales system.
- ☐ Expense control.
- ☐ Petty cash.
- ☐ Government reports.
- ☐ Business security.
- ☐ Insurance.
- ☐ Plan for acquiring a lawyer and accountant.
- ☐ Evaluation of type of business structure.
- ☐ Membership in Chamber of Commerce and Better Business Bureau.

8. Customer Services
- ☐ Credit procedure.
- ☐ Procedure for refunds and returns.
- ☐ Layaway plan.
- ☐ Free services.

9. Competition
- ☐ Description of my competitors.
- ☐ Their strengths and weaknesses.
- ☐ Method for gaining share of market from them.
- ☐ Competitor strengths to be duplicated.

10. Timetable and Schedules
- ☐ Tasks included in timetable.
- ☐ Priorities.
- ☐ Time period for each task.
- ☐ Person responsible for each task.
- ☐ When will monies be needed, and for what?
- ☐ Timetable for capital funds, with reasons for need.

Figure 9-2 presents a detailed timetable showing the activities Bill undertook getting into the business. You'll notice that it took him almost three months to actually take over the operation. Can it be done faster? Yes, but if you move too fast you may create unnecessary problems for yourself.

Finally, Figure 9-3 presents an actual business plan Bill used to acquire bank financing (most banks would be favorably impressed if you did half this planning).

This final chapter of the first part of the book hopefully provides a realistic perspective of the entrepreneurial process. As I've said often, it will not be easy becoming your own boss. Yet the rewards, both personal and financial, can be very gratifying. I hope these chapters have provided a blueprint to make your task easier and more successful.

Purchase and Sale of a Typical Small Retail Business

Bill Edwards, a 32 year-old merchandise buyer for a local department store chain, had been thinking about owning his own men's retail clothing store for about four years. He had checked out several ads in the newspaper and spoken with two business brokers. Nothing really looked right; the chemistry wasn't there. One afternoon while browsing in the Village Men's Store, Bill mentioned to the owner, that if he ever wanted to sell the store, Bill may have some interest. Bill gave the owner his telephone number and left, thinking that the owner didn't appear very receptive.

Sam Jones had owned the Village Men's Store for 12 years. The store had done well, establishing a local reputation for good service and quality clothing. However, during the past couple of years, Sam's attitude had cooled . . . twelve years in retail is a long time. He was less aggressive in merchandising the store, and it showed. The operation looked a little shop-worn. In spite of these factors, the business continued to attract a loyal clientele, and Sam was able to pull about $35,000 in draw and benefits (with sales of slightly over $200,000).

While Sam was relaxing that weekend, he began to think about Bill Edwards' comments. He'd been approached before about selling but never felt ready to retire. Perhaps now was the time to think more seriously about an offer. He recognized that he was probably burnt out. He was spending less time in the store, and while there, his productivity came in spurts. He also recognized that if he didn't find new motivation, he'd watch his store go downhill.

The following week Sam stopped by his lawyer's office to ask a couple of questions about selling a small business. His lawyer, and later his accountant, both admitted that they had very little experience with sales of small businesses. Nevertheless, working together, they placed a preliminary, almost arbitrary value on the store, and gave Sam some guidelines for handling the negotiations.

Sam contacted Bill Edwards and over the course of three weeks, they tentatively agreed on a price and terms. Bill still wanted his accountant and attorney (both neighbors and also unfamiliar with business buy-sells) to review the figures.

During the three weeks of negotiating, Bill had checked with suppliers, the Better Business Bureau, Dun and Bradstreet, and even several merchants in the shopping complex. They all gave Sam and the Village Men's Store a favorable rating. Bill also did a market evaluation of the competition, as well as the location and traffic factors. The Chamber of Commerce was quite helpful, explaining the demographics of the area and the future changes that might occur. After the evaluation, Bill felt that the store's location had considerable stability plus the potential for improvement. Although competition was significant, Bill felt he could increase sales with aggressive promotion and merchandising.

Bill attempted to keep his enthusiasm in check during the negotiation stage with Sam, but he wanted the store badly. He asked a knowledgable friend, who also owned a men's store, to review his analysis. The conclusion was that the Village Men's Store could be a winner with the right person and a lot of work.

Sam originally placed a $145,000 value on the store. He had approximately $45,000 in inventory at cost and $50,000 in leasehold improvements, equipment, and fixtures at replacement value. He wanted $50,000 down and the balance in monthly payments over five years at 12% simple interest. He also had six years remaining on a favorable and transferable lease.

Bill countered with a $95,000 offer; and after lengthy negotiations, they settled on $115,000. Bill would give Sam $25,000 down, retain $10,000 in accounts payable (to be deducted from the selling price), and sign an $80,000 six year note at 12%. The payments on the note would start three months after transfer of the business and would be graduated. The first year the payments would be $800 monthly and during the second through sixth years, the amounts would be increased to $1,750 monthly.

Bill had total cash reserves of approximately $52,000. His father had contributed $20,000 in a non-interest no payment loan, and the rest came from a savings account, sale of stock, and a company retirement plan. Bill knew he could get another $20,000 from a second mortgage on his house if needed, but felt that his cash position was adequate. His wife had a good job, and her salary could almost cover the household expenses. But, this venture did require them to be very conservative, postponing major purchases for a year or two.

One of the major reasons Sam was liberal in his concessions is that he felt that Bill's talents, perseverance, and background could make the store prosper. Bill also had done his homework. He negotiated his position skillfully and made a persuasive presentation. He convinced Sam that he could be trusted not only with the business, but also with a six year $80,000 note, secured only by the store.

Once the contracts were signed, Bill gave his notice at work. He had 45 days to closing, and he had to use this time productively. Despite his visions of a dream fulfilled, this was a period of sheer panic. There were many things to do, and little time to do them. Bill made a checklist of everything he had to accomplish. He then made a detailed schedule. He also started working on a business plan which he finished a week before taking possession of the store. With the business plan, Bill was able to get a commitment of $25,000 from a local bank for short term inventory financing. Although he didn't initially take advantage of this financing, the money would be available if he needed it.

In the business plan, Bill highlighted many of the objectives, backing this up with a binder full of plans and worksheets. With this binder Bill literally had at his fingertips his strategy for success. It was a comforting feeling for him, having things *under control.*

FIGURE 9-3
SAMPLE OF A BUSINESS PLAN

BUSINESS PLAN

Name and Address of Business:
Village Men's Store
1220 Main Street
Palo Alto, CA
(415) 357-7000

Statement of Objective:
This Business Plan will outline the major short and long range objectives for the Vaillage Men's Store. The plan will also describe the changes and improvements anticipated over the next year. The goals are summarized as follows:

1. Within six months show a 20 percent increase in sales over the previous year. Continue that rate for at least 18 months.
2. Within one month, implement an aggressive advertising and promotion program.
3. Within six months, add three merchandising lines.
4. Within six months, increase gross profit to 42 percent.
5. Within three months, remodel and refurbish the store.
6. Within one year, increase turnover to 4.5.
7. Within one month, develop and implement a formal sales training program and incentive pay program.

History of the Company
The Village Men's Store was founded 21 years ago and has had two previous owners. Sam Jones purchased the store 12 years ago and built a good reputation, offering quality merchandise, fair prices and exceptional personalized service. The store is located in a well-maintained shopping area on one of the town's busiest streets. A very high percentage of the local retailers are long-term established businesses. Very few appear to be having any business difficulty.

Until the last two years, the store had a steady sales and profit growth. During this last period, sales have remained constant at $206,000 and $210,000 respectively, while profits (owner's income) slipped from $35,000 to $33,500. Part of the reason for the sales plateau is a lack of merchandising aggressiveness. Sam Jones is now 62 and feels that it is time to turn over the operation to a younger person who would manage the business more vigorously.

Terms of the Sale
The store was purchased on very favorable terms when escrow closed on April 25, 19___. The store's lease has six years to run with no renewal option.

Total cash down payment	$25,000
Buyer retaining accounts payable	$10,000
Balance in a six-year note at 12% simple interest	$80,000
Total price for the store	$115,000

The promissory note has been set up so the first payment is due August 1, 19___. The first year's monthly payments will be $800 and the remaining 60 months will be at $1,750. Security for the note will be personal signatures by both Mr. and Mrs. William Edwards, and a lien on the store's assets, which can be subordinated to any short term bank debt, if necessary.

The store assets are as follows:

Inventory	$45,000
Leasehold improvements	$40,000
Fixtures and equipment	$20,000
Accounts receivable	$10,000
Good will and covenant not to compete	0
Total:	$115,000

The following is a breakdown of the equity cash available and use of funds:

Down payment	$25,000
Improvements to be accomplished in 90 days	$ 7,300
New inventory purchases	$10,000
Cash reserve (working capital)	$10,000
Total	$52,300

Improvements to the store will include the following:

Painting and wallpapering	$ 900
Carpet	$ 5,200
Fixtures	$ 2,000
Lighting	$ 1,200
Total:	$ 7,300

1   2

The Store:	Within the first three months the following improvements will be made to the interior of the store:
	1. New carpets.
	2. Paint and wallpapering.
	3. New fixtures.
	4. New spotlights to highlight displays.
	These will provide the needed "facelift" and should be perceived by the customers as subtle improvements, rather than any major change. It is important to give continuity during the store's transition, in order not to lose built-in customer loyalty.
The New Store Concept	The objective is to build upon and refine the store's present traditional image. The overall ambience will remain. Merchandise will emphasize the "sophisticated look," both in casual and professional wear.
	With a more aggressive promotion and advertising effort, it is felt that the present customer base of upwardly mobile buyers can be expanded considerably. A revitalized interior will help project the new image.
Growth Potential	A major opportunity exists to increase sales as well as gross profit, while reducing expenses. The impact of new merchandise, aggressive promotions, and a motivated sales staff should be felt within three to six months. An increase in inventory levels will have a marked effect in generating greater customer appeal. Aggressive advertising and sales programs will rapidly convert to higher dollar revenues. The six-month objective of increasing sales at the rate of 20% is realistic and may even be conservative. In two to three years the business will probably grow to the point where expansion can be considered.
Product Lines and Pricing	At least three to five major new lines will be added within the next year to build customer excitement and increase sales. Two lines may be dropped. The merchandising objective will be to provide the customer with a unique high-quality selection of both casual and business wear, so that he can purchase his total wardrobe at the Village Men's Store. Pricing will remain competitive.

Inventory	The increase in inventory levels for the next year should provide an additional $20,000 to $30,000 in merchandise. This will be funded by excess cash flow.
	The markdown policy will be aggressive. We will offer at least four publicized sales throughout the year in addition to a continuously rotating selection of high-moving sale items. Department stores have recently found a highly successful sales strategy of perpetually offering 25%-30% off on selected items. We will adopt this technique.
The Local Market	The following factors potentially make the Village Men's Store very successful: a good location; adequate capitalization, and an owner with ten years of experience who will devote total effort to the store.
	The Village Men's Store has already demonstrated an ability to prosper in this market. Its customer profile consists of industry executives and professionals interested in traditional business-oriented attire. A high percentage of college students purchase classic casual wear. The store has established a very loyal clientele while serving this market. The town of Palo Alto is extremely stable, with moderate growth in the surrounding communitites. There appears to be no major change in shopping patterns and no foreseeable entry of a major shopping center. Many of the residents favor downtown shopping because of the unique, relaxed atmosphere.

Competition	A competitive threat exists from local department stores. In recent years, department stores, together with discount houses have secured 40% of the men's clothing market. They offer both price and quality, and are successful at promoting their men's clothing departments. However, these outlets have difficulty providing true personalized service, something that the Village Men's Store will stress.
	There are also approximately 15 independent men's clothing stores within the immediate market area. These stores vary in size, some have a very professional image while others show signs of deterioration. Many are stocked with slow-moving or dated merchandise. These stores tend to lack merchandising skill and sales people. Most have a marginal in-store promotional effort. Very few of these stores are doing any concentrated advertising. With a solid marketing effort, the Village Men's Store will be able to penetrate and increase its share of customers at the expense of these operations.
Advertising	For the first six months of operation, the promotional calendar tentatively includes:
	1. Radio spots — ten week schedule.
	2. Three mailings to the 1,500 customer list.
	3. Display ads in local newspapers to announce three major sales.
	Merchandise reduction to clear dead stock Grand opening Back-to-School Fall Sale
Staff Training and Development	One of your primary objectives is to provide formal training for the staff. A written manual will focus on the multiple customer service factors involved in selling men's clothing. In addition, the staff will be trained in the science and art of selling, with emphasis on personalized service. Furthermore, there will be considerably more direct management support. This combined effort should establish an enthusiastic, customer-oriented atmosphere; that differs from the almost "self-service" image that presently exists. This departure from current sales strategy will be closely monitored so that the staff does not become over-eager, and hence counterproductive.

Administration	The following administrative plan will be initiated.
	1. A new one-write checking account system will be put into effect.
	2. Reports will be generated every 30 days showing sales by major category, promotion items, and sales personnel.
	3. A profit and loss statement will be generated every 30 days, showing sales, expenses, and profits. These figures will be compared to budget and to past performance.
	4. A part-time bookkeeper will be hired for six hours per week to generate the needed reports.
	The business will be initially set up as a sole-proprietorship; an analysis will be undertaken to evaluate the advantages of incorporating.

Business Plan
VILLAGE MEN'S STORE
PROJECTED PROFIT AND LOSS STATEMENT
Prepared April 24, 1984

	May 1984	June	July	Aug	Sept	Oct	Nov	Dec	Jan 1985	Feb	Mar	Apr	TOTAL
Gross Sales	16,000	12,000	24,000	22,000	18,000	16,000	24,000	30,000	20,000	20,000	22,000	24,000	248,000
Less Cost of Goods	10,000	6,000	12,000	12,000	14,000	14,000	10,000	17,000	12,000	14,000	14,000	13,800	148,800
Gross Profit	6,000	6,000	12,000	10,000	4,000	2,000	14,000	13,000	8,000	6,000	8,000	10,200	99,200
Expenses													
Salaries	1,200	800	1,400	1,200	1,200	1,200	1,400	1,800	1,400	1,400	1,400	1,400	16,000
Payroll Taxes	120	80	140	140	120	120	140	180	140	140	140	140	1,600
Advertising	1,000	600	2,500	800	200	200	1,500	500	1,000	200	200	600	10,600
Rent	1,200	1,200	1,200	1,200	1,200	1,200	1,200	1,200	1,200	1,200	1,200	1,200	14,400
Legal & Acct.	200	200	200	200	200	200	200	200	200	200	200	200	2,400
Office Exp.	300	300	300	300	300	300	300	300	300	300	300	300	3,600
Supplies	100	100	100	100	100	100	100	100	100	100	100	100	1,200
Telephone	200	200	200	200	200	200	200	200	200	200	200	200	2,400
Utilities	300	300	300	300	300	300	300	300	300	300	300	300	3,600
Insurance	200	200	200	200	200	200	200	200	200	200	200	200	2,400
Licenses	300												300
Auto/Travel	200	200	200	200	200	200	200	200	200	200	200	200	2,400
Misc.	200	200	200	200	200	200	200	200	200	200	200	200	2,400
Interest			700	700	700	700	700	700	700	700	700	700	6,300
Total Expense	5,220	4,380	6,940	5,640	5,120	5,120	6,640	6,380	6,140	5,340	5,340	5,740	69,600
Net Profit (Loss) Before Owners Draw & Depreciation	780	1,620	5,060	4,360	(1,120)	(3,120)	7,360	6,620	1,860	660	2,660	4,460	29,600
Depreciation	500	500	500	500	500	500	500	500	500	500	500	500	6,000
Net Profit Before Taxes	280	1,120	4,560	3,860	(1,620)	(3,620)	6,860	6,120	1,360	160	2,160	3,960	23,600

Business Plan
VILLAGE MEN'S STORE
PROJECTED CASH FLOW

	Pre-Opening	May 1984	June	July	Aug	Sept	Oct	Nov	Dec	Jan 1985	Feb	Mar	Apr	TOTAL
Cash Available														
Equity Investment	52,000													
Net Profit Or Loss		280	1,120	4,560	3,860	(1,620)	(3,620)	6,860	5,120	1,360	160	2,160	3,960	23,600
Depreciation		500	500	500	500	500	500	500	500	500	500	500	500	6,000
TOTAL	52,000	780	1,620	5,060	4,360	(1,120)	(3,120)	7,360	5,620	1,860	660	2,660	4,460	—
Cash Disbursements														
Down Payment	25,000													25,000
Accounts Payable (old)		5,000	5,000											10,000
Store Improvements			7,300											7,300
Deposits	1,000													1,000
Loan Principle					100	100	100	100	100	100	100	100	100	900
New Merchandise			5,000		5,000		2,000	5,000			3,000			20,000
Owners Drain									2,000			2,000		4,000
Income Taxes									2,000			1,000		3,000
TOTAL	26,000	5,000	17,300	—	5,100	100	2,100	5,100	4,100	100	3,100	3,100	100	
Net Cash Flow	26,000	(4,220)	(15,780)	5,060	(860)	(1,220)	(5,220)	2,260	1,520	1,760	(2,440)	(400)	4,360	
Cumulative Cash Flow (monthly)	26,000	21,780	6,000	11,060	10,200	8,980	3,760	6,020	7,540	9,300	6,860	6,420	10,780	

FIGURE 9-2
BILL EDWARDS', SCHEDULE OF EVENTS

Date	Event
2/1	First negotiating contract with Mr. Jones.
2/6	Mr. Jones provided financial data for review.
2/7–8	Reviewed local market — competition, advertising, Chamber of Commerce, local merchants.
2/9	Second negotiating meeting.
2/20	Third negotiating meeting.
3/1	Tentative agreement on price and terms.
3/5	Received Mr. Jones' sales contract.
3/11	My attorney and accountant reviewed contract and suggested changes.
3/12	Mr. Jones agrees on changes, signs and escrow is set up with 45 days to close (April 26).
3/13	I offered resignation at work, effective in two weeks.
3/14	Initial work on setting up an agenda and business plan.
3/14	Take a hard look at finances — put an ad in paper to sell boat.
3/15	Contact Dad for $20,000 he promised (check is in the mail).
3/16	Contact the bank for information on line of credit (they want financials and business plan).
3/18	Contacted IRS, state and local offices for necessary ID numbers and forms.
3/20	Discuss set of books with accountant.
3/20	Discuss corporation with attorney, agree on sole-proprietorship for at least six months.
3/21	Contact insurance agent for business coverage policy.
3/22	Discuss store with a friend who has a small men's store — many tips, good day!
3/23–26	In-depth field research of competition within five miles, including department stores.
3/29–30	Spend two days with Mr. Jones going over records, suppliers, etc.
4/1–2	Write preliminary draft of business plan.
4/3	Contacted interior designers for ideas on store improvements (preliminary plan to be received in ten days).
4/4–11	Spend one week in store working — experience, evaluating employees, getting to know systems and some key customers.
4/6–7	Drafted formal training program.

FIGURE 9-2 CONTINUED

4/12	Contacted lighting/carpet/remodeling companies for estimates for renovation plan.
4/16–17	Visited L.A. mart to develop contacts and potential suppliers.
4/18	Contacted fixture company for prices on new fixtures.
4/18	Set up one year tentative advertising and promotional calendar.
4/19	Contacted "Safeguard" to set up one-write bookkeeping system.
4/23	Contacted bank to open checking account and Visa, Mastercharge program, and further discuss business plan.
4/24	Worked on forecast, cash flow and profit and loss statements.
4/24	Contacted free-lance window display person to do windows and in-store displays.
4/25	Change name at phone company and utilities, signed new lease.
4/26	**Took possession of the store** (Sam stayed two weeks to help out).
5/1	Started formal training program and incentive pay program.
5/9–23	Began two week massive sale (40–50% off) to move dead merchandise, and generate cash (used direct mail, window signs and newspaper display ads).
6/1–10	Close store for ten days for remodeling (carpet, painting, wallpaper, new fixtures, spotlights, etc.)
6/10–30	Reopened store — three week shakedown to grand opening sale. New merchandise arriving, two new lines.
6/21	Started ten week radio blitz.
6/25	Hired two new sales people, fired one previous sales person.
6/28	Sent out champagne party invitations to customers on mailing list.
7/1	Started one-month grand opening campaign.
8/15	Back to school — fall sale.
10/26	**Six months of operation.** Getting prepared for first Christmas — store looks great! Sales staff eager and well trained . . . inventory increased by about $25,000 (three new lines). Haven't taken any cash out yet!! But 21% above last year's sales. Bank is ready to give me $20,000 for open-to-buy Christmas goods. Sam Jones going to work part time at Christmas.

PART TWO

EXPANDING A BUSINESS

Chapter 10
Should You Expand?

Whether it's a few months or a few years after initially starting your business, you may begin to visualize a larger operation. The motivations can be very strong. Some feel the bold entrepreneurial urge of a new challenge. Others see it as building an empire, and still others recognize the probable financial rewards of large opposed to small. Whatever the reasons, the drive to expand can be very compelling and on occasion, compulsive. It is a very natural tendency to want to enlarge a successful business in one way or another.

This section presents the many issues you must confront in an expansion effort. It evaluates the *benefits* and at the same time defines the inherent *risks*. It also provides a road map to help you navigate through some pretty treacherous waters.

Expansion is, in many ways, the extension of entrepreneurship. The initial step of starting your business was very entrepreneurial. Some of you feel that is the limit to which you want to participate. Others need to amplify the process by expanding, again a noteworthy trait. The important question is: At what level will you feel most comfortable? Hopefully, after reading this chapter, you will be able to evaluate that question and arrive at a personalized expansion strategy.

In previous chapters I have spoken in mostly positive terms about business ownership. Very little has been said about the negative implications. This section will attempt to balance the pros and cons. Prospective entrepreneurs need a positive "go-for-it" type of attitude. Established business people should view major business decisions in a more objective way. This approach is not meant to discourage you in any way. Rather it is meant to provide a more realistic perspective so that you can launch your expansion program and be relatively confident of success. Remember the first rule of business: *to make money you must not lose what you already have.* The only thing more devastating to an entrepreneur than losing a newly established business is losing an established one!

Motivations and Myths

Let's first examine some of the major motivations that launch a business owner on an expansion program and then relate these to some of the realities.

- *If it worked once, it will work twice or three times, etc....* Seems logical, yet there are many variables that contribute to the success or failure of a business. You can't simply assume that by duplicating your operation in another location, the result will be instant fame and fortune.

- *More locations will make more money.* This argument over looks the cost factors in opening other locations: the risk of failure, the possible financial drain of a slow start, and the additional cost of managers to take your place as you start running a multi-unit operation.

- *Starting a chain will provide more status and enhance my ego.* The chance to move from owner to "big time operator" can be very intoxicating. However, if you fail along the way, the trauma can be much more damaging than a bruised ego.

- *A great opportunity has just come up, and I can't turn it down.* Many are lured into expansion by great sales pitches from leasing agents. "The location is fantastic, and we need a successful operation like yours to provide the perfect balance." You will find that as you become successful, many will want you to locate in their developments. The question you must ask, "Is this the right location for me?" There will be plenty of inviting situations but only a few right opportunities.

Benefits and Valid Reasons

I don't want to sell the benefits of expansion short. Certainly you can and should make more money with more locations. You will rarely make twice as much with the second unit, but you do have the potential of improving your income considerably. Additionally, you build *equity*. As you expand your business, you automatically increase its value. Selling a chain of five profitable locations will net you far more than selling just one.

Furthermore, there are other valid reasons why expansion makes sense. If you have the *capacity* and *capability* to handle more than one location, you won't be satisfied until you begin expanding your business. Perhaps you have become bored with your operation. You have developed it to its highest potential; it's running profitably and you need the challenge of something new to rekindle your managerial fires. If your business can be duplicated and if you select the right spot, you can achieve financial as well as emotional benefits from an expansion process.

You may find it *necessary* to enlarge your operation. In a partnership situation, one location may be able to support one family, but not two. The logical move is to find an additional opportunity.

The valid reasons for growth are obvious. However, it is important that you carefully and deliberately examine both pros and cons so as not to be propelled into expansion for the wrong reasons.

Disadvantages

Expansion is not for everyone. It is not easy or inexpensive. The risks, although not as strong as initially starting a business, are still very real. Expansion is hard work and some entrepreneurs simply say "It's not worth it". To determine whether they touch a nerve ending, consider these reasons for not expanding.

- *There's a "comfort zone" feeling in one location.* Some owners feel very secure in their single operation. They know their customers, and their business expansion presents too many unknowns.

- *The risks far outweigh the rewards.* It's like starting from scratch. You have to worry about traffic, building lease negotiations, construction costs, staff recruitment—too many potential down-side problems for an unknown upside return.

- *Some entrepreneurs know their limitations.* They say that having one location is hard enough and that two locations would be stretching themselves too thin and would be flirting with disaster.

- *Others enjoy doing it by themselves.* They recognize that in multi-unit operations they would have to delegate. They don't trust others to perform the job as well as they do and are unwilling to relinquish control.

- *The pursuit of happiness* is perhaps one of the best arguments for not expanding. Some owners are content with status quo. They are unwilling to test the expansion waters. Being rich and famous is not all that important, being happy is.

Best Argument for Expansion

Probably the best argument *for* expansion relates to the notion that you simply can't afford not to. This doesn't mean that you have to open a nation-wide chain. But perhaps, sooner or later, you may have to grow in order to survive. This could involve only remodeling or refocusing your product direction. Perhaps it is not as dramatic as opening several new outlets, nevertheless, it takes careful planning and execution to shift your business concept.

You must remember that the marketplace is changing constantly. If you don't recognize the signals or are reluctant to move accordingly, you may fail. The auto industry was slow to understand that consumers' tastes had changed to smaller cars. In spite of their economic muscle and sophisticated marketing apparatus, the automobile manufacturers were totally out-flanked by their foreign competitors. Other vivid examples of a changing marketplace relate to the downtown shopping areas when suburban enclosed malls were built, and the independently owned gas stations when self-service chains were introduced. These examples highlight the need for every entrepreneur to be sensitive to the dynamics of the market and to *adapt* or *grow* before it becomes too late.

Many Options Available

Expansion means different things to different people. Let's examine some of the options available to you:

1. **Expanding in your present location:** This could include adding more space (building a mezzanine or leasing adjacent space) or even extending the concept (pizza to full Italian menu or card store to card and gift store).

2. **Trading up:** This option considers the possibility of selling your present operation and buying someone else's larger one. You have gained the valuable experience, and yet you may be unwilling to open a second location. By trading up, you can accomplish and your objective.

3. **Multi-unit operations:** Once you are convinced that your concept is highly successful and profitable, adding one or more additional locations is a natural extension.

4. **Opening a different business:** Some entrepreneurs are not content simply running one type of business. Their expansion strategy includes different types of businesses. Their theory is that if you can successfully operate one small business, you can do the same in virtually any business. You may take the opportunity to wholesale merchandise in your field or perhaps get involved in manufacturing. That's called vertical expansion. Or you may look completely outside your present business and open a totally different type of operation.

5. **Franchising:** If you feel particularly adventuresome and your concept is exceptionally successful, you may consider franchising it. Although the legal requirements are considerable, many entrepreneurs have made fortunes by allowing others to "buy in" via franchising.

FIGURE 10-1
CHECKLIST TO DETERMINE
IF YOUR CONCEPT IS FRANCHISABLE

	Yes	No
1. Can the business be duplicated in other locations at affordable costs?	☐	☐
2. Can other people be trained to successfully operate the business concept?	☐	☐
3. Is the consumer demand for the product or service adequate to justify expansion?	☐	☐
4. Does the business offer substantial margins for the franchisee to make a profit and also pay ongoing fees?	☐	☐
5. Is your business "prototype" generating the profit and concept appeal necessary to attract franchisees?	☐	☐
6. Have others been successful in franchising similar concepts?	☐	☐
7. Do you have or can you acquire enough capital to finance a franchise expansion?	☐	☐
8. Can standardized procedures and policies be developed and enforced?	☐	☐
9. Do you have or can you acquire the experience and expertise necessary to handle a franchise expansion?	☐	☐
10. Are there enough financial and personal benefits to you to warrant the time, effort and investment?	☐	☐

Chapter 11
Getting Ready to Expand

Before you launch your expansion program, you will want to develop a clear and precise understanding of what you presently have and where you want to take it.

To help you develop this perspective, consider the following questions. Although this exercise may appear to be somewhat academic, it does make you examine the basic fundamentals of your business. Write out your answers in as much detail as possible.

- What business am I really in? You must carefully define your business and look at all its aspects so that you can determine exactly where and how it has been most successful. When expanding, be able to abandon those things that do not work and concentrate on those that do.

- Am I capable of running a larger operation? Can you handle the difficult tasks of an expanding business? Do you really want the extra pressure? What management skills need improvement? Recognize additional income will probably be a long time coming.

- Is my present business in good shape? Before you decide to expand, evaluate each phase of your operation to determine whether it's running at peak efficiency. Consider your present location as a prototype. This is where you have put the systems in place, made the mistakes, and refined the concept. Each additional site should be an improvement over previous locations.

- Do I have a plan? Expanding without a plan is like driving across the country without a map or a clue as to which road to take. You will probably get there but it will be very frustrating and you will make a lot of wrong turns. The foundation of your expansion effort will be your business plan.

It is also important to analyze areas that may not be included in the business plan. For example: What are your personal motivations? Do you want to grow? What are your resources, Do you have the capital, people, and talent to do it right? What is the future of the industry? Is it a fad or will it be around for a long time? Also consider where you want to be in two years, five years, and ten years.

The Business Plan

The expansion business plan performs two major functions. First, it is an internal blueprint for your expansion effort. Second, it provides the documentation for outside financing. In many cases, it's the major factor in getting a bank or investor to help fund the project. Chapter 9 discussed business plans in detail, so I will not repeat the information. However, it is important to highlight several areas that are not normally part of a start-up plan. If you must attempt to persuade lenders to finance your expansion, the following areas should be developed:

1. Include major factors involved in your expansion. Briefly describe your overall objectives and then cover the amount of money that will be needed. Specify where the funds will be used and state how you plan to repay the financing. This summary should be the opening part of the plan. Later sections will provide backup detail but it is important to give the lender a preliminary perspective of the who, what, when, where and why of your expansion program.

2. Add a brief profile of your business. Include the uniqueness of your product or service and why you feel it is an expandable concept.

3. One of the more important parts of the plan is your sales history. You must prove that your past success can be duplicated with expansion. Otherwise, you're presenting an unproven, high-risk situation that few lenders will want to consider. Begin by defining the market and showing how you have positioned yourself within it. Demonstrate, with actual percentages, how your sales have expanded. Then present a persuasive argument on how you plan to accomplish your future sales projections.

4. Past financial data will be the most important aspect of your plan. It should include historical profit-and-loss statements, balance sheets and a projected cash flow statement. This financial analysis will be carefully scrutinized by the lender. So, unless you are a financial wizard, it is vital to get some assistance from an accountant. The past financial data will be analyzed to establish the soundness of your business. Most lenders will use ratios to determine whether your operation is healthy. Your accountant can provide industry averages for comparison purposes. It is highly impressive to include these key ratios in your plan, but only if they are favorable.

The formula for current ratio is:

$$\frac{\text{Total current assets}}{\text{Total current liabilities}}$$

(2:1 is considered healthy)

GETTING READY TO EXPAND   139

The formula for liquidity ratio is:

$$\frac{\text{Cash} + \text{marketable securities} + \text{accounts receivable}}{\text{Current liabilities}}$$

(1:1 shows the company is in good shape)

The formula for debt ratio is:

$$\frac{\text{Long term debt}}{\text{Owner's equity}}$$

(3:1 is a desirable ration)

5. The financial number that is most crucial, however, is the *additional cash flow* necessary to service the proposed debt. That must be proven in your business plan. Today's computers and current software packages make this cash flow projection quite simple to perform. Your accountant should be able to generate a comprehensive cash flow spread sheet. You provide the projections and the little semi-conductors do the rest. One note of caution, bankers are becoming skeptical of these printouts. They would much rather see a type-written two-year projection, accompanied by solid and realistic assumptions.

Even if you determine that you do not need outside money, take time to generate an informal business plan, if only, hand written in a three ring binder. By writing down the essential elements of your program, you can begin to organize the multiple tasks and variables. You also will be able to foresee most of the potential problems, allowing you to pre-determine the possible solutions. It may take a few hours, or perhaps a few weeks, but it's time well spent. A well thought-out written plan will significantly improve your chances of success in an complex expansion effort. (See Figure 9-1 for a checklist of important areas to cover.)

Analysis of the Marketplace

Despite the fact that you have a successful operation now, there are no guarantees that it can be duplicated and that you can enjoy the same level of profitability in another location. This situation was clearly demonstrated by a retailer I spoke with who owned a chain of sporting-goods stores. Over a period of twelve years Frank (not his real name) had successfully operated one and then two stores within twenty miles of each other. He skillfully repositioned his business as changes occurred in the marketplace. He added ski and tennis equipment when the sports became popular. He even added a full line of running and aerobic shoes and sportswear. His stores were well established and profitable.

Frank then decided to open another store in a new but growing suburban area. He found a location in a shopping center with similar characteristics to his existing locations. However, only 50% of the center was presently leased.

Frank decided to put in a larger store with 30% more merchandise. The cost of lease-hold improvements, fixtures, and opening inventory seemed to grow far beyond budget. Still, Frank knew the sporting goods business, and the store reflected his years of experience. It was clearly the best stocked, most attractive store of its kind in the area. Unfortunately, Frank's store failed! It did so, not quickly, but slowly. It drained the successful stores as it went. In retrospect, Frank was able to identify a number of the problems. The population in the area was not yet able to support a sporting goods store of its size, it would in five years, but Frank couldn't wait. The shopping complex continued to stay half leased, and the low traffic caused tenant turnover problems. The cost of opening was far more than anticipated, causing severe cash flow problems. This had a compounding effect since Frank was unable to adequately stock the other stores during peak season. As Frank continued to spend more time trying to solve the crises of the new store, problems at the other two stores went unsolved.

The end came when Frank unceremoniously pulled a truck up to the store, loaded the merchandise, shut the doors, and walked away. He is being sued by the landlord, but even if he loses the case, he will be better off than if he had remained open.

Frank's story points out the importance of doing a thorough analysis of the market before committing yourself to a long term lease. Too frequently an entrepreneur will see a successful business as an invincible vehicle. Cookie-cut the concept and put it any place and it will succeed—*wrong!* Remember, "location, location, location". Sometimes all it takes is a few subtle flaws in a particular site and a successful concept is doomed. In order to analyze a location potential, you must be skeptical, objective, and analytical. If you don't approach the task objectively, you will discount the problems and over-emphasize the benefits. Take time, find the right site, and, above all, be objective. You have too much to lose with a careless decision (see Chapter 3 for location analysis).

A Case For Incorporation

The previous example of an expansion plan that didn't work highlights the inherent advantages of incorporating your business. Fortunately, Frank had separately incorporated each store. When the problems became unsolvable, he used the corporations to form a wall of protection around his two successful stores. Although he didn't declare bankruptcy, he did put pressure on suppliers to provide the extra time for paying off his debts. The only area that became a major problem was the store lease, which he had signed personally.

Look at your business as a ship made up of several water-tight containers. If a ship springs a leak, doors can be shut effectively limiting the flooding to that section and saving the ship. Attempt to do the same thing with your expanding business. Plan for the worse and set up corporate protection around each part of your operation.

It is also important to maintain a separate set of books for each location. In this way, you can compare performance and measure key areas. Otherwise, one location could be operating unprofitably pulling down the entire business, and you would never know which one. If you initiate this bookkeeping approach in the beginning, a couple of years later you'll find it was one of your better decisions.

If you shift money back and forth between locations, it should be done with no interest loans. These loans should be recorded on the books so as not to co-mingle funds, which could create a problem in your corporate protection.

Time Table

The process of expansion takes time, in most cases, far more than you would imagine. Too many people are involved to make the task quick and easy. Each participant has his own time table which may or may not conform to yours.

One of the best ways to manage the time element is by use of a simple, but effective, flow chart (see Figure 11-1). This is a flow chart with activities and a timetable. It uses the example of a retail store from the investigation stage to the opening.

Charts like this are extremely helpful for projecting and managing a multi-task project. When you initially decide to expand, many of the time factors will be guesses. As the project gets underway, you will be able to refine these numbers. The flow chart gives you a graphic way of visualizing the entire effort.

Begin by using a large sheet of accounting or graph paper. Divide the sheet by individual activities, e.g. construction, fixturization, etc. As you receive time estimates from the various contractors and suppliers, plug these in by writing the dates on the flow chart. If the project gets delayed or accelerated alter the future activities accordingly. In other words, if your lease negotiation takes an extra two weeks, all of the future tasks will have to be pushed back two weeks. If you must meet a certain deadline, for example, the Christmas season, the use of this flow chart will gauge how much pressure you must exert on various people in order to meet your time objective. It is also advisable to use a pencil to provide ease in making changes; there will be many!

Following is a list of the major tasks of opening a retail operation. These minimum and maximum estimates are just approximations—activities could involve months instead of weeks.

FIGURE 11-1
TIMETABLE FOR OPENING A BUSINESS

Months

Activity	1	2	3	4	5	6	7
Market Research	Competitive Survey —— Chamber of Commerce						
Location Analysis Site Selection		—— Study of Potential Location					
Lease Negotiation			—— Negotiation and Signing of Lease				
Selecting Contractor and Plan Development				—— Assigning Bid			
Construction			Blueprints of Leasehold Improvement		—— Construction		
Inventory		Contact Suppliers for Opening Order		—— Arrival of Opening Order			
Fixtures and Equipment		Plans and purchase of Fixtures			Fixturization		
Financing	Development of Business Plan —— Presentation to Bank			—— Funding			
Promotion and Opening						—— Grand Opening	

Retail Start-up Tasks	Weeks Low	Weeks High
Site Selection	1	4
Lease Negotiations	1	4
Plans for the Store	3	6
Construction Contract Bidding	2	4
Construction	6	10
Fixturization	1	3
Stocking	1	3
Hiring/Training Staff	2	3

Cash Flow

Cash is the lifeblood of a business. Its care and maintenance is crucial to your success. When you decide to expand, you must constantly be aware of your cash flow position, otherwise, you can easily *jeopardize* your entire operation. Expansion has a way of simply consuming cash. What happens, is that costs normally exceed budget, and the time it takes for you to break even is usually longer than anticipated. Those two factors alone place a considerable strain on an existing business. If you don't factor "worst-case scenarios" into your planning, you can quickly slip into negative cash flow. The problem becomes acute when you are unable to replenish inventory as cash becomes short; sales drop off and the downward spiral begins. Inventory replacement cannot be ignored.

During expansion or any other time when there is an unusual demand on cash, learn to operate with a cash flow projection. This will help you forecast your cash surpluses and deficits. It is a relatively straight-forward exercise. It allows you to monitor and scrutinize cash on a monthly basis. While a profit-and-loss statement shows the health of a business, a cash-flow projection helps you analyze the endurance factor and provides you the time to take corrective action before you get into any trouble (see Chapter 9 for Cash Flow Analysis).

Finding Money for Expansion

Expansion is *expensive*. Funding the growth of a business is perhaps one of your most difficult entrepreneurial tasks. Nevertheless, with imagination, careful planning, and calculated risk taking, you can develop a successful strategy for acquiring expansion capital. Consider some of the following money sources:

Investors. If your business is successful, others may be willing to invest in your expansion plans. Setting up a corporation and selling stock privately or as a public offering provides an opportunity to generate the necessary capital. Be careful to observe the regulations of the Securities and Exchange Commission for publicly held companies. If you seek money from strangers, it will take a more elaborate presentation, usually a written prospectus. If you obtain money from people you know, it will require less.

If you plan to expand by purchasing an existing business, you might consider this approach: Offer the owner of the business stock in your corporation as a down payment. That way you can avoid an up-front cash outlay. The seller receives a tax free exchange (stock for stock) and becomes a minority share holder in your corporation. Be sure to use your attorney, to structure this one. (Since the paperwork is rather complicated). Furthermore, this is a form of venture capital, you should definitely present a plan showing how your shareholders will recoup their investment. You can still control your business by retaining 51% of the stock.

Partners. You may not be able to expand successfully on your own, but with the financial and managerial help of a competent and compatible partner, you may be off and running. Operating two or more locations is a favorable approach for a partnership. Remember, you are the one providing valuable expertise and the successful concept; the newly acquired partner may be just providing the money. Don't sell your equity interest cheaply!

Bootstrap Financing. This term describes the use of internal cash flow to finance your expansion. Normally this is a slower way to move forward but has fewer strings attached. In fact, most growing companies bootstrap at least part of their growth. If you plan to take this approach, you must be dedicated to cash preservation. In other words, you have to build your bank account.
The first consideration, if you haven't done so already, is to incorporate. The corporate tax structure allows you to retain more dollars in the business than if you were to save the money personally. The second step, using a cash-flow projection is to determine when enough funds will be available. Since it takes time to expand, your funds will be growing while you are in the planning stage. You will also find banks very receptive to a company with a strong cash position. It demonstrates solid management skills and discipline. Even a moderate cash balance can provide leverage for a much larger loan. Be sure to put your money in a bank that offers the best chance for financing your expansion needs.

Creditors. Your suppliers will undoubtedly play a major role in your expansion. Having the cooperation of your creditors will give you everything, from the needed breathing room, to financing your entire expansion effort. Extending your payables from 30 days to 90 days can give you considerable positive cash flow. Let's say you presently pay inventory purchases within 30 days. If you can convince your suppliers to extend that to 90 days and also give you 60 days on opening inventory, your surplus cash flow during that period could be significant. It may even be enough to finance a good part of your construction equipment and fixture costs.

If you plan to try this approach, be prepared to give a persuasive presentation. Have a plan for bringing the accounts current within a year and offer buying loyalty. It is to the suppliers best interest to consider such an arrangement. First, they obtain another outlet to move their product and then they can often pass on the payment delays to manufacturers.

Conversion of an Asset. To generate expansion cash, you may be able to liquidate an asset that isn't being properly utilized. For example, if you own your business property, you may be able to sell it and lease back on a long-term basis. Perhaps you have a vehicle in the business that isn't necessary or accounts receivable that can be speeded up. If your inventory is heavy, consider selectively reducing it and converting it into cash.

Additionally, when you begin to consider expansion, it's vital that you trim any excess cash flow. "Lean and mean" is the name of the game. You may even have to reduce your personal income for a temporary period of time. And you should scrutinize each expense to uncover any savings opportunity. If you're presently running a successful operation, you may have become complacent. Now is the time to refocus and operate at maximum financial efficiency.

Leasing and Other Cash-Saving Opportunities. In order to preserve cash, consider leasing some of your assets. For example, leasing companies, banks and commercial finance companies will provide lease arrangements for fixtures, equipment, furniture, and vehicles. By leasing these business assets, you conserve your cash. The payment may eventually total more than a conventional loan, but most banks will only provide partial financing for such purchases and a lot more red tape. Consult your local yellow pages for firms that will lease business assets. Be sure to insist on the investment tax credit. Otherwise, the leasing company will take it. Since that amounts to 10% of the purchase price directly deducted from your tax liability, it is well worth requesting.

Negotiating deposits can be another way of saving cash. Most commercial real estate owners want a lease deposit. If you have a successful track record, as well as a solid financial position, landlords will consider a reduction and even a waiver if you simply ask. Remember, with a successful operation you are dealing from strength, and your negotiating tactics can change dramatically.

Commercial Banks

Needless to say, banks will look more favorably on a successful established business than they will a start-up. However, bankers by nature are conservative. They would much rather lend to an individual who doesn't need the money than to one who does. Your chances of getting a long term expansion loan (three to five years) will improve considerably if you use the following strategy.

1. *Prepare a written plan* detailing your present business condition and future plans. Most bankers get verbal loan requests from

small business owners and are very impressed with a written business plan, backed up with solid financial data.

2. *Find a banker that can make a decision.* Some loan officers have very low lending limits, while others can literally give the bank away. Ask up-front whether your loan request fits into that banker's lending authority. If it doesn't, you want to talk with the person who is going to make the decision. If the individual is reluctant to introduce you to that banker, move to another bank. It is imperative that you gain a personal rapport with the lending officer who controls your company's destiny.

3. *Have a positive but not arrogant attitude.* Don't say, "If I get the money", say, "When I get the money". Bankers will believe in your project if you believe in it, and you may have to do some subtle selling.

4. *Take your request to more than one lending institution.* But, once you have received a commitment, transfer all your business to that bank. You must show loyalty to those who put trust in you. Smaller banks seem to be more approachable than larger ones. However, it's still an individual who says . . . "yes" or "no".

The critical decision for a bank in reviewing a business loan is the ability of the borrower to *repay* the money . . . sounds straight forward. The problem is that many loan requests do not show enough evidence that repayment is feasible. Business owners frequently fail to show how the business can generate enough extra money to service the debt. Again, this is where your cash-flow projections enter the picture. With a well documented cash flow chart, you can demonstrate the firm's capability to generate excess cash flow. A banker may scrutinize your numbers, but in the end you will be the one making the projections. Unless the estimates are totally absurd, you can usually sell the package. Ability to repay the loan is the banker's number one criteria, and your request should be structured around it. If you then prove that your experience qualifies you to undertake this project and your past credit record is positive, you should be able to borrow money from almost any bank.

Expanding Without Money

Can you expand *without* any money? The answer is *yes!* But, it's not for the fainthearted. Chapter 17 on Financing A Sale outlines a number of creative tactics that allow people to purchase an existing business with little or no money down.

If you feel that you know your business to the point where you could significantly improve marginal operations, or you have developed some secret recipe of success, then start looking for businesses in your field owned by people who are tired, burnt-out, unhappy, or unsuccessful. Prepare a presentation that outlines a plan whereby they can "bail out." Initially you may have to overcome some of their ego problems. Nobody wants to think a competitor can come into their business and do a better job. Tact, diplomacy, and patience are essential if you want to successfully pull off this strategy. However, you can acquire marginal businesses with little or no cash. The important question that must be addressed is whether or not it's worth it. Bringing back a troubled business can be difficult and costly. Be cautious with this approach to expansion.

Finding Your Next Location

Finding the best expansion site is somewhat similar to a balancing act. You cannot locate too close to your present operation, or you'll steal your own customers. If, on the other hand, you locate a considerable distance away, you will be on the road all the time.

The basic criteria to use for selecting a second location is exactly the same as is your first. However, also consider how you want to spend your time. One retail entrepreneur I know opened three stores within the same number of years. They made almost a perfect triangle. Each was separated by 200 miles of boring driving (or very expensive plane trips). He was forced to spend three or four nights a week in motels. Although the "on the road" thing didn't bother him that much, it was expensive. Additionally, he was too far away to quickly respond to crises, and the business ultimately slipped away from him. He is now down to one store and was fortunate to be able to salvage that.

Consider your personal and family commitment, in addition to location availability, when you start exploring additional sites.

Chapter 12
How Do You Manage the Expanded Business?

There is no doubt you will be tested and challenged by the decision to expand. If you are like most small business owners, when you opened your first location, you did most of the work yourself. As you expand that will change. A fellow entrepreneur clarified this situation well. "When I had one store, everything was under control, because I did it myself. When I opened the second and third stores, I couldn't believe how difficult it became. I had to delegate and then live with a lot of mistakes. I also had to be much better organized, because I had to cover many more bases . . . there never seemed to be enough time."

As your expansion project gets underway, you will find your management role changes. You will have to *delegate* a great deal of the day-to-day management activities. This presents you with an entirely new set of tasks. You must learn to successfully recruit, train, develop, and motivate other people. The people you place in key jobs will determine your level of success. This is an extremely critical factor in retail and service businesses, but the same criteria prevails in virtually any business. Successfully operating an expanding business means successfully handling the people who work and manage that business.

It doesn't stop there. You must have the organizational aspects under control. If you have flaws in the operational systems, whether it be in bookkeeping, purchasing, merchandising, or promotion, they will only become magnified if you add additional outlets. It is imperative that you run one location well before launching an expansion program. You may not have time to rework the fundamentals once you get started.

The other managerial skill you need to develop is the ability to identify and solve problems quickly. Too often an entrepreneur becomes so involved in the "roll out" of the expansion program, that he or she neglects to handle the on-going problems until they become crises. Become skillful at immediately handling small problems before they grow into bigger ones. In expansion, you must always keep one eye focused ahead, and the other looking behind. What have you accomplished, if you expand your business only to see it unravel because your day-to-day problems remain unsolved?

People Management Programs

Expansion requires a successful development of people. As your business grows, you must rely more and more on people to assume important responsibilities. If you create a team of loyal, well-trained, honest people, there are virtually *no limits* to your expansion possibilities.

As I expanded my business, my major role became the recruitment, development, and motivation of people. Once I accomplished that task, all else seemed easy; now I had *help*.

A few individuals are naturally gifted in providing leadership. Most have to work at it. If you feel it's an area you should improve, consider seminars, courses, or a variety of books to sharpen your "people" skills. The concepts can be learned. Following are three programs I found particularly helpful in developing and motivating people.

Manuals. Shortly after I opened my second store, I wrote a training manual for sales personnel. Later, this was followed by an operations manual and a manager's manual. At first, these were rather simplistic. They represented a basic "how-to" guide for new employees and a reference guide for seasoned personnel. As the business grew, so did the manuals. The sales manual finally reached 60 pages of specific sales techniques and product knowledge. It was our "bible". It provided the new employee with a blueprint for immediately becoming productive. Remember, as you expand, you can't be at each location all of the time. I believe these written manuals were one of the key factors for establishing a smooth running and profitable business. Still, nothing takes the place of personal one-on-one or group training sessions.

Management Meetings. Developing managers will be one of your major challenges. There are differences between supervising managers and supervising employees. It is difficult to keep from giving mixed signals to managers. On one hand you want them to function in a certain way (your way). Yet, it is also important they have the freedom and autonomy to operate effectively on their own. If you use loose controls, they tend to select their own priorities. As you tighten up, they become less willing to make necessary decisions. A balance must be reached, and a good way to achieve that is the use of effective management meetings. The program I found most successful was as follows:

1. Meetings would be held at least every three months and last for a full day. The climate of the meeting would be open, allowing each manager to voice opinions, make suggestions, and offer fellow managers recommendations or personal insights.

2. Although most topics were preset in a written agenda, important issues or problems could be introduced for discussion.

3. The discussions on each issue always started with brainstorming. (Remember, no negative opinions are allowed during this process.) When the managers were encouraged to voice their creative thinking, a number of imaginative solutions were introduced.

4. The solutions were arrived at in a democratic manner. Each manager then felt that he or she had made a personal contribution and, therefore, was more willing to implement the plan.

5. Test projects were developed and assigned to those individuals who seemed most interested in the topic.

These meetings created a team environment among independent and competitive managers. They had the opportunity to see the total picture and also gain a better perspective of their roles. The style and openness of the meetings created a climate where each member participated in joint decisions, yet each felt personal responsibility for implementing the solutions. They were also encouraged to communicate with each other after the meeting. I believe this program helped considerably to create a high morale among the managers and within the stores.

InterStore Competition and Rewards. As the operation grows, you will have an opportunity to measure one location against another in sales, expenses, staff productivity, etc. Since your business uses duplicate formats, this is one of the most effective ways to identify problems. These comparisons also create an opportunity to effectively motivate your employees. Individuals and groups want to excel and will work harder if given some kind of challenge, recognition, or reward. As you begin setting up various contests or department awards programs, consider the following guidelines.

1. Make the program fair.

2. If you set up performance goals, be sure almost everyone reaches target.

3. Keep the program short, imaginative, and stimulating.

4. Somehow allow everyone to participate.

5. Provide some type of extra award for really outstanding performance.

6. Ask your employees for feedback and suggestions.

Relocation

Even if you decide that expansion is not worth it, you may be faced with relocation at some point in time. The reasons vary: your lease is expiring and new rent is unaffordable, or the neighborhood has changed, or your shopping complex is starting to deteriorate.

Probably as many as 30% to 40% of all retail or service operations are forced to consider relocating their business, and the prospect of moving always presents major problems. Although you are not starting from scratch, you must consider a number of important factors in order to preserve your established business. Your major concern is to bring as many customers with you as possible. If you have enough advance warning, you can do several things to ensure a smooth transition. For example:

1. Tell every customer in as many ways as possible when and where you're moving. Put signs in the store and flyers in their bags. Make a personal comment to customers - "Drop by the new store and see the improved operation."

2. Have a spectacular "We're moving sale" to bring in customers and tell them of the move, and a grand opening promotion to do the same after the move.

3. If you don't have a mailing list, consider starting one. The opportunity of highlighting your move via a promotional mailer has a number of advantages. Don't forget to include a map showing your new location.

4. Don't move too far away unless you have the type of business that retains a number of loyal customers.

5. Don't stay out of business too long. If people can't find you the first time, they may not try again.

Remember that your customers have a lot on their minds, and your move will not be their priority. You must *repeat* your plan often to them simply to have it register.

When you decide to move, attempt to achieve a couple of important objectives. Try to improve your location in order to capture additional customers and concentrate on refining your operation. Moving a business is the ideal time to do a massive spring cleaning. In other words, reshape your business by eliminating those things that don't work and expanding those that do. If you keep a positive attitude about relocation, it can become an opportunity, rather than a disaster.

Expansion . . . A Real Experience

I would like to share a personal experience about expansion. The story has a relatively happy ending, but while it was happening, it certainly provided some of the most stressful times I've ever experienced. It was a classic case of rapid expansion, numerous problems, near disaster, and finally success.

My partner and I opened our first store in an enclosed mall in Sacramento, California, during the summer of 1971. Since the mall was still under construction, our sales were very slow the first year, and we didn't even take a salary. Finally in the summer of 1972, a Penney's department store opened, and the mall was completed. Things finally started to improve. Since there were two of us and we didn't get along all that well, we decided to open another location.

The second store was immediately successful. Now we had two stores making a profit, and we thought we were invincible. The third and fourth stores were added the following year (two more within another year). There was only one minor problem - we didn't have any money!

The next couple of years were difficult, to put it mildly. In addition to the cash flow crisis, we had other major growth problems. We expanded so fast that our operational controls were not functioning very efficiently and in some cases were nonexistent. We had people problems because we couldn't get around to the stores often enough. However, the most severe problem was cash. Too many creditors wanted too few dollars. There were times when, if we had had a major problem in the system or an economic downturn, or even three weeks of bad sales, we would have been out of business. There was simply no backup position or slack. We were stretched too thin. I bought a book on "How To Go Bankrupt" and kept it in my briefcase. Somehow I felt that if things really got bad, I could pull out that book, wave it around like a sixshooter, and the creditors would run away.

We finally saw some light after a particularly good Christmas season, and the creditors began to have faith and patience. I paid off a construction contractor on New Year's Eve, three years after he built the last store. As we sat in his office drinking a glass of champagne (which I had brought along because he was the last creditor to be paid), he told me two important things. He said he began to believe in us when we told him honestly just how things were, and we didn't lie. When we said a check was in the mail, it was in the mail. Second, any time he asked for money, we sent him something. It may not have been what he wanted, but it was something. Those are the two rules for playing this particular game of hardball: *communicate often and send something!*

We made it, but it took three years of very modest salaries, and operating from crisis to crisis. It was hard on the nerves, but, in retrospect, it was well worth it. You too can expand a successful business, but you must be prepared for your blood pressure to increase a notch or two.

PART THREE

SELLING A BUSINESS

Chapter 13
Should You Sell Your Business

Every one's business is for sale . . . *at the right price!*

There probably isn't an entrepreneur who hasn't frequently considered selling his or her business. It has been said that the two best days in the career of an independent businessperson are the day the business starts and the day it sells. During the twelve years I was a retailer, there were times I thought of selling at least weekly and, depending on the pressure, occasionally the thought crossed my mind daily. It was not because I didn't enjoy the business . . . actually, I received a great deal of personal as well as financial gratification from it. Nevertheless, the pressure of owning a business is particularly difficult, and the stress of the day-to-day operations becomes overwhelming at times. The possibility of selling "to get out from under" occasionally presented a very enticing option.

For most entrepreneurs, however, the urge to sell usually passes. You eventually find solutions to the problems that are bothering you. Besides, there is always the fear of the unknown. What would you actually do if you sold your business? "The devil you know may be better than the devil you don't know." Still, as the motivation to get out increases, and it becomes more difficult for you to run your business with enthusiasm, it may be time to explore the realities of selling.

What we are about to discuss is *timing*. The objective of this chapter is to help you determine whether or not now is the time to seriously consider selling your business. You cannot minimize this decision. It will have a profound effect on your future. In addition, once the decision is made and the process begins, it may be psychologically difficult to stop.

After reading this and the next few chapters, you may decide the time is not right. Still, you have taken an important step. You have moved from the urge stage to the exploration stage, and you have decided to return to your business and run with it with renewed dedication. That is not to say that you won't pick this book up a year from now and execute the plan . . . it's simply a matter of timing.

This chapter also helps you determine your emotional, physical, and financial attachments to your business. Frequently an owner will fail to properly assess all of the side benefits the business provides. Perhaps the grass looks greener on the other side of the fence, but after you check, you find the water bill is twice as high. Will you be able to replace the freedom you now enjoy? What about the perks . . . the car write-off, medical insurance, travel and entertainment through the business . . . and let's not forget the cash! If you sell, will you find it difficult to duplicate those benefits, and if so, how important are they? What you don't want to do is to wake up 48 hours or four months after selling and say "I really shouldn't have done that!" You probably will have occasional second thoughts, but hopefully you will decide that it was a good decision because you examined all of your options before making it.

If you are like most owners, you have devoted your energy to the business. When you start to consider selling it, you find yourself in very unfamiliar territory. Chances are you have never sold a business before. Many a small business owner acts hastily and sells on an emotional basis—"I just can't handle this business any more, I'll take anything to get out". Or, because of inexperience, you may end up with the wrong buyer and eventually a law suit to collect your money. How can you avoid these pitfalls? Like all major tasks, your chances of success increase with the amount of planning you put into the project. Planning in this case can be divided into three steps:

1. Obtain a good understanding of the business buy-sell process.

2. Determine precisely what you want to achieve from the sale.

3. Develop a strategy for reaching those objectives.

You'll find that the following pages prepare you for dealing effectively with each of those steps.

To begin this decision making process, you must answer some thought-provoking questions. The answers may push you to some uncomfortable conclusions. You may find that you are burnt out, in the wrong business, not making enough money, or just plain unhappy. The more honest you are with this self-analysis, the clearer will be your final decision. Someone once said, "All of the major decisions in life should be made with one's intellect, rather than one's emotion." The decision to sell one's business is definitely a major one. What we will be doing is examining facts to help you make that decision based on objective thinking. Feelings, emotion, and ego are important but sometimes they cloud the real issue. It's far better to carefully evaluate facts and then rationally select the best option.

Motivation Changing to Frustration

At one point in time you were highly motivated to start your own business. Stop and reflect on exactly what led you to risk your capital, expend great amounts of energy, and put yourself on the line to become an entrepreneur. This examination of your past will give you valuable insight into your present situation. If the expectations you had when you first started the business have not been fulfilled, you're probably experiencing some degree of frustration.

For example, if you started the business because you thought it presented a real opportunity to make a lot of money, and you have only been able to survive, your present frustration may be running very high. Perhaps you were driven by the feeling that you just had to start something on your own. The challenge of opening a business and succeeding was so important to you that you were ready to risk everything. But now, the work may have become far less challenging and in fact downright boring. The future may not appear to hold the excitement you need to be happy and content. The dream of owning your own business has been illuminated by the light of reality, and its not what you expected, nor what you wanted.

There are numerous other motivating factors that launch people into their own businesses. Unfortunately many of their initial expectations prove to be less appealing in reality than they were in fantasy. I had an acquaintance who left a high-paying managerial job in which he felt very confined. Although he had considerable responsibility, he felt that having a boss, as well as a rigid corporate structure, left him virtually no freedom. So he purchased a retail business. After a little more than two years, he sold his store and returned to corporate life. His expectations of freedom in his own business never materialized. In fact, the store seemed more restrictive to him than the pressures of his previous job.

Many people think that having your own business opens the door to a free life, where you are the boss and where you can do pretty much as you want. They fail to consider the pressures that come as a result of the *four-wall syndrome*. Yes, you can do anything you want with your own business, as long as it doesn't alienate your employees, customers, suppliers, landlord, and banker. You don't have one boss—sometimes you have several, and the situation provides anything but freedom.

As you examine your past motivations and expectations against present day reality, you begin to see whether your frustration level is high enough to explore the possibilities of a sale. The key here is *happiness*. You can never be happy all of the time, it's impossible! But, if you find that the happiness and satisfaction you once achieved has turned into unhappiness and constant frustration, you may have reached a point where you could be more content doing something else with your life.

Small Business Pressures

No matter how many people you talked to prior to getting into your own business, no one really prepared you for the pressures. They may have attempted to explain to you the long hours, paperwork, employee problems, or inadequate cash flow. But, until you experience it personally, you have no idea of how stressful it can be.

Stop and reflect on the past few months in the business. Have you worked harder or longer hours than you anticipated? Have your employees frequently disappointed you? Has your cash flow been less than adequate? Have the customers been particularly unreasonable lately? If the answer to these questions is no, you might consider closing this book and putting it on the shelf for a later date. You might even consider going back to Chapter 10 on Expansion. On the other hand, if the answers are yes, join the ranks of the typical entrepreneur.

Some people actually thrive on the entrepreneurial pressures, while others feel overwhelmed. When you first start a business, energy and desire have a way of overcoming most problems. As time evolves, patience and motivation slowly seem to dissipate. What previously may have been acceptable pressure now becomes more difficult to handle. Time changes businesses, but most of all, it changes the people who run them. In analyzing whether you should sell your business, you must recognize that change is inevitable, and see things in the present, rather than the past.

On balance, you should also consider the positive side. It's yours—the business is all yours! Nobody tells you what to do or when to do it. Some of your employees may be very loyal and are doing a remarkable job. There is definitely a genuine excitement when your business is running well and making money. It tends to rekindle your desire and recharge your battery. These factors— the good and the bad—will influence your decision to sell or not to sell.

The Two "C's"

The two "C's"—*Capital and Capability*—are the major fundamentals of a successful business. Without the proper amount of capital and cash flow, the business struggles and frequently fails. Without the owners capability in managing the various tasks, a small business is equally doomed. Since these two factors, or the lack of them, are so important to an operation's survival, they become equally vital when you consider selling your business.

First, let's consider capital. There are two rather important questions to answer. 1. Are you receiving the type of return on your investment and time that you expected or need? 2. More fundamentally, do you have a major problem paying your bills?

The pressure of trying to make a living from a small business has become increasingly more difficult over the past couple of years. If most business owners divided the dollars they take out of the business by the hours they put in, some would qualify for government assistance. If you factor in the investment, risk, time, and energy, the financial return can sometimes be very disappointing. Despite all the rumors, few people actually become rich in small businesses. Very simply, if making money is one of your major personal objectives, and the business is not helping you reach that target, then you must determine if you should do something else to achieve your financial goals.

Many small businesses have continuous problems with *cash flow*. Not having enough cash to pay the bills definitely takes the fun out of being your own boss. This particular pressure probably forces more people to sell than any other single reason. Most small businesses are under-capitalized to start with. Unless the business takes off immediately, the problems become increasingly acute. When cash is scarce, inventories suffer, customers find fewer choices, sales drop, and the spiral continues downward. If cash flow is a major, relentless, problem for you, this may be the time to consider directing your valuable time, talent, and money into another opportunity.

The second fundamental ingredient of successful businesses is the owner's capability. Although most small business situations do not require formal education, they do require some specialized knowledge and experience. Dun and Bradstreet has determined that the major cause of business failure relates to the owner's lack of competence . . . unbalanced experience, inadequate managerial expertise, or insufficient specific knowledge in the chosen field.

You can learn to operate a business, but if your learning becomes an "on-the-job training program", serious problems may be developing along the way. Your learning time-table may take longer than the business can afford.

Additionally, some owners find that they are not very comfortable with key elements of their businesses. For example, selling is a major task of most successful operations. But, not all people can sell effectively or, for that matter, want to do it at all. If selling is essential to the success of your operation, and you don't learn it, or teach it to others, problems are sure to arise. The same applies to purchasing, record keeping, merchandising, etc.

Therefore, if either of the C's, Capital or Capability, presents critical problems for you, you may seriously consider exercising the option of selling your business and moving on to a more comfortable career.

Other Valid Reasons

Some may think the only reason you are selling your business is because it's losing money. Frequently that's not the case at all. My business was making a good profit, far more than I ever expected when I first started. I was simply burnt out. After twelve years, there was nothing new to challenge me. I probably didn't make a major creative contribution to the operation for its last two years. I was complacent, and the business literally ran itself. The stimulation and enjoyment were gone. I finally figured out that if I didn't get out and do something else, my brain would turn to oatmeal. I had become a bored, over-stressed caretaker. So I sold, in order to revive my entrepreneurial need to accomplish something.

The best way to visualize other valid reasons for selling your business is to review the following list. You may have additional more compelling reasons. The important thing this list points out is that you don't need to be losing money to sell, in fact, it helps if you're making a profit, you'll get a better price.

Other Reasons

1. Competitive pressures are increasing and will get worse before it gets better.

2. The business needs remodeling and you don't have the capital or inclination to do it.

3. You don't want to go through another recession.

4. You want to retire and travel.

5. You have no heirs to leave it to.

6. There's another business opportunity that will make more money or more sense.

7. You want to collect your investment and become liquid.

8. The lease is running out and you don't want to renew at the proposed terms (although someone else may).

9. A buyer has surfaced and seems very interested (every business is for sale—at the right price).

10. You can't get good people any more.

11. You just can't stand the customers any longer.

12. There is an unresolved partnership dispute.

13. The theft factor is getting to you.

14. It's impossible to take time off; you haven't had a vacation in years.

15. The composition of the neighborhood and customers has changed.

16. You are getting a divorce.

17. Your wife is threatening a divorce unless you sell the business.

18. All of the aggravations just aren't worth it.

19. Your health is failing and you don't want the pressure any longer.

20. Your trusted manager just quit.

As you can see, there are several valid reasons for selling a business. Perhaps you can identify with more than one or even add to the list. Still, it's not really the numbers that are critical - it's the *intensity*. If one issue is causing you sleepless nights then that may become your reason to sell.

Stress

As an entrepreneur, you have probably found that stress comes with the territory. There are a number of factors that contribute to this phenomenon. The life of an independent business person can be a lonely existence. You can't totally confide in your employees, and after awhile, you bore your spouse with the same old problems. Entrepreneurs do not have support systems. In large corporations you can rely on your peers for input. There is considerable shared responsibility and group activity. When you have your own operation, it's you at the top, absorbing all of the pressures, with few people to turn to for help. That can be very stressful.

Some entrepreneurs find this stress acceptable, others even find it stimulating. However, some have backaches, tension headaches, insomnia, and a rash of other physical and psychological ailments. If you are experiencing a high level of stress, is it worth it?

Excess stress may also manifest itself other ways. Some people will pass on the pressure to the employees, causing alienation and a variety of related problems. Others will absorb the stress, until one day they blow up. Others will find a few martinis seem to solve the problems . . . until tomorrow.

We live in a stressful competitive world, but when anxiety fills the day, then it may be time to examine one's life and lifestyle. If the unacceptable stress is the direct result of an uncompromising business, think about making a change. Life is too short!

Figure 13-1 is a stress chart. It provides a way to gauge your business stress and tension. Your score and its interpretation will give you valuable insights for your decision.

What Are Your Instincts Saying

Entrepreneurs, for one reason or another, tend to have a more intuitive nature than the average person on the street. The entrepreneur usually develops a highly sensitive "gut feel" to certain things in the business. It probably comes from being forced to make quick decisions or being on the line all of the time. It's important that you listen to your instincts. You get the first messages regarding your future from your subconscious. One ex-entrepreneur told me he recognized the symptoms when he realized that the employment want-ad section was the first part of the newspaper he looked at each day.

Often owners who are deciding whether to sell, telegraph their intentions by dropping hints to close friends or relatives. They may not be totally convinced they are going to get out, but they are starting to hedge their bets. There's usually a psychological pattern that develops when a person is coming to grips with whether or not to sell the business. It starts when:

1. One becomes preoccupied with all of the problems of the business and spends less time on the solutions.

2. You start to feel, and even comment to people, that the business isn't fun any longer, or that you're tired and bored with it.

3. It's much harder to go into the business every morning, and much easier to leave earlier.

4. You start thinking, or even fantasizing, about what you would do if you didn't have the business and how you would feel . . . free!

5. You talk with somebody that's knowledgeable about selling businesses or you read a book like this one. You're now in the exploration stage.

6. You make an informal plan about the sale of your business.

7. You finally make a firm decision and commitment to sell the operation.

This pattern may take a couple of months or a couple of years. Some owners perpetually cycle in and out of the process. However, if you have reached the last two stages, or if you are just plain curious, read on. The next five chapters will provide a step-by-step plan to exercise this option and to sell your business successfully.

FIGURE 13-1
ENTREPRENEURIAL STRESS CHART

In the morning I feel tense about getting down to business:

☐ 1. On occasion; but most of the time I feel pretty good about starting the day.

☐ 2. Frequently, particularly where things seem to be up in the air.

☐ 3. Everyday, no matter what the current problems are.

During the day, in the business:

☐ 1. I enjoy the work and leave only when I have something more important to do.

☐ 2. The place is stressful at times, but I tend to hang in.

☐ 3. I find it almost impossible to remain for any length of time and will use any excuse to leave.

In relationship with the staff:

☐ 1. We're almost like a family, and I have people that have been with me for a long time.

☐ 2. I can get uptight with the staff, but they understand...most of the time.

☐ 3. I'm irritable and tense with my employees and have a high turnover.

Considering my income . . .

☐ 1. I'm making good money. I'd like more, but I don't think I could be as happy in another job.

☐ 2. Money is tight and I wish I could make more, but things are tight for everybody.

☐ 3. I never have enough money either inside or outside the business. I could probably make more money doing something else with far less stress.

In my search for happiness and contentment:

☐ 1. I am basically very happy and find that having my own business contributes to this feeling.

☐ 2. I am relatively happy, but find that something is missing that I can't put my finger on.

☐ 3. I am very unhappy and frustrated most of the time.

Regarding my ability to sleep and relax:

☐ 1. I sleep quite well and feel refreshed when I wake up.

☐ 2. When things are difficult, I may wake up thinking about the business, but I still find I can "get away" mentally.

☐ 3. I don't sleep well and find myself worrying about the business. There doesn't seem to be any time to relax.

FIGURE 13-1 CONTINUED

When a customer walks into the business with a problem:

☐ 1. I see most problem people as challenges and try my best to convert them to happy, long-term customers.

☐ 2. Customers cause me some frustration and stress, but that's business.

☐ 3. I find myself getting very irritable and sometimes try to avoid the situation.

At home the atmosphere is:

☐ 1. For the most part very positive. That's probably in part because I'm happy with my work.

☐ 2. On difficult days I find that I can strain relationships at home if I'm not careful.

☐ 3. Basically a mess. I bring the business home and stress everyone. There is going to be a real problem if I don't change.

Regarding eating, drinking, or smoking:

☐ 1. I seldom have to resort to over-indulgence to relieve the pressure.

☐ 2. I've been known to have a couple of drinks to relieve the pressure.

☐ 3. To balance the pressure I probably eat too much, drink too much, and basically over-indulge.

If I sell the business:

☐ 1. I'd be unhappy because I really enjoy the business.

☐ 2. I'd be able to get another job or another business and be careful to find one with a little less stress.

☐ 3. I would be very happy and relieved.

This chart simply addresses personal stress and does not consider the many other valid reasons for selling a business.

Scoring Interpretations

Value each answer with the number preceding it. If the total is:

10 – 17   You are probably happy in your business and controlling the pressure. Unless there are some pressing problems or another valid reason (e.g. you want to retire), then consider continuing.

18 – 23   You are experiencing some stress, at times rather serious. You should isolate and solve the problems in order to get more satisfaction from your business.

24 – 30   You are experiencing considerable tension and stress running the business. If this continues, you should consider all your options, including selling.

Chapter 14
Preparing to Sell

Many an entrepreneur would sell the business "in a flash" if someone came into the office and offered to write a check. Unfortunately it usually isn't that easy. If you thought making the decision to sell was difficult you may find it was only the first in a series of tough decisions.

- What price should I ask?

- What terms should I be able to accept?

- Who would buy my business?

- Should I tell the employees?

- Should I use a business broker or try to sell it myself?

- How long will it take?

The next chapters will answer these questions and several others that are equally important. The balance of the book actually provides a road-map, preparing you for what will be an exciting and somewhat frustrating experience. The business buy-sell process can be simple or extremely complicated. The size of your operation may have some bearing on the complexity of the sale. However, it is difficult to predict before-hand how many problems will arise or how long it will take. The best way to approach it is to prepare for the worst and be pleasantly surprised if it goes well.

The first thing you must realize is that you are not the only owner who has sold a business . . . some estimates indicate that 2.5 million are sold annually. Therefore, have some comfort in the knowledge that you are not alone with your concerns and fears.

Your Involvement

Selling your business should be taken very personally. After all, you were the one who built it, and you should be closely involved in its sale. It is far too important a task to totally delegate to someone else, whether it be a qualified attorney, accountant, or business broker. That's not to say you shouldn't retain professional help. But, you must maintain control and constantly provide important input, so the professionals can be most effective.

However, becoming closely involved in the sale presents a couple of problems. First, it will take you away from the day-to-day operations, and second, since selling a business is probably unfamiliar territory, you will have to *do your homework*. To recognize the importance of these issues, consider how critical a successful sale will be to you. If you are like many owners, your business is one of your largest personal assets. Getting the right price and terms will have a profound effect on your financial future.

Second, you probably have little or no experience in selling a business. You know how to purchase, promote, and sell your products, but you probably don't know how to successfully sell a business. This is understandable since it is not something you do every day. I will attempt to take the mystery out of the process. It's actually not that overwhelming. Much of it is common sense. Nevertheless, a lot is at stake, and you should spend the time necessary to develop a working knowledge of what is involved. This knowledge will be crucial if you attempt to sell the business yourself. It will also be extremely valuable when discussing your needs with attorneys, accountants, or business brokers. These outside professionals will have your interest in mind, but they will have several other clients absorbing their energy simultaneously. You will never find anyone more interested or affected by the outcome of the sale than yourself. It therefore is vital that you participate in every major decision and even orchestrate the effort.

The major reason why some owners fail, in attempting to sell their businesses, is that they have done very little preparation or planning. If you consider the consequences, I'm sure you will agree that you want to be well prepared with an effective plan. Four areas are critical to the success of selling your operation.

1. Pricing the business (Chapter 15).

2. Determining who will sell the business (this chapter).

3. Locating and negotiating with qualified buyers (Chapter 15 and 16).

4. Getting paid (Chapter 17 and 18).

We will explore each of these areas in depth. When you have finished this book, you will be prepared to deal knowledgeably with all four.

Prepare Yourself . . . Mentally

For some, selling the business may mean some psychological adjustments. Entrepreneurs frequently become emotionally attached to their operation. Many owners who decide to sell really don't want to but have been forced into it. Some actually set up unreasonable barriers for potential buyers - they will establish the price too high or make the terms too difficult. Others will totally involve themselves in the business and be reluctant to talk with prospective buyers, thereby postponing the tasks involved in the sale. For many, the prospect of selling something they have worked so hard to build becomes a psychological trauma. The tendency is to avoid confronting the situation, in the hopes it may go away.

But if your reasons for selling the business are valid, don't postpone the inevitable. Once you have definitely determined to sell your operation, recognize that the job must be done and get on with it. If you find yourself doing things that are not helping sell the business, sit down and have a serious talk with yourself in order to refocus on the objective.

During the sales process it will sometimes be difficult for you to determine precisely what is going on. While you wait for people to react to offers, counter-offers, contract signing, etc., you can easily become immobilized. Fear of the unknown often creates real panic. This type of tension has a way of draining your energy and creating self doubt. You may even start to question your strategy. Don't let your anxiety show - it will look like negotiating from weakness. Additionally, your tension over the outcome of the sale will limit your performance in the day-to-day management of your operation.

How can you control this fear factor? Learn to relax! A somewhat simplistic answer, nevertheless very helpful. Also, try to focus in on the task at hand rather than on your hopes and fears. Concentrate on what is happening rather than what might happen. Doing something is better than worrying—particularly if it's about something over which you have virtually no control. If the buyer has until next Thursday to accept your counter-offer, there is nothing you can do about the sale until next Thursday. You might as well be productive in the business.

You must also prepare yourself mentally for the negotiation process. In most cases, when buyer and seller get together, there is mutual respect and fair play. However, each has very different objectives, a frequent cause of conflict. This is one of the major reasons for using an attorney or business broker as an intermediary. They tend to absorb the personal reactions of the parties and keep the sale moving ahead. Nevertheless, you should prepare yourself for emotional reactions in the negotiation stage . . . it's only natural. You must make sure, however, that you quickly get back on track and return to rational thinking. Some buyers can be very shrewd and use confrontation as a negotiation tactic. Be aware that keeping your mental composure is of prime importance, and if you start to feel yourself becoming too emotional , call "time out" and temporarily back away.

Finally, be prepared for things to go wrong. As an entrepreneur you are only too familiar with Murphy's Law: "Whatever can go wrong, will go wrong, sometimes precisely at the wrong moment." You may plan every last detail of the sale but if you don't leave room for error, delays, misunderstandings, or for people to be just plain slow at making important decisions, you will become very frustrated. In selling the business, you will frequently draw on your reservoir of patience. The calmer you are during the process, the stronger your negotiating position, and the better your chance to reach your financial goal - *getting a good price!*

Business sales take time. It is not uncommon to see a firm on the market for six months, a year, or longer. Your personal motivations and the quality of your business will influence the time-table. If you are highly motivated to get out, you will probably under-value your operation, and perhaps get a quick sale. If you set your price high and your terms restrictive, you narrow your potential market. If your business is particularly successful and is priced fairly, things will normally move rapidly. It's hard to find a good business priced right these days, and a number of people are looking for them.

To visualize a typical time-table of a sale, review the example of the Village Men's Store in Chapter 9. Recognize this example does not include the marketing phase (finding the buyer). The most important thing to remember, whether you price high or low, is that the process takes time. Mentally adjust to that fact and while you're waiting, continue to operate your business as effectively and profitably as possible.

Think Positively

As part of the preparation stage, look at your business in positive rather than negative terms. Some owners fail to see value in their operation. Typically, this is the result of financial difficulties. Owners know their operations inside and out. They see all of the flaws and all of the problems. They begin to think, "How could anybody possibly see value in this business?" Well, value is in the eye of the beholder. There is case after case of a marginal business being turned around after a sale. The enthusiasm and capital of the new owner often performs miracles over what appeared to be a terminally ill business.

Instead of being openly critical about the problems, be enthusiastic about the opportunities. Instead of being demoralized about the lack of business, see it as a temporary and curable situation. In other words, mentally visualize your business as an asset rather than a liability. If you remove the negativism, it will be much easier for you to price the business fairly and negotiate successfully to obtain that price.

Establish Your Reasons for Selling

Some potential buyers think the only reason the business is for sale is that it is losing money. As a seller, you must convince them that is not the case.

Every prospective buyer will want to know why you are selling the business. It's important that they believe your reason. You must create a certain degree of credibility early in the negotiation process. The subject of why you are selling can be a way of establishing that credibility - or conversely, a way of making everything you say in the future sound untrue. It pays to be honest. Most people really don't lie well. If you're tired of the business, tell them that. After all, people get bored with their jobs and careers and make changes. Entrepreneurs should have the same luxury. Incidentally, boredom or the need for change sounds very realistic to a buyer who is doing the same thing by leaving a career and buying your business. Avoid giving reasons like, "I am sick and my doctor told me to sell the business", or "My wife wants me to sell and spend more time at home". They may be valid, but they sound like excuses covering up the real problems.

If the business is not making as much income as you want, tell the buyer. But also explain that, because you are burnt out and not spending time in the business, you had to hire more employees and therefore your payroll is up. Remember, some small business owners bring in a spouse or even the kids to make things go. Another buyer may need only a limited salary because of a two-income family. Review the valid reasons for selling a business (in the previous chapter); then spend time making those reasons sound very believable, because you are going to be asked about them.

Operate All Out!

Once you're committed to the sale of your business, don't quit. On the contrary, pour it on. Perhaps you're burnt out and would really rather be someplace else. Well, in a few months you will be. Right now the business is still yours, and these may be the most critical months you have spent operating it. The extra push will be easier than you think. Since you have made the decision to sell, you can see the light at the end of the tunnel. You should be able to endure almost anything. Furthermore, your constant activity will be contagious to the employees. The sales will probably increase, providing you with better cash flow and giving the prospective buyer a better sales picture.

Also, remember that potential buyers, their friends, relatives, and assorted advisors are going to be around the business. A vibrant operation is going to be more attractive than a depressed one. If things are on the up-beat, you can honestly say to the buyer, "Look at these sales figures; last week we were up 15% over the previous year. You're buying a great business with a bright future!"

In addition, operate straight! Until the sale, all cash should go through the books. I realize that concept may be difficult for some entrepreneurs to handle, but consider what happens when you say to a potential buyer, "Well, I don't record all my cash, my true sales . . . that's another story." Guess what? You have just admitted to a felony. This will create more problems in the future than you ever considered. Non-verified sales simply do not exist. Business brokers will never represent sales that cannot be verified. If the buyer experiences hard times after the purchase, you have opened yourself up for a potential lawsuit based on fraud.

During the last months record all the cash. You won't have to give excuses or create two sets of books. Potential buyers, unless totally naive, will readily understand the increase of cash. Your only alternative may be to significantly reduce the price of the business to reflect the lack of verifiable sales.

Finally, run promotions, increase advertising expenditures, and, in general, attempt to generate business. Consider offering bonuses to the staff for extra sales performance. Do whatever you have to do to create new business (within reason). At the same time see if you can reduce expenses. Look around for ways to cut costs, trim non-productive payroll, and pay for travel and entertainment out of your own pocket. Reduce or postpone any non-essential expenses. Your objective is to show profit. People buy businesses because they make money. So develop a plan to improve your bottom line and start yesterday.

Cleanup Campaign

Early some morning, before anyone arrives, go into your business with a clipboard and a critical eye. See the operation from the perspective of the potential buyer. Make a list of those things that should be changed to make the operation more visually appealing. A retail store's checklist might look like this:

1. Rearrange floor displays for maximum visibility.

2. Redo the front window display.

3. Replace the point-of-sale and window banners with fresh pieces.

4. Paint that ugly wall.

5. Clean the carpets.

6. Replace dirty price tags.

7. Clean up the cash-and-wrap counter and the storage areas.

8. Dust the merchandise.

9. Order rent-a-plants to brighten up the store.

10. Etc.

11. Etc.

You'll be surprised how long the list will get when you take an objective point of view. Now, split the list among the staff and over the next few weeks turn the operation into a showplace. Then make sure that you have an ongoing procedure to keep it that way.

Selling the business is somewhat like selling a house. Home buyers want to move furniture in and start living in a clean environment. A business buyer will be more inclined to pay top dollar for a business they can walk into and start making sales. If they have to close for two weeks to repaint and refurbish, then your price will reflect that interruption.

The best way to handle the financial impact of the clean-up campaign is to set an affordable budget. How much cash can you devote to the project? Look at your list and attempt to pick out those items which will provide the highest visual benefit for the lowest dollar cost. Set priorities. When the budget runs out, that's all you can do.

Improvement Plan

If you had the money, time, interest, and energy, exactly what would you do to improve your business? You're probably saying to yourself, "If I had all those things, particularly the money, I wouldn't be selling." Well, if you get a call telling you a long lost relative passed on and left you a bundle, this list will come in handy. If that doesn't happen, give the plan to potential buyers. You know your operation better than anyone else. You know precisely what should be done to increase sales and profit. You may not have enough money or inclination, but the new owner will. This improvement plan, if brought up at the right time in negotiations, could be just the thing that turns on a buyer and makes a sale.

This improvement plan has another potential use. A retailer, who was in the process of selling his store, asked if I would help him handle a major problem that had just surfaced. He had a buyer for his operation, the price and terms were settled, but unfortunately the shopping center's leasing agent was creating a stumbling block. The seller had less than a year remaining on his lease, and the center was being particularly unco-operative in discussing a new lease. When you have a soon-to-expire lease, you don't really have a business to sell. Buyers are extremely reluctant to purchase a business that doesn't have a good long-term affordable lease.

I asked the seller to put together an improvement plan with a reasonable time-table and budget. The prospective buyer reviewed it and made a few minor changes. He then presented it to the shopping center management as "his" proposed plan of improvement if he purchased the store. The center was impressed enough to sign a new lease with similar terms. Everybody won and the sale was made. The improvement plan was the catalyst that made it happen.

Consider Your Selling Strategy

When you sell a business, you are faced with making decisions on several alternative sales strategies. You may be surprised at the options available to you. Before you set any plan in motion, it's critical to take time to evaluate all the alternatives. Once the sales process starts, the business will change, simply because you will change. You want to try to avoid making major adjustments in strategy. That's not to say that if one method doesn't work, it's impossible to shift to another, but it does take time and you lose momentum.

In fact, like many business owners, you may make the decision, at some point in time, to pull your business off the market. One owner I spoke with did just that after finding no one wanted to pay his price. He was making a good income from the business but felt that he should be doing something else. After six months on the market and only a few unqualified buyers, he decided the business was more valuable to him than a sale at a low price with a risk of future payments. He not only returned to running the business, but he made a decision to expand and open a second operation. He stated that the expansion gave him an entirely new challenge and renewed his interest in the operation.

As you develop a better understanding of the sales process begin writing down the advantages and disadvantages of various strategies and options. Keep a file and make notes as you research the project. Write comments in the margin as you read this book. Your reactions and inputs will help you select the best selling approach. You may even want to consider an alternative to an outright sale. For example:

1. Take on a partner. Silent or working partners may offer the capital and expertise to make the business flourish.

2. Sell part of the business to a key employee with a long-term buyout provision.

3. Work part-time in the business and hire a manager.

4. Get another job, hire a manager and keep the business.

5. Walk away—many people do it. But before you do, try to sell it. There is a buyer for almost every business.

6. Go bankrupt. Bankruptcies under Chapter 7 and Chapter 11 have increased dramatically over the past years. (See Chapter 19).

When your business consists of multiple locations, additional options are available. You may consider selling one location rather than the entire operation. Supervising a chain of anything is difficult. Absentee ownership entails multiple management problems. Frequently, one location is losing money and draining others. Consider selling the losing one. Since prospective buyers readily accept absentee ownership as a valid reason to sell, they may not be overly concerned about the poor performance.

If you let your imagination work, I'm sure you can think of even more options or perhaps a variation that will offer a better outcome than an outright sale. If you're unsure, give more time to the evaluation stage. Talk to other owners who have sold their businesses. Contact a few business brokers. They will, of course, want to list your business. Simply explain to them that you are in the "thinking stage" and ask them to give you a feel of the market. If necessary, take a vacation. Sometimes getting away from the day-to-day activity will enable you to evaluate all of the factors more clearly.

How to Handle Employees

As the old saying goes, "People are your most important asset . . . or, occasionally, liability." At no time will that be more accurate than when you decide to sell. As your business changes, after you make the decision, your employees will also change. No matter how loyal they are, their immediate reaction is going to be "how does it effect me?" People get very self-centered when their world is threatened. Your employees will feel endangered no matter how you sugar-coat the message.

Basically you have two choices. Don't say anything - or tell them exactly what you are planning to do. I've done it both ways, and there are advantages and disadvantages to each. First, consider the pros and cons of saying nothing. If you are using a business broker or have a special telephone number for inquiries, you may be able to keep it under cover for a period of time. I sold two stores with a total of thirty employees and didn't announce the fact until the day before the sale closed. I took two people into my confidence prior to the final days and that was only because some correspondence was inadvertently sent to the store instead of my home. In retrospect, I was very happy I kept it from them. The negotiations took six months and I'm not sure that I could have retained some key employees during that period if they had known. Nobody was hurt by not knowing; as a matter of fact, almost all stayed. The transfer to the new owner was quick and smooth and the employees didn't have time for unnecessary fears.

If you don't tell your staff and it gets out (you'll be very lucky if it doesn't), some of them may feel betrayed. Now you're going to have to talk fast. You must reassure them that the sale was in the very preliminary stages, and you didn't want to say anything until you knew for certain; you didn't want to worry anyone unnecessarily.

If you decide to tell the employees, it is important that you do it effectively. If not, you will have some major problems on your hands. Follow these tips. Try to tell each employee individually. They have put faith in you and deserve extra consideration now. This is particularly true of any long-term staff members. Be honest, tell them why you are selling the business, but don't raise their fears and don't go into detail about any financial problems. Simply explain the business is too difficult for you to handle, and that a new owner would be beneficial to it's operation and would provide them with a more secure and stable future. If you are burnt out, tell them that too. They probably know it already, and you will only be confirming their observations. That's the path I took on the sale of one of my stores, and it worked well. I also set up a small bonus plan for all the employees who stayed until the store sold. Whether it was my approach or the fact that they recognized the store needed new ownership, a positive attitude prevailed during the three months it took to sell the operation.

As a final consideration, if you find that some employees show resentment or negativism, don't hesitate to make changes. If there are problem staff members, let them go. Recruit some new people. A new employee is interested only in learning the job and getting along and less concerned with the long term.

Probably the best strategy is to keep the sale confidential until it's absolutely necessary to tell everyone. Then do it as effectively and gently as possible, reassuring them that they have no reason to be concerned about their jobs. You will provide excellent recommendations to the new owner, and furthermore, they will be needed because of their experience.

Business Brokers

You must also make the decision whether to sell the business yourself or use a business broker. Since this is the era of do-it-yourself, you might be inclined to try it on your own initially (you can always change your mind and list later). The major advantage is that you save the broker's fee. However, depending on the situation, a broker's fee may be the best investment you ever made. It was surprising to learn that only a small percentage (5-10%) of sales actually go through business brokers, although the figure is growing rapidly. Five years ago there were 3,000 business opportunity brokerage firms - today, there are over 7,000

Most business sales are made directly between buyer and seller with an attorney or accountant acting as advisor. Sales occur this way because either the buyer or the seller approaches the other directly. Frequently, the buyer and seller know one another. Whether you decide to use a business broker will depend largely on how adventuresome you are, or whether you know potentially qualified buyers. When you finish this book, you will be prepared to do it yourself. One major recommendation, if you proceed on your own, obtain the services of a qualified attorney . . . there are just too many legal pitfalls.

A business broker, like a real estate broker, works on a commission basis. However, most business brokers now charge either a minimum fee or a percentage, whichever is greater. Typically, a minimum fee for the sale of a small business will be $5,000 to $7,500. The percentage would normally be 10 to 12 percent of the sale price. In other words, if you sell your business for $40,000, you would pay a minimum fee. If your price is, say $75,000, the percentage would exceed the minimum and you would pay 10-12% of the sale price.

But, remember, if they don't sell the business, there is no commission or fee. The broker is paid strictly on performance. A business broker, if qualified and skilled, will offer a number of important services. Carefully consider the following to determine whether they meet your specific needs.

1. *Confidentiality.* A business broker provides a degree of confidentiality that you would not be able to achieve if you attempted to sell the business yourself. Insist on strict confidence; and ask the broker to require each prospective buyer to sign a statement that they will not contact the employees, customers, suppliers, or otherwise make known their intent in the business. Despite all precautions, the sale may be exposed, but this approach does give you some extra protection.

2. *Availability of Buyers.* Business brokers have a reservoir of potential buyers. They recognize the importance of an ongoing file of qualified individuals and may have someone actively seeking your type of business.

3. *Screening.* Business brokers will screen buyers so as to provide you only with "qualified prospects". That doesn't eliminate your investigation, particularly if the sale terms include a note from the buyer. People will occasionally misrepresent themselves. It will be up to you to verify they are what they say they are and have the financial ability to handle the payments.

4. *Expertise.* A broker specializing in business sales (not just an occasional business opportunity between home sales) will offer considerable expertise. He or she should be qualified to take the sale through the entire process—marketing, negotiation, and closing. The broker will have the expertise to advise you on pricing, buy-sell contracts, and selling terms.

5. *Negotiations.* Since the buyer and seller have very different objectives, the possibility for conflict is high. A qualified business broker will provide an intermediary relationship to both parties. The broker will carry offers and counter-offers back and forth without the buyer and seller having to confront one another. A broker, by law, has a fiduciary relationship to both parties and must be honest and forthright in negotiations.

6. *Pricing.* Seeing the marketplace at firsthand, a broker can be very helpful in establishing a "salable" price. It is important, though, that you take a direct involvement since you know the business, and you'll be the one most affected by the pricing outcome.

If you decide to use the services of a business broker, attempt to interview as many as possible. Talking with these individuals will greatly enhance your knowledge of selling a business and give you valuable comparisons. Questions you may want to consider asking are:

1. What method will be used to value the business?

2. What specific services will be provided as part of the fee?

3. What type of listing contract will be required?

4. Will the broker provide a sales brochure?

5. What will be the format for the buy-sell agreement (ask to see a typical sales contract).

6. How will potential buyers be handled? Will the broker accompany each prospect to the business?

7. What information will the broker need?

Sometimes it's more important, when trying to evaluate brokers, to listen to the questions they ask, rather than the answers they give. A truly professional broker will want to know in depth information about your business. Also be skeptical of a broker who attempts to place an unusually high price on your business with a long-term exclusive contract.

Typically there are three types of broker listing agreements:

1. *Open Listing* - With this type of contract you may list the business with as many brokers as you wish. Whoever sells the business receives the commission. If you sell it personally, there is no commission. As you can appreciate, brokers are not happy with this type of contract and will be reluctant to put too much time into the sale - unless, of course, there is a potential buyer waiting in the wings.

2. *Agency Listing* - This listing provides a broker with an exclusive right to sell your business. However, you can still sell it personally and not have to pay a commission. This arrangement normally presents the broker with a fair compromise and gives you the flexibility to pursue buyers on your own.

3. *Exclusive Listing* - No matter who sells the business, the broker is paid a commission. All brokers will attempt to persuade you to sign an exclusive listing. Don't do it. It leaves you with little or no flexibility and virtually no control. The broker will also ask for an extended time, period -6 months to a year. A more reasonable time schedule is three to four months. If a broker can't find a buyer in that period of time you have the wrong broker or a major problem with your business. If you have to sell your business fast, consider giving a 30 day contract. This way if one broker can't sell it, someone else might.

After signing with a broker, you might consider inviting the broker's office sales staff to your location for a "get acquainted party". Be prepared to tell them the advantages of owning your business. It's also helpful to provide a few photographs of the site. Above all, be pleasant, but persistent. If you don't hear from your broker in a week, phone and find out what's happening. Make sure your business is that broker's priority.

Chapter 15
How Much Is Your Business Worth

Assign prime importance to determining the accurate value of your business. An owner is particularly vulnerable when on the brink of selling. This "true story" will graphically illustrate why.

An acquaintance owned a retail operation for about three years. Although he had made money in the business, he had also experienced a number of problems. The final straw came when his manager resigned to start a similar business in the same area. Up to that point, he had been insulated from the day-to-day hassles. With the loss of this key employee, he became openly negative about the operation. He recognized that it was time to get out before the business suffered major harm.

He contacted a business broker and perhaps because of his psychological state, signed a selling agreement on the initial visit. Number one mistake! Always put some time between the initial contact and the commitment. The broker will still be there in a couple of weeks.

The price was set based on the broker's recommendation and "expertise" in the field of valuing businesses. In fact, the price was set to produce a quick sale. A potential buyer appeared within a week, and a contract was signed in three weeks. Although the owner was pleased about the prospect of selling his business, he was ambivalent about the price and terms. Nevertheless, he went through with the sale.

As he later described his business to me and produced year-end financial statements, it became apparent that he had sold his firm for 30-40% less than fair market value. Considering the total dollars involved, that was a significant sum. Whether the broker was negligent or inexperienced is probably difficult to determine. Regardless, the sale is now history. But the point remains; you have so much at stake when you sell your business, that you must take an active and educated role in the major decisions. Pricing is definitely a major decision.

What makes the task of valuing a business difficult is that there are no ironclad rules and very few meaningful formulas. However, there are some basics. That's what this chapter is all about—*basics*. You won't emerge as a certified business appraiser, but you will know how to call the plays. If you follow the guidelines in the next few pages, you will get very close to the true value of your business. Since there is no exact right price, getting close will be just fine.

Definitions

Before we begin the actual task of developing a valuation formula, it is important that we cover some fundamental definitions and concepts. As you become involved with the professionals in the field of selling businesses, you will hear a number of terms. Your ability to deal with the "pros" on their level at the outset will serve notice that you know what you're doing. This edge will provide you with the control you need to avoid being stampeded into a poor decision.

Book Value (Net Worth). This is an accounting term that describes the business owner's equity in a very limited way. If the total liabilities at full face value are deducted from the cost of all assets less reserves for bad debts and depreciation, the difference is what the business is worth on the books. The balance sheet shows this as owner's equity. There are three problems in using this figure to determine the value of a business.

1. It does not take into consideration the profitability or the earnings potential of the operation.

2. The tangible assets, leasehold improvements, and fixtures, etc., are shown at their depreciated value rather than their current fair market value.

3. Debt is considered at its full face value, even if it may be worth less or can be settled for less.

Good Will. This term is applied to the intangible value of a business beyond its book value. It won't be shown on a typical balance sheet, so some people feel that it does not exist as a measurement of value. It appears on the balance sheet only if the current owner bought the assets of the ongoing business from somebody else and part of the price was allocated to goodwill.

Goodwill can probably best be explained as the business's ability to generate a profit. What contributes to this ability includes such intangible assets as general reputation, brand name recognition, technical know-how, location, unique concept, and historic ability to retain customers. But because it can't be counted like inventory or valued like equipment, its dollar amount is subject to negotiation. This is covered in greater detail later in the chapter.

Duplication Value. This is what it would cost to replace your business at current market prices. Since a buyer always faces the option of starting a business similar to yours from scratch, this figure represents a foundation for establishing value. What it does not take into consideration is the amount of money it would take to bring a new business up to your earning capacity—that's where good will comes in.

Spendable Cash Flow Versus Profit. In many ways cash flow—the money the business generates above operational costs—is more important than profits. This earning capacity is what you are selling. This is the money the buyer will use to pay any debt (probably to you), pay his or her salary and improve the business. Profit, on the other hand, is the bottom line on the P&L statement and what taxes are paid on. Most alert small business owners tend to minimize profits and maximize spendable cash flow.

Real Estate. Although most of our discussion concerns business owners who lease their locations, some firms actually own their buildings and property. This situation presents an additional dimension to the sale. You have the option of selling the property and the business as a package or retaining the real estate and leasing it to the new owners. Frequently, this leasing arrangement presents the best alternative. The price of an on-going business plus real estate is often so high that few buyers are able to afford the deal.

Economic and Non-Economic Factors Effecting Price

There are a number of additional factors, other than assets and good will, that will effect the value and hence the final price of your business. Actually, valuing a business is part science and part art. The science lies in knowing what to do with the numbers. The art is knowing how to use the variables to apply upward pressure on the price. Consider, for example, how each of the following will effect the value of your operation.

Terms of the Sale. If you demand all cash, there will be fewer qualified buyers capable of handling the purchase. As you become increasingly liberal in the terms, more potential buyers become available. An all-cash sale may have a downward pressure of 30% or more from fair market value. But 30% down, with 70% to be financed, will normally get what your business is worth. (See Chapter 5 for a table on down payments.)

Risk. If your business has been operating for five or more years and you consistently show favorable earnings, then a buyer will perceive and ultimately pay for "lack of risk." On the other hand, the risk factor is increased and the perceived value decreased if earnings have been erratic, or there is a major competitor in the area, or the buyer doesn't fully understand the business.

A potential entrepreneur who lacks experience wants to minimize the chance of failure and will pay a premium to a seller who can verify that the risk is low. However, if your buyer is a competitor who knows the business, a lack of bottom-line profit may not be of much concern. The competitor is focusing on your gross sales, which he can reduce to a net income figure through combining operations. I personally believe the best potential buyers for a going business are the people who are already in the business.

Motivation. Motivation is a door that swings both ways. If you are highly motivated to get out of your business, and you demonstrate this in the negotiations, your price will fall. If you have patience and are willing to stick with a realistic figure, someone will recognize the value and purchase the operation. Buyers are faced with the same dilemma. If they find a business that is attractive and delay too long, then someone else may move in ahead of them. As a seller, attempt to read the extent of a buyer's motivation. At the same time attempt to portray confidence and patience.

Ease of Management/Training. If you have a bar, liquor store, or fast-food business, then you will attract a large pool of potential buyers. These businesses are easier to run than a shoe store, pharmacy or appliance outlet. Whether your business is difficult or easy, offering a buyer training is essential to most sales. Buyers see the opportunity to learn a business as a valuable factor and will pay accordingly. Reluctance to stay on and help a new owner may create mistrust and will often lower the price.

Economic Times. Timing can be extremely important to a seller. If the economy is in a recession, your business probably is too. If you want top dollar, then you may have to ride out the hard times. If you want someone else to shoulder that burden, then your price will reflect the state of the economy as well as your P&L.

The Future. Although it's like looking into a crystal ball, if your industry, business location and city appear to have a bright future, the value of your operation will remain strong. If any of these factors look doubtful, buyers will want to hedge their bets and lower the price.

Supply and Demand. The most advantageous position for a seller is two or more qualified buyers interested at the same time. Essentially you have an auction. When two people start bidding, the selling price will often exceed the asking price. However, if there are a number of businesses similar to yours on the market, some comparison shopping will occur. Then, the better your business looks externally and internally (the books), the better chance you will have of capturing an available buyer.

Negotiation/Preparation. The selling price often reflects the skill and preparation of the buyer or seller. This factor is highlighted in a typical sales situation in Chapter 9. The buyer was prepared to negotiate strongly. He persuaded the seller to trust him and reduce the selling price based on his logical reasons. If you, as the seller, are prepared to justify and substantiate your figure, showing that it represents the true value of the business, you will find a buyer willing to pay your price. It may be one of your greater selling efforts. If you don't feel strong in this area, hire a pro. A good business broker will supply this expertise, but you have to supply the ammunition.

Tax Implications. The tax implications of a business sale have always been rather complex. With the passage of the Tax Reform Act of 1986, the tax consequences to both buyer and seller have changed dramatically. The biggest factor affecting this issue is the repeal of capital gains. Before 1986, a business owner could receive very favorable tax treatment if the sale was structured in certain ways. Much of that advantage has been lost. However, there are still several areas that affect taxes, and skillful negotiations plus a knowledge of the tax law will provide you with an edge. Taxes and legal considerations are covered in Chapter 18.

How to Perceive Value In a Business

Think for a moment of your business as an apple orchard. There are really two valuable parts in the orchard. First, there is the crop of apples that is sold each season—call that the annual profit. Then there are the trees that produce that crop—call them the tangible assets. When you sell a business, you sell both parts. You're selling assets (trees) and earning potential (annual crop).

The key to getting a fair price for your business is to show its earning potential, or what I call *Potential Earning Power*—P.E.P. That's really what buyers are buying. It provides the future, both for them and their families. If you have a well-located, well-stocked business, but no earning power, getting a good price will be difficult—not impossible, but difficult. Having all the above plus earning power provides a very salable business.

Most buyers will purchase a business if it has the potential to return 20-30% on their investment after a fair salary is deducted. In other words, if a buyer invests $100,000 (cash or terms), and takes a $25,000 salary to run the business, that business should be able to provide an additional $20,000-$30,000 in annual earning power before taxes. Remember, if the buyer puts the same $100,000 in U.S. Treasury Notes, the return would be about 6-8% with virtually no risk.

If you cannot show earning potential in your business, then you are faced with the task of finding a potential buyer who is simply interested in buying a job. Then the central issue becomes whether you can get paid for anything over the market value of your tangible assets. Even if you have never shown a profit, don't despair. You may have hidden earning power in your business which can be shown to a prospective buyer.

Traditional Methods for Valuing a Business

Typically, there are four ways to value a going concern. Remember, we are discussing small businesses. These firms are not traded on stock markets where their value will be set on supply and demand, industry multipliers, or someone's expectations of future earnings. We're concerned with the small retail, service or manufacturing business you see up and down Main Street, U.S.A. - a business just like yours. The four general methods are:

1. *Asset or replacement-cost approach:* This method involves appraising the fixed or tangible assets at market value. That value is what it would cost to replace them in the same condition they presently exist. For example, replacing a drop ceiling would cost "X" dollars. Since a drop ceiling normally does not come used, the replacement cost would become the asset value. However,

used furniture or fixtures would cost less than new and would reflect the depreciated value. Relying solely on this method of valuing a business would totally ignore the profit or earning potential of the operation.

2. *Income or earning approach:* This method considers only the net profit of the operation. For example, if a company produced a profit of $10,000, and an investor wished to receive 20% on his investment, the price of the company would be $50,000. But this approach has two major disadvantages. First, it doesn't consider the tangible assets, which may be of considerable value. Second, since most small companies tend to minimize profit for tax purposes, this method fails to consider owner's salary, fringe benefits, and depreciation.

3. *Formulas using multiples:* In Chapter 5 the subject of multiples was discussed in detail. This approach has many drawbacks and rarely provides anything but a vague starting point.

4. *Comparison approach:* This method, which considers the price paid for similar businesses, may be suggested when you list your firm with a business broker. It has serious drawbacks. Very few businesses are exactly alike. They simply cannot be appraised like residential real estate; there are far too many variables. For example, if you are a skillful negotiator, are willing to carry back paper, and have patience, you will get a strong price. None of those factors can be related to the assets or earnings of comparable businesses.

As you can see, each of the traditional methods for valuing a business has its limitations. It takes a more innovative approach to accurately determine the true value of a business operation. It also takes time. But because you're dealing with real dollars—perhaps your source of income in future years—your time and thought will be well worth the effort.

When you finish the exercise outlined in this chapter, you may discover the hidden value in your business. More important, you will have established a method to substantiate and verify your price when negotiating with potential buyers. You will now have valid reasons to justify the dollars you're asking. This preparation and validation will provide you with an invaluable edge at the negotiating table.

Innovative Approach to Valuing a Business

First, let's consider the profit aspects of valuing a business. Ideally, a small-business owner will write off everything possible to reduce taxes. One of the major attractions of being an entrepreneur lies in paying a number of business-related expenses out of the operation's income. When you review the Profit and Loss statement of a typical small business, it may appear to be marginally profitable. Only after the statement is *adjusted* or *normalized* can you gain a true perspective of the firm's potential earning power (P.E.P.) or precisely how much *spendable cash* is available. Adjusting or normalizing the Profit and Loss statement to reflect a true picture of your company's financial health becomes your first major task.

Profit, for most small companies, is a misnomer. Far more important is the excess cash the business will provide. The owner can then make decisions on how to use that cash, e.g. more inventory, fancy cars, huge salaries, even expansion.

Figure 15-1 shows an example of how a typical business P&L statement can be normalized. This firm generated only $6,300 profit on sales of $460,000—a somewhat anemic performance. However, when each expense was scrutinized and the owner's spendable cash was analyzed, the earning power of the firm jumped to $122,220. That is a significant improvement, making this company very salable. The following section explains each adjustment.

FIGURE 15-1
TYPICAL RETAIL PROFIT AND LOSS STATEMENT

	Actual	Adjusted	Difference
NET SALES	$460,000	$460,000	
Cost of Sales (inc. freight)	235,500	235,500	
Gross Profit	$224,500	$224,500	
Operating Expenses			
Employee wages	$ 62,600	$ 42,600	$ 20,000
Officers wages	42,500	—	42,500
Payroll taxes	11,800	4,800	7,000
Rent	24,500	20,900	3,600
Advertising	10,800	7,800	3,000
Auto expenses	9,200	5,200	4,000
Donations	2,100	—	2,100
Dues and subscriptions	1,200	—	1,200
Insurance	3,300	3,300	—
Insurance (officers)	2,900	—	2,900
Accounting and legal	4,600	2,100	2,500
Telephone	4,200	4,200	—
Utilities	3,100	3,100	—
Office expenses	3,800	1,600	2,200
Store supplies	1,400	1,400	—
Repair and maintenance	6,300	1,100	5,200
Taxes and licenses	400	400	—
Postage	300	300	—
Profit sharing plan	2,400	—	2,400
Outside labor	5,600	—	5,600
Misc.	2,900	1,400	1,500
Travel & entertainment	4,100	2,100	2,000
Depreciation	10,200	—	10,200
Total Expenses	$218,200	$102,300	$115,900
Net Profit Before Taxes	$ 6,300	—	$ 6,300
Earning Spendable Cash			$122,200[1]

(1) The $122,200 represents the cash available to an owner after the Profit and Loss Statement has been "normalized" or adjusted

The objective of this exercise is to examine each expense and determine whether the money was passed through to the owner in the way of compensation or fringe benefits. Additionally, adjustments should be made where the new owner could minimize or eliminate the expenditure once the sale is completed.

Employee's Wages: This figure includes a manager's salary. With a new owner working full time, the manager could be eliminated, providing an annual savings of $20,000.

Owner's Compensation: $42,500 is the owner's draw.

Payroll Taxes: There is a reduction of taxes on $20,000 (the manager's salary). In addition, the new buyer may elect not to take a salary, reducing payroll taxes further. Re-calculate the payroll taxes carefully.

Rent: The business reimburses the present owner $3,600 a year as rental for his garage (used for storage) and a room in his house used as an office.

Advertising: During the preceding year, the owner spent $3,000 more than his normal outlay for radio promotions. This was a one-time test-oriented expense that would not be repeated.

Auto expense: The owner expenses both a car and a van. Since the business could get along with one vehicle, this cost could be reduced by $4,000.

Donations: This is a voluntary cost and could be totally eliminated.

Dues and Subscriptions: Memberships to a club and service organizations could be eliminated.

Insurance/Officers: This expense includes medical, disability, and key-man life insurance—such benefits may be reduced.

Accounting/Legal: This figure includes one-time costs for preparing the business for sale.

Office expense: Included in this figure is a monthly payment on a personal computer no longer used in the business. The purchase of some office furniture was also added in. The furniture was expensed, rather than depreciated; this one-time cost would not be repeated.

Repair and maintenance: Again, this includes a one-time expense for preparing the store for sale (painting, decorating, etc.).

Profit Sharing: This is a fringe benefit that could be eliminated.

Outside Labor: This item includes payment to a daughter in college for typing and other work-related activities. Non-employee compensation could be reduced in the future.

Miscellaneous: After reviewing the individual payments, the owner determined that $1,500 was for one-time or extra-ordinary expenses.

Travel and entertainment: Eliminating optional business travel reduced this expense to $2,100.

Depreciation: Since depreciation is simply a book entry rather than an actual expense, it could be regarded as spendable cash. (Other expenses that could be adjusted are—interest on loans and any lease payments.)

Remember, the new owners may not want to reduce some of these expenses e.g. health insurance, profit-sharing, or the extra car. But, leave that up to them. Your purpose in normalizing the P&L is to show how the monies in the business have been used. Furthermore, you should be prepared to justify your figures. To simply say that you can cut advertising in half probably will not be convincing. You will have to explain and validate your adjustments. Be careful to show in this normalization ways to minimize taxes, but never tax evasion.

FIGURE 15-2
RESIDUAL LEASE VALUE

1. Years remaining on the present lease ⟶ *5*
2. Current annual rent for similar space (comparable square feet and desirability) — *40,800* $ *3,400*   (*1,700 ft - 2 locations*)
3. Present annual cost of existing space, including all extra occupancy charges) — *21,600* $ *1,500*
4. Annual savings (line 2 minus line 3) — *19,200* $ *1,900*
5. Total savings over the length of the remaining lease (line 4 multiplied by line 1) — *96,400* $ *9,500*
6. Estimate value of the lease considering "present discounted value". $ *$5,700*

Explanation
1. **Short Term Lease:** A lease with one to two years remaining has practically no extra value since it will soon expire. The unknown future actually presents a negative factor offsetting any dollar gains.

2. **Mid Term Leases:** A lease with three to five years remaining has value and should be multiplied by a factor of 60% to arrive at "present discounted value" (e.g. if the total savings for a five year lease was $5,000, the value of the lease to the buyer would be $3,000 – $5,000 × 60%.) As a seller you could build that amount into the price of the business and validate it by using this analysis.

3. **Long Term Leases:** Five or more years remaining on lease presents an even more favorable situation considering rents are increasing in most areas. Multiply the total savings by 70% to arrive at a present value.

The next step is to determine if there is value in your lease. As previously mentioned, a transferable lease is one of the most important aspects of a business sale. Figure 15-2 provides a worksheet for developing the lease asset value.

The rationale for attributing value to a lease relates to the present cost of leasing similar space. In other words, if you signed a lease some time ago, and since then the per-square foot cost of comparable space has increased by 20%, there is asset value in your lease. This assumes that the lease conditions remain the same for the new owner.

In order to sell this concept to a potential buyer, you must do your homework. First, determine what similar space is currently costing. If it is higher than your transferable lease, complete the worksheet and be prepared to explain your analysis. Recognize the lease asset value is not the sum of the annual savings. Rather, it represents a reduction based on the inflation and risk factors affecting the future value of the money saved. Future dollars saved must be discounted to provide a realistic current value. The discounts used in the worksheet are arbitrary. If the amount saved is significant, you might consider a more thorough analysis. Contact a local community college or university to find an expert capable of producing a present/future value analysis.

Assets and Other Tangibles

Your next step is to determine the value of the other business assets. This includes your equipment, machinery, inventory, fixtures, leasehold improvements, supplies, accounts receivable, work in progress, and mailing list. Some of these assets may be difficult to value. For example, how do you value a used cash register? Is it what you paid for it, what it would sell for new (replacement), its depreciated cost (book value), or what you could sell it for (fair market value)? You may, in fact, look at all of these values. But it is the fair market value that most experts consider in the sale of a business. Nevertheless, to substantiate fair market value you may have to have perspective on these other values.

Let's examine each of these asset categories separately. (Note: Figure 15-3 provides a worksheet for developing the value of a business. The following asset categories are included in the worksheet.)

Tangible Assets: (Line 1, Figure 15-3) List all the tangible assets in the business (equipment, machinery, fixtures, leasehold improvements, signs, vehicles, office equipment, furniture, etc.); then place a fair market value on these items. Remember, the better you can validate your estimates, the less opportunity the buyer will have to negotiate and reduce your figures.

Inventory at Cost: (Line 2) Estimate the closing inventory at cost. Typically, the final price of the business will be adjusted based on actual inventory figures on the closing date.

Supplies at Cost: (Line 3) Estimate the cost of all supplies, and make a detailed list of what the buyer will receive.

Work in Progress: (Line 4) Estimate the cost of the work in progress at the time of closing.

Accounts Receivable: (Line 5) Some businesses transfer the accounts receivable in the sale. If this is done, some reduction must be made for doubtful accounts. The "age" of the account and the kind of debtor affect the likelihood of collection. A rule of thumb is that any billings over 30 days are discounted by 25%, and any over 60 days by 50%. Accounts beyond 90 days may be viewed as worthless. However, the strength of the account and the history of collections may offset such "normal" discounts. If you have accounts over 90 days old, can you show a payment history from the customer that indicates that the receivable will be collected? If the buyer requires too steep a discount, you may also want to consider taking the accounts receivables and collecting them yourself. Or let this part of the price be contingent. For example, let the buyer collect them in the ongoing business and turn over to you 70% of what he actually collects. You both may win, and you have reduced the buyer's risk. Risk goes down—comfort goes up.

Licenses/deposits: (Line 6) Some businesses (bars, restaurants, liquor stores, etc.) have valuable licenses or permits. These typically have a market value. Local business brokers will be able to provide this information. Also add in any rent or utility deposits that will not be refunded at the time of the sale.

Customer Mailing Lists: (Line 7) A seller often overlooks the value in a customer mailing list. However, there is a problem in determining a realistic value. What is the response to mailings. How much do sales increase following a mailing? How many coupons are turned in? Average sale? Can the list be rented to others? How much? The key is to prove how effectively these names and addresses are in generating increased sales. Give the list a value comparable to the dollar profit that would be lost over three years if it did not exist. Again, this analysis may take time, but the dollars should be well worth the effort, and it is information that should be gathered during the conduct of your business.

Lease Value: (Line 8) If there is an asset value for the remaining part of your lease based on the analysis in Figure 15-2, then place that amount in this space.

Other: (Line 9) This could include any trademarks, trade-names, and prepaid expenses.

Figure 15-3
Business Valuation Worksheet

1. TOTAL MARKET VALUE OF TANGILE ASSETS
    Leasehold improvements, equipment fixtures, etc.)

    Itemize 1. _____ $_____
            2. _____ $_____
            3. _____ $_____
            4. _____ $_____
            5. _____ $_____
            TOTAL $_____

2. Inventory at Cost (Closing Date) $_____
3. Supplies at Cost (Closing Date) $_____
4. Work in progress (Closing Date) $_____
5. Accounts Receivable (Discount
    for Doubtful Accounts) $_____
6. Licenses and Deposits (Itemize) $_____
7. Customer Mailing List $_____
8. Lease Value $_____
9. Other (Trademarks, Patents, Etc.) $_____
10. Average Annual Cash Flow
    Total Spendable Cash $_____
    Less Managers Salary $_____
    Less 10% Return on
    Tangible Assets $_____
    SUBTOTAL $_____
    Capitalization Multiplier (4 x)
    Cash Flow Value of Going
    Concern $_____
11. Additions - Intangibles Value $_____
12. Total Value of the business $_____

Justifying the Price of Your Success

When attempting to set a realistic price on your business, valuing the tangible assets is a fairly straight-forward process. Inventory, fixtures, lease-hold improvements, etc. can be appraised with a certain degree of accuracy. A more difficult problem arises when you try to justify the value of intangibles or the *success factor*. Basically, the success factor can be thought of as the difference between the earning power of a successful enterprise and one that has not yet established itself. For you, the seller, that difference has real monetary value. Your task is to convince potential buyers that they should pay for it.

You can't fall into the trap of seeing the success factor as the time and energy you put into the business. But it does relate. If your efforts were effective, and your business achieves significant earning power, then you should be compensated. However, if your business simply returns a fair salary to you, the success factor value will be limited.

Perhaps the best way to visualize the success factor is an example of the choice you would have as a typical entrepreneur, deciding on whether to start or buy a business. Assume that you would like to go into the dry-cleaning business. You check with a number of suppliers, leasing agents, and others in the industry. You determine that it would cost a certain amount to open a store. Then you discuss your plans with a couple of business brokers. They inform you that there are some established businesses on the market. One that looks particularly attractive shows a consistent bottom line profit . . . plus the owners have a good income and fringe benefits. Of course the price is higher than it would be if you started a store from scratch. But is it? What do you face if you start your own business? You must find a good location, arrange for an acceptable lease, develop the business to a profitable level (may take months or years, but it doesn't happen overnight, nor is it cheap), and finally weather all of the mistakes associated with a new business. In other words, that established business for sale has done those things for you. In essence, the price the buyer pays for that "known profitability and risk reduction" is the value placed on the *success factor.*

When you attempt to sell your business, you must justify the success factor value by convincing potential buyers it's really a savings. They will save that money, or perhaps more, by purchasing your operation, rather than starting their own from scratch.

Capitalizing of Your Spendable Cash

In order to account for the positive value or success of an ongoing business, it is appropriate to include a capitalization value for the annual cash flow, or spendable cash. Essentially, that means you're asking to be compensated for your ability to create a successful business. Traditionally, this process takes the form of a multiplier. For most businesses that multiplier will range from two to six times net spendable cash, depending on the risk factor. The higher the risk, the lower the multiplier. A high-risk business, like a specialty manufacturing firm, may have a low multiplier of two. On the other hand, a low-risk business that can be easily managed and has a guaranteed return, may have a high multiplier of five or more.

Another way of looking at this issue is to determine how many years a buyer should be expected to pay for the lack of risk built into your operation. An example at the end of the chapter will cover this concept more clearly. (This value is included on Line 10, Figure 15-3)

Additional Hidden Values

Many sellers feel after valuing the assets, estimating the inventory, and even capitalizing the cash flow that there are other important intangibles that add value to their business. Granted, many of these intangibles cannot be accurately appraised. Nevertheless, it's important to consider them in the overall valuation process. Of course, there is one problem—these intangibles can have a positive or negative side. Take for example down payment. If a seller will accept 20 or 30 percent down and carry a note for the balance, there is a value, and the seller should be compensated. However, if the sale is to be all cash, then the seller must be prepared to deduct some amount from the price. The question on all of these intangibles is how much?

Remember, valuing a business is perhaps one of the most difficult parts of the selling process. If you value it too high, it will languish on the market as buyer after buyer walks away. Value it too low, and someone gets a great deal, and you're out. Take care in valuing these additional intangibles, but at the same time, don't ignore their existence. Figure 15-4 provides a list of positive and negative intangible values.

Typical Situation

Perhaps the easiest way to visualize the valuation process is to show an example of how Fred and Betty valued their successful retail gift store, which they had owned for seven years.

Fred had decided to make a career change late in life and had purchased a gift and card shop when he was 52 years old. Since he and his wife had backgrounds in business, the task of running the operation didn't present unusual problems. Earnings over the past few years were good, and they had enjoyed the business. However, both Fred and Betty were now close to 60 years old and thoughts of retirement started to enter the picture. They wanted to move closer to their daughter and grandchildren, and the business was starting to stand in the way.

Here's how Fred and Betty developed a fair price for their business. First, they determined from an analysis of their Profit and Loss statement exactly how much spendable cash (Potential Earning Power) the business provided. Even though their P&L showed a low net figure, they found considerable spendable cash when they adjusted, or normalized, the statement. Following is a recap of their annual cash flow.

Salaries (Fred & Betty)	$38,500
Employees (over-staffing of 1)	$ 6,000
Auto expense (car written out of business)	$ 4,000
Donations/dues/subscriptions	$ 1,000
Insurance (medical, dental, disability and life)	$ 4,000
Telephone (personal use)	$ 1,200
One-time expense (new plumbing)	$ 1,700
Depreciation	$ 4,600
Profit before taxes	$ 5,000
Total	$65,900

Using the capitalization concept of spendable cash, Fred and Betty did the following exercise. They felt that the business success factor could use a capitalization multiple of four times because of the low risk factor. This capitalization concept must take into consideration two other important factors:

1. **Deduction of Manager's Salary.** You must deduct the salary cost of a qualified manager. The rationale for this deduction is important for the overall valuation concept. A buyer may decide to run the business as an absentee owner. A manager would have to be hired. Since the value of a business represents a return on investment, the manager's salary would be an operational expense. Even if the buyer assumes an active role in managing the business, a fair salary should be deducted from the business's value.

2. **Deduction of Return on Assets.** Since the assets of the business should produce their own return, it is important to deduct a percent for this factor. Typically, the amount used is 10%.

Figure 15-3
Business Valuation Worksheet
Fred & Betty's Gift Store

1. TOTAL MARKET VALUE OF TANGILE ASSETS
    Leasehold improvements, equipment fixtures, etc.)

    Itemize 1. Leasehold

improvements	$19,700	
2. Fixtures	$ 4,900	
3. Office Equipment	$ 600	
4. Sign	$ 1,000	
5. Cash Register	$ 800	
TOTAL		$27,000 ✓

2. Inventory at Cost (Closing Date) — $24,000 ✓
3. Supplies at Cost (Closing Date) — $ 600 ✓
4. Work in progress (Closing Date) — N/A
5. Accounts Receivable (Discount for Doubtful Accounts) — N/A
6. Licenses and Deposits (Itemize) — N/A
7. Customer Mailing List — $ 5,000 ✓
8. Lease Value — N/A
9. Other (Trademarks, Patents, Etc.) — N/A
10. Average Annual Cash Flow

Total Spendable Cash	$65,900
Less Managers Salary	$30,000
Less 10% Return on Tangible Assets	$ 2,700
SUBTOTAL	$33,200
Capitalization Multiplier (4 x)	
Cash Flow Value of Going Concern	$132,800 ✓

11. Additions - Intangibles Value — $25,000 ✓
12. Total Value of the business — $214,400

After these deductions are made, the sub-total is then capitalized. In this example (Line 10, Figure 15-4), the total is $132,800. This was arrived at by deducting a salary of $30,000 for managing the business and $2,700 (10% of tangible assets) from the spendable cash of $65,900 and then multipling by four.

Fred and Betty estimated the fair market valuable of their tangible assets (leasehold improvements, fixtures, office equipment, sign, and cash register) was $27,000. This amount was entered on Line 1 of the worksheet.

Inventory at closing was estimated at $24,000 (Line 2), and supplies at cost were estimated at $600. The business did not have work in progress, accounts receivable, or license/deposits. However, there were 1500 loyal customers who responded eagerly to his quarterly promotional mailing. They placed a value of $5,000 on the mailing list.

Fred and Betty felt, as many other business owners do, that there were other intangible values associated with the business. They made a list and placed a dollar value on each item.

Positive Factors

- They were willing to finance the sale over five years, taking approximately 25-35% down. (Value—$5,000)

- They were also willing to consider an interest rate on the note of 4% below what a bank would charge. (Value—$10,000)

- The lease was transferable with seven years remaining, but at market rate. (Value—$3,000)

- They were in business over five years, showing profit, but more important, considerable cash flow. (Value—$10,000)

- The location was good, but not excellent. (Value—$2,000)

- The business was easy to run with efficient systems. (Value—$3,000)

- They were willing to spend one month training the new owner. (Value—$4,000)

- The store needed no improvements and was ready to operate. (Value—$3,000)

Negative Factors

- Fred and Betty would require that the loan be secured by the buyer's other real property. (Negative value—$15,000)

Net Added Value $25,000

This amount was entered on Line 11 on the worksheet, Figure 15-3.

When Fred and Betty added the figures, the total was $214,400. Now, they were ready to sell. They had established a value that they were able to substantiate and validate. Each tangible value was backed up with documentation, and each factor in their intangible checklist became a major

FIGURE 15-4
ADDITIONAL INTANGIBLE VALUE FACTORS

Positive Factor   **Dollar Value**

1. Willingness to finance the sale. The lower the down payment, the higher the value. $_____

2. Interest on loan—calculate the savings based on prevailing rates. $_____

3. Term of seller's loan. The longer the loan, the higher the value. The average is 4 to 5 years, beyond that there is value. $_____

4. Lease: Transferable with a substantial period remaining. e. g. over 5 years there is value $_____

5. In business over 5 years. $_____

6. Consistent profit over 3 years. (More importantly consistent spendable cash.) $_____

7. Excellent location (bright future for the area). $_____

8. Easy business to operate. $_____

9. Willingness to train. $_____

10. No remodeling or other changes necessary $_____

11. Attractive, appealing atmosphere and image compared to competition. $_____

12. No additional working capital needed to get started. $_____

TOTAL ADDITIONAL VALUE $_____

Negative Factors   **Dollar Value**

1. Cash deal only. (This can reduce the overall value by as much as 60%) $_____

2. Large down payment. (40% to 75%) $_____

3. Short term lease. (Since the future of most businesses rely on a lease this can have a major impact on value) $_____

4. In business less than 2 years. (Lack of track record creates risk unless buyer is experienced in business) $_____

5. Low profitability and little spendable cash.) $_____

6. Poor location (declining area) $_____

7. No books or financial records. $_____

8. Difficult business to operate. $_____

9. Business in need of refurbishing. $_____

10. Working capital needs $_____

TOTAL MINUS POINTS $_____

NET ADDED VALUE $_____

benefit for the buyer. They were willing to pull these worksheets out in negotiations and show a prospect just how they arrived at the price. With this type of analysis, Fred and Betty were well prepared to convince a buyer of their *concept of value and get their price*. Being a realistic couple, Fred and Betty understood that they had to be flexible. After negotiations, they settled for $175,000.

Checking the Price

Over the years there have been a number of basic business valuation *rules of thumb*. These are not very scientific or accurate. Nevertheless, they are accepted ball-park approaches. Let's check these against Fred and Betty's valuation exercise.

- A business should return 20-30% to buyers on their investment, depending on the relative risk. If a buyer purchased Fred and Betty's business for $175,000 and received $33,200 in net spendable cash, the return would be approximately 19%—within the margin, especially considering how easy the purchase is and the relatively low risk.

- A business should be able to pay for itself in five years out of excess earnings, plus provide an adequate income for the owner. If Fred and Betty found a buyer who put 30% on the purchase price, the monthly payment would be approximately $2,500 (a five-year note at 8.0% interest). This payment would be affordable with the current cash flow, and the business would be paid off in five years. After the note is paid, there is a handsome return left for the buyer.

Contingent Purchase Price

There may be a number of reasons why a buyer will be unwilling to pay what you may perceive to be a fair price. Perhaps your earnings history, though good, is relatively short (i.e., less than five years). Perhaps there has been a recent strong upward trend, and you want to sell the later years rather than the average. Perhaps you are basing cash flow on gross receipts that your buyer is unsure can be reduced to net income. Don't be insulted—be creative.

Your prospective buyer may be unwilling to pay now what you reasonably believe the business is worth. Let the price be adjustable. Perhaps the buyer can agree to pay for the value of all assets other than cash flow. Let the payment for cash flow depend on gross receipts actually realized, or gross receipts reduced by direct cost of sales. (You need some measure that is not subject to manipulation or your buyer's management ability.)

Of course, if the price is going to be contingent, you are taking some risk of the downside. You should try to both negotiate a floor below which the price cannot fall and avoid a ceiling above which it cannot rise. That is, if you are taking an additional risk, you should have some opportunity to get a final price higher than you're asking if things go better than projected.

Chapter 16
Marketing Your Business

Selling a business yourself is not an easy task. Still, it can be a very interesting and quite challenging experience. When I decided to sell my business, I found the idea of selling it myself irresistible. I felt that if I could successfully build it, I could darn well sell it . . . and for a good price!

Once you make the decision to sell, you begin to visualize yourself outside the business. Take care that the operation does not show any signs of change for the worse while you carry out your three major objectives:

1. Sell it as fast as possible.

2. Get as much money as possible . . . but more important, be sure you get paid.

3. Set up the necessary protections for any future events.

As you develop your marketing strategy, you must remember that selling the business is going to consume time. You will be negotiating with buyers, and meeting with attorneys, accountants, and escrow officers. This will take you away from the day-to-day activities of running your operation. As you review this chapter and consider the demands on your time, you may decide the job should be delegated to a business broker. A broker may provide a faster sale and will certainly eliminate much of the legwork. However, we will approach this as if it were a "do-it-yourself project".

You must be prepared to devote time to each of the four major phases in a business sale:

1. *Preparing for the sale:* Essentially this involves getting the business ready (cleanup campaign), and preparing all the supporting documents (financial records, lease, sales records, etc.). This is the stage when you create "the package".

2. *Finding the buyer:* This includes advertising, interviewing, screening and selecting the best potential owner for the business.

3. *Negotiating the sale:* This is the give-and-take stage where you are persuading the potential buyer to accept your concept of value or price.

4. *Wrapping up stage:* This is when the sale is completed, contracts are signed, and preparations are made for the new owner to take over.

This chapter is devoted to creating an effective marketing strategy, to help you move quickly and efficiently through that process.

Packaging is All-Important

The critical question becomes: How can I best present my business so that a potential buyer sees *value,* and so that his or her *needs* and *motivations* will be satisfied?

Packaging has become the name of the game in our consumer-oriented society. Packaging a business opportunity and marketing toothpaste have more in common than you might think. You have to present your business in the best possible light, focusing on benefits and showing potential buyers how their lives will be enhanced when they buy your operation. How does this differ from advertising and marketing Crest toothpaste? You may have a bigger ticket item, a more complex transaction; but in the end, the sale creates a satisfied buyer as well as a satisfied seller. The satisfaction is a result of meeting the buyer's needs and sets of expectations. You, as a seller, present a package (a business) with certain promises (expectations). The better you present the package, the better your prospects of selling quickly and getting your price.

Packaging also creates *image.* You can improve the business image in two basic ways. First, make the operation look good by doing a thorough house-cleaning. Second, make the figures look good. A business buyer is purchasing an opportunity to make money. By all means, don't alter the figures to make them look better, that will create a potentially explosive problem of fraud. However, consider taking your books to an accountant for the preparation of a recap of three years sales and expenses and a current balance sheet. You may even want to request a Pro Forma Cash Flow Statement to show a prospective buyer the true cash benefits in the business. If you provide an accountant with the input, a very impressive financial package can be generated. Even when your profitability is marginal, effective packaging can improve the buyer's perception.

The next step is to prepare a written history of the business, highlighting the positive factors—superior location, economic climate of the area, lack of major competition, steady clientele, quality line of merchandise, appeal of store design, lease conditions, etc. This information can be presented as a brochure or simply as a fact sheet. When I sold a store (priced at $85,000), I prepared a four-page brochure with pictures of the interior and exterior along with a description of the business, shopping center, and local area. I then sent the brochure, with a cover letter, to similar businesses within a hundred-mile radius and to all suppliers serving the industry. The cost was $800. I found a buyer directly from the mailing, and closed escrow within a couple of months. Although the financial picture was not that bright, the packaging (brochure) was First Class. It generated *interest* and *desire*—the necessary forerunners to a successful sale. Incidentally, this was a store that six months earlier I had thought of shutting down and walking away from.

There's an interesting phenomenon worth mentioning, concerning financial data. Some buyers, for a variety of reasons, won't ask for sales and expense records. When I sold two stores to a national chain, they simply asked for sales by month for the past two years. However, they were sophisticated buyers. They recognized that my profit and loss statements were less meaningful than the overall sales volume. I have discussed this factor with a number of ex-owners, and several have related similar experiences. The point is: Don't volunteer financial records (unless they are very good), until requested.

The Typical Buyer

Business buyers come in all shapes and sizes, with various levels of experience, diverse backgrounds, and different financial capabilities. Consequently, the typical buyer is almost anyone.   But, you are not looking for anyone . . . you are looking for the *Right* one. Ideally you are looking for someone who can run the business better than you. This is particularly important if you are planning to carry back a loan. Unfortunately, statistics show that new owners have a difficult time initially duplicating the previous owner's profits. Only 25% were able to improve the income picture, another 25% held things even, while half experienced a drop in earnings. It therefore pays to pick your buyer carefully—assuming you have that option.

First, it's important to understand what a typical buyer is looking for in a business. The needs and motivations of small business buyers today are probably no different than they were when you entered the business. Primarily they want independence. They also feel that owning their own businesses will improve their lifestyles, income, and prestige. They look forward to more happiness and job satisfaction. Some look at owning their own business as a way of securing their futures - they are buying jobs. In a few words, they are somewhat naive, yet determined.

As you prepare to sell, you must acquire a sensitivity to those entrepreneurial needs. You will be most effective presenting your business in ways that show buyers how their needs and motivations will be satisfied. Some say that the decision to buy a business is 80% psychological and 20% financial. If that's the case, identify the psychological needs, show how your business meets those needs, and you have a sale.

Finding A Buyer

Estimates indicate that up to 25% of the working population would like to be in business for themselves. That would indicate that 25 million people are potential candidates for your business. Even when you introduce geographical limitations, experience, financing, and other requirements, there still remains a large pool of possible buyers. Now the task is to find them.

Essentially, you have to get the word out. You cannot be reserved or shy about it. Don't be embarrassed that you are selling. On the contrary, be open and enthusiastic. After all, most people will envy you. You built a business and now you are about to cash in on the "the big payday". If you want to keep the sale confidential, this presents some problems, but not insurmountable ones. You must be more discreet when contacting people. If you ask for their confidence, very few will divulge any information.

Begin by making a list of everybody you believe will have even the remotest interest in purchasing your business. Frequently, the person who makes the commitment is the one you least expect. This initial step is simply a way of identifying all of the possible players. Consider the following list of prospects:

Employees (past and present)	Competitors
Suppliers	Sales Representatives
Friends	Relatives (including sons or daughters)
Former or Present Entrepreneurs	People who showed interest in the past
Club Members	Customers

You may be able to add to this list. Right now you are not looking for quality, but for quantity. You want to put as many candidates in the race as you can. You may also consider contacting local real estate agents, lawyers, accountants, chambers of commerce, small business consultants, trade associations, bankers, and the local SBA office. If you explain you have a business for sale, these individuals may know of someone interested in business ownership, and your contact will provide a referral.

Once you have a list of prospects, start making phone calls. You may want to approach certain individuals with a slightly different tact. In some cases, you may indicate up front that you are planning to sell and if they are interested, you would be happy to meet with them. In other cases, you may want to approach them by explaining that you are going to sell, asking if they know anyone who may be interested, and indicating that you would appre ciate their passing on the word. If that person is interested you will know quickly; otherwise, you have someone out bird-dogging for you.

Advertising Your Business

Ironically, advertising may not provide the results you would expect. It will attract a diversified group of people, most of whom won't be qualified or, for that matter, serious. It also takes considerable time to screen the prospects. Nevertheless the cost is not prohibitive, and therefore you should give it a try. It's important that you realize the limited pulling power of advertising and use other methods of finding buyers simultaneously.

You have three basic advertising options:

1. Major local newspapers.
2. Trade journals.
3. *The Wall Street Journal.*

Local newspapers may include several that are located some distance away, if they have broad circulation. People will relocate for the right business opportunity.

Trade magazines in various industries offer classified sections where you can advertise a business for sale. The problem with trade journals is the lead/lag time. You may have to place your ad two months prior to the issue reaching its readers. You may have sold the business during that time. In addition, trade journals are typically national in circulation. People will move, but not usually across the country.

The *Wall Street Journal* has various regional editions. Thursday is business-opportunity day in their classified section, and a regional ad is a "must" to generate potential buyers.

Writing a good classified ad is important. The words you select to describe the business must make readers want to reply. Your only objective with this ad is to persuade people to contact you . . . nothing more. Here's how to approach your ad writing task:

1. Get copies of the *Wall Street Journal* and other major papers, to review what other businesses in your general category are doing.

2. Write down every benefit or feature your business offers. For example, good location, high profit, excellent lease, substantial cash flow, excellent profit history, priced for a fast sale, easy to manage, fantastic potential, new fixtures, etc. (not all of these benefits will be in your ad).

3. Create a headline (first words in bold type) that will catch people's attention. Headlines are the most important part of advertising. For instance, "IMMEDIATE PROFIT AND CASH FLOW FROM LONG ESTABLISHED HARD-WARE STORE".

4. Don't tell everything in the copy of the ad. Remember, all you want to do is generate enough interest for prospects to call.

5. If you want the sale to remain confidential, install a separate phone in your home temporarily or use your attorney's number. P.O. boxes normally don't have the same level of response as the telephone, but you will get a more qualified prospect.

6. Keep your ad relatively short and change it slightly each time you place it. Don't run it for more than ten days. You don't want readers to think that your business is not selling.

7. Sometimes you will get more of a response if you eliminate specific references to your type of business . For example, "specialty retail store" or "unique service business" are good phrases for classified ads.

Screening Buyers

After you have developed a program to generate prospects, you face the task of screening them. Use some method to qualify those who express interest or you will find yourself frustrated by people lacking the money, experience, or sincere inclination to purchase your business. Some individuals find pleasure in "stroking" business owners. Perhaps they hope some day to buy a gold mine . . . cheap. Early in the game, determine who is a serious viable candidate. Ask *pertinent* and *penetrating* questions; then request certain documentation of financial status. Consider for a moment what you would do if you were renting an expensive home. You would want to know if your future tenants could afford the rent. Now, you are parting with something much more important—your business—and you have the right to check out the financial resources of your prospects.

If a prospect telephones, you can tactfully ask such questions as:

*   What is your background and experience?

*   Do you intend to run the business yourself?

*   Have you been looking long for a business?

*   Have you ever owned a business before?

*   Will you be prepared to provide a financial statement and references?

You can preface your questions by explaining how careful you must be. You have had a number of people interested, and you want to narrow the field, so as not to waste their valuable time or yours.

You must also be prepared to answer most questions on the phone. Refrain from getting into any detail about financing. Explain that that subject can be best discussed in person, and then make an appointment . . . away from the store. You may have to meet with a prospect several times before you know whether a sale can be made. Therefore, it pays to negotiate simultaneously with as many individuals as possible.

At the first meeting, but only after developing a comfortable rapport, ask the potential buyer to fill out a non-disclosure statement (see Figure 16-1). This will add professionalism to your approach and achieve a certain degree of confidentiality. After all, you don't want your income-tax returns or sales figures floating all over town. Provide general information about sales, expenses and profits, but don't volunteer too much or provide written documentation, at least not at this first meeting. If the prospect is interested in pursuing the discussions, ask that a *personal financial statement* be filled out. You can get these forms at a stationery store or from your bank. Indicate that you would be more than willing to provide additional written data after you receive the personal financial statement.

You must maintain a friendly, business-like relationship in these early discussions. Frequently a seller immediately becomes too demanding or too conciliatory, with adverse affects on the future negotiations.

In these early meetings, you want to assess whether the prospect:

1. Can afford your business.

2. Can successfully manage it.

3. Is compatible - a round peg for a round hole.

4. Is serious.

These are very subjective questions. Nevertheless, you must somehow determine whether serious negotiations should take place. If there is any doubt, by all means pursue the possibilities. However, if a prospect has no cash and you want $50,000 down, it's important to clarify that issue before both parties expend considerable time and energy. Serious reasonable buyers will respect your frank and candid position.

FIGURE 16-1
NONDISCLOSURE FORM

Explanation: This form can be typed up and copies made to be signed by potential buyers.

Date_____

Confidental information about (name of busines) is being disclosed to me in connection with my interest in purchasing (name of business). In consideration of this disclosure, I promise not to disclose any information about (name of business) to any person at any time, nor to use such information in competion with (name of business). I understand the information, financial records, and other pertinent data are valuable to the ongoing success of the business, and that use of this information by me or others could damage the business. Should any legal action be initiated as a result of this agreement, the prevailing party will be entitled to attorneys' fees and legal costs in addition to any other damages proven.

_____
Signature of Potential Buyer

Negotiating from Strength

When selling your business, you will have to sharpen your negotiating skills to a fine edge. The lack of an effective negotiating strategy could erode your price and might even jeopardize your ability to convince a buyer to purchase the business. Fortunately, negotiating skills are simple to learn and, with some practice, easy to implement.

Rarely does a business sell for the asking price. Usually the price is finalized only after both parties agree to compromise their perceptions of value. The important point is that you stay in control of this give-and-take process. The most effective way to do that is to assume the *power* position in the negotiations.

Power is based on perception. If you think you have it . . . you have it. Furthermore, the other party may also believe you have it. The definition of negotiating is the ability to use power, together with information, to affect the behavior of others. You do this all of the time with your employees, spouse and children. You probably relate it to every day trade-offs. Nevertheless it's negotiating. Begin the sale process by saying to yourself, "I am in control of this event!".

Your power is greatly enhanced by information. The more you know about a given subject, the better you can project power and maintain control. Consider the sale of your business. You have infinitely more information about your operation than the prospective buyer. You also probably know about the process of buying and selling a business, from reading this book. However, the most critical information you have is your understanding of the available *bargaining chips*. As the negotiation process speeds up, there will be a series of give-and-take decisions. You will give up something to get a concession from the buyer, and vice-versa. Before you seriously discuss selling your business with anyone, you must know and understand your limits on each chip. Following is a list of your bargaining chips:

- Price.

- Terms (down payment, duration, and interest).

- Security.

- Assets to be sold.

- Liabilities to be assumed.

- Tax structure of the sale.

- Information to be provided.

- Timing.

- Costs involved in the sale (escrow fees, broker commissions, etc.).

As you approach the selling process, develop a clear perspective of each of these bargaining variables. Know precisely (write it down on paper) where you will give ground and where you will draw the line. For example, if cash is important to you because you are investing it in another business, you may have to take a hard position on down payment.

However, you may be willing to reduce your price. Once your know your upper and lower limits for each of your chips, you know exactly how to maneuver your bargaining position—that's power!

In addition, successful negotiation is built around finding out what the buyer wants, showing how it's attainable, and at the same time getting what you want. How do you do this? Continue to ask questions—pertinent and penetrating questions.

- Where will the down payment come from?

- Why are you interested in this type of business?

- What do you expect from owning an operation like this?

- If we reach an agreement, when could you take over the business?

Questions like those above will provide valuable information on the buyer's financial status, motivation, time pressure, and real needs. With this information you can begin to relate the benefits of owning your business to the individual needs of the buyer.

To determine whether you are dealing with a phony (a small percentage does exist), ask for business and personal references, then check them out. Your banker or attorney can do a credit check if you have the prospect's social security number. The banker may not want to provide you with an actual copy, but he will certainly comment if any major problems are uncovered.

The Negotiating Climate

Despite the fact that buyers and sellers have opposing interests, negotiations can move forward if a positive climate is developed. Establishing the climate is essentially your responsibility since you are in control of the sale. Here are some do's and don'ts that will help you create the right climate.

Do build an atmosphere of trust. Typically people might think the only reason you're selling the business is because you're losing money. To counter that perception, some sellers talk only about positive things. Be honest and candid and also discuss the flaws. This disarms and builds trust. "This is a great business. I've been able to make a good income from it, and I'm going to explain the good and the bad so that you fully understand what you're in for." Don't overwhelm, but do balance your discussion so they believe and trust you.

Do compromise. You know where you're willing to make concessions; the buyer doesn't. The key is, understanding what you give up is not critical to you, but valuable to the other guy. (This is where the bargaining chips come in.) If you show unwillingness to compromise, the buyer is forced to accept your position or walk away. That's the risk you take.

Do be patient. The most advantageous outcome doesn't occur quickly. You achieve it by carefully evaluating all of your options and moving cautiously. Leave room for delays and problems . . . very few sales are without them.

Don't be abrasive. If you are too heavy-handed, you will force distance and stifle communication . Listen to what the buyer has to say. Put yourself in his or her shoes without necessarily accepting that position yourself. Try to avoid a win-lose situation; your goal is always a win-win.

Don't be pretentious or superior. Don't take yourself too seriously. Buyers will react poorly if you seem arrogant. Try to look at the process as a game; step back and take a "who-cares" attitude. By doing that, you will automatically portray power and confidence.

Don't appear to be in a rush. You may still have a sense of urgency; but if you try to make buyers move too quickly, they will start to develop mistrust. You can keep control by setting an agenda and timetable, but always ask if it is convenient for the other side too.

Selling Is Necessary

Selling and negotiating have many similar characteristics, yet they are different. Negotiating involves give-and-take, maneuvering for position. Selling involves moving through the process, toward a conclusion.

Selling is a skill of persuasion. Hard-sell tactics probably won't work too well in this situation. Most important, you must be a good listener. Ask questions and let the buyer do most of the talking. If you dominate the conversation, you run the risk of overselling, saying the wrong things, or simply irritating the prospect. Furthermore, by listening, you uncover motivations and buying needs - information that's invaluable to you in the selling process. Following is a brief description of how the business sale flows through the five basic selling steps.

Get attention . . . by an effective ad, brochure, or fact sheet. Show a clean and efficient operation by being well prepared to present an attractive package.

Build interest . . . by describing benefits. Determine the buyer's needs and motivations, then show them how the business can fulfill their financial dreams.

Meet criticisms . . . anticipate all possible objections by knowing your business well. Be prepared to answer objections and problems effectively, maintaining the control and the momentum of the sale.

Objection: "If the business is so good, why are you selling it?"

Your Response "Yes, it is good, but I'm ready to move on to other things. My entrepreneurial spirit is telling me to try something else. The same thing may happen to you in a few years."

Objection: "I don't think some of the merchandise is salable."

Your Response "I understand your concern. When we take the final inventory, I'll give you half-price on 20% of the stock. This will enable you to "special out" that merchandise and generate some immediate cash."

Recognize buying signals . . . so you know when the customer is ready to buy. Read the verbal and non-verbal communications, telling you that the prospect wants to own your business.

Buying Signal: "Are you sure I can hit those sales figures?" The buyer has been sold; confirm that the figures are realistic and close the sale.

Buying Signal: "I don't think I could come up with the entire down payment, but I'm close." Figure out a solution; you have just sold your business.

Buying Signal: "Well, my wife's ready, but I have a few questions." He's ready too; answer the questions and close the sale.

Close the sale . . . by knowing when to stop selling, negotiating, and discussing the business. Stop talking and close the sale!

Closing Technique: "After interviewing a couple of other buyers, I really believe you can do the best job with this business. Why don't we set up an escrow account? I can stop negotiating with the other individuals."

Closing Technique: "I really believe you want this business, and I want to see you get it. I will concede to your last condition, but now I need a good faith deposit so we can wrap-up these negotiations."

Businesses do not sell themselves. They need help from a knowledgeable, motivated salesperson—the owner. You must be pleasantly persistent. You can't stop until the contract is signed. And during the escrow period, constantly reaffirm to the buyer that the decision to buy your business was a good one.

How To Handle Price

Since price is a key ingredient in a business sale, you need to develop an effective strategy for dealing with it during the sales process. Typically, price is adjusted in the form of offers and counter-offers. If a prospect is serious about the business, he or she will propose a lower price or a change in terms. As the saying goes: "If we can't talk price, let's talk terms."

You can effectively retain control of the pricing negotiations by being prepared to *substantiate* and *validate* your price early in the discussions. By doing that, you will put the prospect on notice that you are not interested in reducing the price substantially. "The price on the business is $120,000, and let me explain exactly how I arrived at that figure. I'm fairly firm on this price, but I will consider terms if you want to make a reasonable and realistic offer."

The ball now bounces over to the buyer's court. It's important to get all of the offers and counter-offers in writing. Once the offer comes in, you are now negotiating from the buyer's position. It's always advantageous to negotiate from the buyer's numbers. You can then counter-offer or accept. If the offer is ridiculously low, counter-offer with your original price or don't respond. Some people try to steal businesses, and are occasionally successful.

As a matter of tactics, give up price and terms slowly, and only by asking for concessions in return. Also attempt to close the sale on each counter-offer. "I've received your counter-offer. If you are willing to agree to . . . then I will accept, and my attorney can draw up the papers."

Most serious buyers do not go into long drawn-out negotiations. They want to know how the deal can be structured within their framework of money, time, and talent. If you find the prospect continually trying to negotiate fine points or seeking major concessions in the price, terms, or security, it's time for you to find another prospect.

Chapter 17

Financing the Sale and Avoiding the Deal Killers

Developing a successful strategy for financing your business may be as critical as developing the marketing strategy. The problem relates to the prospective buyers. There are many people who want to be independent small business owners. Unfortunately, not many of them have a great deal of cash. Although the statistics are difficult to uncover, probably 70-80% of all small business sellers carry back some form of note on their businesses. The average sale consists of 20-30% down and the balance financed over 5-7 years, with interest slightly below the prevailing rate.

The *benefit/risk equation* is the first factor you must address when working out your financing strategy. Essentially, that equation relates to the benefit of selling your business versus the risk of getting paid. If you recall, *Getting Paid* is one of the major objectives in the sale process.

To understand the benefit/risk equation, you must take an objective look at your business. If you own a highly profitable, easy to run business, and you have priced it fairly, there will be a large pool of potential buyers—perhaps some willing to pay cash. On the other hand, if you own a business that is difficult to operate, with little or no profit, you may have difficulty finding prospects at any price. You then have to determine whether there is more benefit in getting out than in getting paid. If you take the risk and accept a shaky sale, at least you're out!

Most businesses fall somewhere in the middle. That's why you must determine how much risk you're willing to accept, and how you can protect yourself (another major objective in selling a business, to be covered in the next chapter).

Creative Financing

If you decide to finance your own sale, you can develop a creative financing package that would make the recent residential creative home buying programs look like kid's stuff. Consider these options for down payments and monthly payments. But be sure to consider them *carefully*. They are all high risk.

Down Payments

1. Part of the down payment can be made by the buyer, using the first few months' excess cash flow. If the buyer doesn't assume

any debt, there will be an initial surplus of cash. You can set up short-term (weekly) promissory notes or even post-dated checks to provide part of the down payment proceeds.

2. Let the buyer assume your liabilities. Normally, it would be your responsibility to clear any debt, but if you can get your suppliers to agree, simply have the buyer assume your liabilities, reducing the down payment accordingly. A business broker may even take a note for his or her commission.

3. Retain some of the assets - car, furniture, etc. - and sell them yourself.

4. If the business is debt-free, consider building up liabilities in order to let the buyer assume them. You can take the cash during the last 30-60 days that would normally have been used to pay off these liabilities.

5. Take something in trade for the down payment or for the entire purchase price, e.g.: income property, another business (may qualify for a tax free exchange), boat, vacation home, etc.

Monthly Payments

1. Use a graduated plan, e.g. first year-$1,000/month, second year-$1,250/month, third year-$1,500/month.

2. Use a 20 or 30 year amortization schedule to develop the payments. This lowers the monthly amount by making it mostly interest. Set up a balloon payment in five years for the unpaid balance (the buyer will then have to refinance).

3. If the business is seasonal, consider an annual supplement payment along with the smaller monthly payments, e.g. $1,000/month and $5,000 at Christmas. You have to set up two separate promissory notes.

Now that you know some of the alternatives, don't be too anxious to use them - *cash* is still king! If you can get cash for your business, reduce the price and grab it. In spite of what may appear to be a good win-win financing package, anything can happen, creating future problems for you. Unless you're willing to come back and run a run-down business, get as much cash as you can so that the buyer is committed to the sale. Low or no down payments, with little or no security, makes it too easy for a buyer to simply walk away. If a buyer is going to use personal property such as his house, as collateral, consider having him take out a second mortgage and apply the proceeds to the sale. This way you get the cash, rather than the security.

No-Cash-Down Sales

Should you ever consider a no-cash-down sale? Yes, if the conditions are just right. For example, if your business will be difficult to sell (few potential buyers) and your prospective buyer is very experienced and capable (he or she will have to be), and you can get collateral other than the business, and if you don't need the cash and you won't be out-of-pocket when you turn over the business, then it may be convenient for you to accept a no-cash-down sale and walk away. It's back to the evaluation of the benefit/risk and only you can judge that. Do businesses sell with no-cash down? Everyday!

Before you start thinking of taking 10% down or no-down payment and financing the rest with monthly payments sent to you in a Mexican fishing village, consider what your business can *afford*. Some buyers operate on the concept of OPM (other people's money). That's fine, but when it's your money, you should first determine if it's possible. Theoretically, a business should pay for itself out of excess profits or cash flow. Objectively review your profit and loss statement to determine how much a buyer would have in excess cash to make monthly payments. Say that figure is $1,000, then structure your financing package around that number. You, as the seller, create the financing program. The buyer may influence or negotiate, but you know the business; the financing program is your ball game. If you develop and approve a payment plan that the buyer can't meet, then you have sold a business and bought yourself trouble. Most sellers want to walk away and never be bothered by the business in the future. If that's your objective, structure an affordable deal.

A Typical Financing Deal

Say you own a restaurant. You have a steady positive cash flow. You want to sell; and one of your talented, trusted employees wants to buy but has no money. You know the individual will make it, perhaps do an even better job than you. He is very young and eager. You structure the sale like this:

- Buyer assumes present outstanding liabilities of $15,000

- You arrange with your bank to grant a loan for $10,000(you may have to guarantee it personally). It's a 36 month note to be paid by the buyer and you get the funds.

- Monthly payments (personal note to you) for the first year are $850.00; second year, $1,000; third year, $1,200. Payments are calculated on an amortization schedule of 20 years, with a balloon for the unpaid balance due at the end of the third year (this is also when the bank loan is to be paid off).

- The buyer's father secures the note with real property.

You have basically given your business away. However, if you have selected a qualified buyer, the risk may be low and the benefits great. You have freed yourself to do something else, and you have some cash and a monthly check. If the buyer falters, you'll be able to move in on the security.

Deal Killers

There are going to be problems during the course of negotiations. That's normal. In a sale, there are just too many conflicting interests and objectives. Furthermore, the purchase or sale of a business can be an emotionally charged experience.

When the problems escalate to the point where good communications can't seem to solve the dispute, you have a deal killer. The buyer and seller part company, and the process, with a new prospect, must start over again. Of course, there are valid reasons to discontinue negotiations. If the buyer and seller have much different perceptions of price, or if one party is dishonest, or if the buyer simply cannot afford the business, all are logical reasons to end discussions. However, too frequently, buyers and sellers will get into conflicts and not know how to resolve them, other than terminating negotiations. You can avoid this simply by anticipating the typical deal killers and learning how to sidestep them.

Here are a number of potential problem areas that should and can be avoided.

1. When you *hold back information* on major problems until the end of the sale, you are creating a deal killer. All businesses have problems. Perhaps that's why you're selling.   Buyers will understand and accept flaws in a business, if they are presented throughout the discussion in an honest and straight-forward way. If you wait until the end to unload, you can watch the buyer disappear.

2. Sellers must be *willing to bend*—particularly with price and/or terms. If you are absolutely inflexible, "I want cash and that's it," you have placed most buyers in a box. They have nowhere to go except away. If you want the negotiations to continue, you must always leave an opening however small.

3. If you *refuse to show* records to a potential buyer, you create an atmosphere of distrust, and often kill the sale. In selling a business, you have to provide full disclosure. Occasionally some records are difficult to put together. Explain this candidly to the buyer and seek a compromise. The safest way to approach records is to prepare them in advance of the sale and present them only upon request.

4. If you wait until the last moment to discuss the impending sale with your *landlord,* you run the risk of unraveling the entire program. Landlords can be very unreasonable. Be sure you deal with the lease issue well in advance of a final discussion with the buyer. Get a firm commitment in writing that the lease transfer will not be unreasonably withheld.

5. Sometimes you don't have to kill a sale. Your *attorney, accountant or broker* will do it for you. Yes, your pros can create deal killers just as well or better than you. Consider, for example, a sales contract drafted by your attorney which has 36 clauses, all

protecting you, and none protecting the buyer. How will the buyer feel about that? What about an accountant who puts together your financial record showing a loss in the business, but fails to explain how, through cash flow, you were able to personally pull $50,000 per year. Then there are business brokers who neglect to follow up or actively pursue potential buyers. Qualified buyers will stay on the market for a limited period of time. Someone will find them and sell them a business. Don't let your professionals kill your sale. Control them, explain upfront what you expect, and closely monitor their activities.

6. Be sure that *both spouses agree* to the program. Sales have been killed on the eve of a closing by a spouse who refuses to sign a contract or a security agreement. If you are dealing with just one member of a family, tactfully interject, during the discussions, the importance of husband and wife agreeing to the conditions of the sale.

7. A sale can be destroyed when one party *misinterprets or forgets* what was agreed on in previous discussions. There will be several topics and a number of issues discussed during each session. Relying on one's memory for this important data is too much. Make notes during meetings as well as phone conversations. Confirm important points in writing and be prepared to bring out written documentation when the buyer disputes what was previously said. People have a way of adjusting their memories to meet current conditions. It's called selective recall.

8. *Don't make plans* about your future until the sale is completed, or at least don't tell the buyer. Sometimes a seller will have the moving truck at the scene on the date of closing. The whole world knows the family is moving to sunny California. This creates the perfect opportunity for the buyer to leverage a major concession right before closing. Remember the business is still yours until you get the money and turn over the key.

What happens if negotiations do fall apart? Can a qualified buyer be salvaged? Yes, but the degree of difficulty depends on the circumstances. First, you must determine precisely what went wrong. Be as objective as possible. If it was the chemistry between you and the buyer, you may be faced with bringing in a third party to help put the sale back on track. You can use an attorney, business broker, even a friend, but the individual must be skilled in negotiation tactics. The person you select can contact the prospect, explaining that he or she represents you and would like to make an effort to resume negotiations.

If the deal fell apart because you were too rigid, then you will have to make a concession in order to get the buyer's attention. Obviously you are not dealing from strength. Still, what do you have to lose by sending a letter or making a phone call to explain your new position and your willingness to reopen discussions? Nothing!

Attempt to use some *"winning friends and influencing people"* skills when you try to salvage a particularly qualified buyer. Explain that you have interviewed a number of potential candidates and it is just as important to you to find the right person as it is to get your asking price. Then go on, and convince the individual how he or she is just perfect for the business. If the prospect is willing to resume discussions, you would be willing to provide some major concessions.

Chapter 18
Tax and Legal Considerations in a Business Sale

One thing I want to make clear before you start this chapter: the discussions of the legal and tax ramifications in the following pages are meant to provide an overview, and not legal or tax advice. Lawyers, accountants, and even business brokers are in a much better position to advise you on specifics. The potential tax liabilities and legal hassles resulting from a poorly structured business sale make it mandatory that you seek advice and direction from a professional. Furthermore, the tax law has gone through several major changes since 1980, the most recent being the Tax Reform Act of 1986.

Different Interests

Selling a business involves a series of trade-offs or compromises. Typically, problems arise when a buyer and seller realize that their objectives are very different. Often a sale may be near completion when one of the parties rejects a clause in the contract, causing a stumbling block or even a major stalemate. This chapter helps you understand and overcome these potential obstacles. An awareness of some of the various roadblocks to closing a sale is frequently as important as the negotiations involved in the sale.

First, consider the major motivations of the buyer and seller. You will readily see the potential for conflict.

Seller's Interest:
1. Getting the best price and terms.
2. Structuring a favorable tax treatment.
3. Eliminating past and future liability.
4. Developing a sales contract that has binding and rigid protection.
5. Receiving the entire price (even if it has to be over a period of time).

Buyers Interests:
1. Getting the lowest price with the most favorable terms.
2. Structuring a tax treatment that allows the purchase price to be amortized or expensed.
3. Eliminating problems with the previous owner concerning title, leases, or liabilities.
4. Receiving protection against any false or misleading information provided by the seller.

If both parties want the transaction to happen, they will agree to the necessary compromises on every issue. The previous chapter discussed methods of reaching agreement through negotiations. This chapter focuses on two areas: how to structure the sale so that you retain as much money as possible (the tax implications) and how to protect yourself to assure that you get paid. However, since this is not a one-sided situation (There is a buyer on the other side.), all these areas have to be approached so major conflicts may be avoided. After the Tax Reform Act, a seller can be somewhat more flexible in areas like allocating purchase price, and this flexibility can be a means of gaining other points (e.g. price) that are important.

Tax Impact

Selling a business is a tax event. There are certain ways to structure the sale to minimize the tax impact. However, in order to structure the sale properly it pays to *plan ahead* and be careful. The consequences of making an error, to be discovered by the IRS a couple of years later, can cause you a real problem. The penalties and interest on outstanding tax liabilities have become very expensive.

If you operate as a sole proprietor, then the transaction is normally straight forward. The sale will involve the assets of the business, and you will be taxed on the gain or loss between the sale price and your tax basis (what you originally paid, less depreciation).

If you operate as a partnership the sale almost certainly will be an asset transfer, although it could be structured as a sale of the partnership interests. If the partnership ends as part of an all-cash sale, then whether assets or partnership interests are sold won't usually matter. In effect, the individual partners will be taxed on the difference between their individual shares of the sale price and the basis in their partnership interests. Frequently partners have different bases depending on their investment shares.

If you operate as a corporation, then things get somewhat more complicated. You have essentially three ways to sell your interest in the business.

Option 1. Have the corporation sell the assets to the buyer; then have the corporation distribute the proceeds to you as the stockholder.

Option 2. Sell the stock in the corporation directly to the buyer.

Option 3. Have the corporation first distribute or transfer the assets to you, liquidate the corporation, and then you sell the assets to the buyer.

If you elect to take the first or third alternative, you will be faced with double taxation. In the first alternative, the corporation will be taxed on gain experienced at the corporate level, and second, you will be taxed on the after-tax proceeds as they are distributed to you to the extent they exceed your basis in the stock.

Before the Tax Reform Act of 1986, option three offered considerable advantages. You could liquidate the corporation to the shareholders prior to a sale and avoid double taxation. That is no longer possible. Now if you use the third alternative, the corporation will be taxed on the gain when it is distributed to the shareholders, and the shareholders will be taxed again on the gain over their basis. (For an important exception, see the next section.)

Although selling the stock in your corporation (option two) offers advantages to you, it represents major disadvantages for the buyer. If you do sell the stock, the profits are taxed to you only once—no double taxation. Unfortunately, most buyers will resist this approach once they have discussed it with their attorneys or accountants. The buyer's risks are much greater. Generally, if the buyer buys assets rather than stock in a corporation, all liabilities are cut off. However, when buyers purchase the stock they assume all past, present, and future liabilities, *known* or *unknown*. If a hidden corporate liability surfaces, the corporation (and therefore indirectly the new buyer) is liable, and that includes any taxes, liens, etc. Very few buyers are willing to take that risk. Furthermore, the buyer assumes the depreciated value of your assets, without the chance to reallocate them on a stepped-up basis. This has a significant impact on the buyer's ability to minimize the company's future taxes. Fortunately, there are strategies that can be taken to avoid or lessen this problem.

As the seller, you could offer some extremely attractive concessions for the buyer to consider a stock sale. Recognize that a seller can indemnify (protect) the buyer if future liabilities surface. This indemnification can be backed up by personal guarantees or the right of the buyer to deduct any claims from notes due you. Additionally, a portion of the sale price could be held in escrow for a period of time to ensure against claims. Furthermore, you can simply lower the price of the business if the buyer will buy stock— share the benefit. This is where a good tax consultant becomes valuable. The alternatives can be penciled out, and when you know the tax impact, you can negotiate price or terms with the buyer so there's a win-win. Here are some factors which may encourage a buyer to buy corporate stock:

1. If the lease is held by the corporation and the landlord is resisting a transfer, then purchasing the stock would avoid negotiating a new lease. The same situation could prevail if the business were a distributorship or a franchise. Unfortunately, such distributor or franchise contracts often include restrictions on stock transfers. Most have personal guarantees and are therefore null and void if a transfer or sale is made.

2. If the corporation has a tax loss carry-forward, it may provide the buyer an opportunity to benefit by maximizing future taxable profits. However, the Tax Reform Act of 1986 severely restricted the availability of loss carry-forwards where more than 50 percent of the stock is transferred.

3. If the buyer plans to assume a large part of the existing debt, it may be necessary for the sale to include the corporation. Because suppliers lose all claims once ownership is transferred, they will normally want to be paid off if the assets are sold. However, if it is a stock sale, then the assets remain part of the corporation, and the suppliers normally have no cause for concern.

NOTE: For an example of the Actual Tax Implications see page 107

Liquidations Prior to 1989—

Special Opportunity to Avoid Double Taxation

Prior to the Tax Reform Act of 1986, it was possible to make an election that would allow a dissolving corporation to avoid much or all of the inherent gain when property was distributed to the shareholders. The only tax occurred when the shareholders sold the assets received in liquidation. Double taxation was avoided. This favorable election was repealed by the 1986 Act.

However, a special transitional rule in the new law applies to small corporations with a value of $10 million *or less* and which have 10 or fewer shareholders. These corporations (and shareholders) can take advantage of the old rules if the corporation is liquidated *prior to 1989*. Only corporations with a value not in excess of $5 million receive the full value of this exception. There is a phase-in for values in excess of $5 million. So most small businesses qualify. It may be time to take advantage of this exception whether or not you intend to sell.

In other words, even if you don't plan to sell your business in the foreseeable future but want to avoid the problems of double taxation or trying to sell stock, you may want to consider becoming a sole proprietor, partnership, or S-Corporation. These forms of business not only avoid the seller's double taxation problem but also make it easier for the buyer to purchase the assets. Since there are other implications to this strategy, it is important that you consult a tax specialist to help you evaluate this option.

Tax-Free Reorganizations

Tax-free reorganizations again have limited application to small businesses. Nevertheless, some years ago I used one of the six separate sections to split up my business. Because of a number of problems, my partner and I decided to go our separate ways. We had two corporations holding various stores. We exchanged stock in a rather elaborate agreement, and each became the sole shareholder in a separate corporation. Each of us then owned separate stores and paid no taxes in the exchange. Again, you need a tax specialist to draft the plan and even submit it to the IRS for a ruling before you enact it. The consequences are disastrous if the IRS refuses to recognize your reorganization after it has taken place.

Capital Gains

Prior to the Tax Reform Act of 1986, obtaining income that would be treated as capital gains rather than as ordinary income had significant tax advantages. No more.

In 1984, the capital gains provision of the tax law reduced the holding period from one year to six months on assets acquired after June 22 of that year. That meant selling an asset held more than six months would result in a maximum tax impact of no more than 20 percent, as opposed to a maximum of 50 percent tax on ordinary income.

This distinction between capital gain or loss and ordinary income or loss continues, but the 1986 Act removed the capital gains exclusion which ended the favorable tax treatment. What the government giveth, it sometimes taketh away!

Unless the tax law is changed again (and it probably will be), whether *gain* is characterized as capital or ordinary income will no longer matter in most cases to the business seller. Simply stated, now there are no tax advantages of capital gains over ordinary income since both are taxed at the same rate. (In the phase)in year of 1987, however, there is a rate differential of 28 percent for capital gain and 38.5 percent for ordinary income.)

However, there is one area where capital gains (or losses) can shelter taxes effectively. At this time, an individual can only deduct a maximum of $3,000 in capital loss against ordinary income. The remaining loss is then carried forward to future year(s). But if you have capital losses from other sources (e.g. sale of stock, real property), then these losses can offset capital gains dollar for dollar. The same shelter can occur if you are selling a business at a loss. You can offset any capital gains from other sources in the same way. Again, it pays to plan a sale so all opportunities are explored to minimize your tax impact.

Allocation of Assets

In all business sales, whether you are operating as a sole proprietorship, partnership, or corporation, you must allocate the purchase price among the assets, or the IRS may do it for you at a later point in time. Essentially that means you must put a dollar value on each business asset. Because there are present and future tax implications in how the assets are allocated, it is important to understand the process and the impact. Still, if the allocation is done with a proper give and take it can be fair to both parties. With the current tax law (removal of capital gains advantages), properly allocating the asset value is more a concern for the buyer than the seller. Consequently, this gives the seller some additional negotiating leverage.

Table 18-1 provides a breakdown and explanation for the possible options in a business sale allocation. (This will give you insight into the areas to avoid, or at least minimize, and those areas that offer the best tax advantage.)

In most cases, allocations have flexibility and can be arbitrary within

Figure 18-1
TAX IMPACT ON THE BUYER AND SELLER
ALLOCATION OF PURCHASE PRICE

Allocation	Seller	Buyer
Inventory	Any amount over cost is ordinary income.	The higher the price the less ordinary income on sale.
Fixtures, Lease-hold improvements, equipment and machinery	Capital gains treatment	Must capitalize and amortize over useful life even if longer than lease term; go item by item.
Goodwill	Capital gains treatment	Deductible as paid generally.
Lease Valuation	Capital gains treatment	Ordinary income (be careful, the IRS may reallocate between interest and purchase price if rate too high or too low.
Real Estate Building	Capital gains treatment	High allocation; depreciable asset.
Real Estate Land	Capital gains treatment	Low allocation; non-depreciable.
Trade Name or Franchise trademark	(If all rights are relinquished, capital gains treatment.)	Low allocation; cannot claim anything; asset remains on books.
Accounts Receivable	Ordinary income	Rate of Interest on Notes (affects price - higher interest, lower price).
Customer List	Ordinary income	Probably amortized over useful life, but IRS may attempt to lump it into Goodwill.
Interest on Notes	Ordinary income	The higher the allocation, the less gain as receivables are collected
Covenant not Compete	Ordinary income	Amortized over length of covenant.
Employment Contract	Ordinary income	High allocation; direct expense write-off as paid

reason and prudence. For example, if most of the purchase price is shifted to fixtures, lease-hold improvements, or lease value, it could be written off by the buyer in a depreciation or amortization schedule and still not have a negative effect on the seller.

Let's consider a couple of other examples. suppose you, as a seller, want to allocate $100,000 of the purchase price to goodwill. Unfortunately, the buyer cannot depreciate or amortize goodwill. It remains on the buyer's books as an asset and can only be recovered when the business is sold. However, if you were to allocate that amount to a combination of leasehold improvements, fixtures, and even part to a mailing list, the buyer would have the benefit of annual deductibility. Since the tax implications to you, as the seller, are the same, you can use the allocation issue as a bargaining chip in negotiations.

Perhaps you're not able to justify allocating the entire purchase price to depreciable assets. Rather than using goodwill, it may be better to allocate part of the price to lease value, which can be amortized over the remaining term of the lease. It may also be more advantageous for the buyer to pay a higher interest rate, which is deductible, and reduce the purchase price. All of these alternatives should be viewed as ways to legally minimize the tax burden and create a beneficial deal for both buyer and seller.

Sales Contract

We now shift from taxes to contracts. At some point in time, certainly prior to closing the sale, the contract must be drafted and introduced. Often this provides the basis for a whole new round of negotiations. Most business sales contracts are multi-paged, multi-sectioned documents full of legal jargon. They have warranties and indemnification clauses, and in general, intimidate the reader to the point of fear. Yet once you pick them apart, they simply provide protection for both parties to transact a complicated business deal.

Typically, the seller will have an attorney draft a preliminary contract. In the Appendix, you will find a sample business sales contract. A word of caution: use this as a guide only. Each transaction has its own concerns, and the law varies from state to state. This sample is meant only to educate the potential buyer and seller about the kinds of provisions they should be ready to consider. Most business sales have a number of important and unique factors that must be included in the sales contract, and an attorney experienced in business buy/sell transactions is the best guide for this legal maze.

Important Contract Conditions

The contract will have multiple sections; yet there are important areas that you should be familiar with. By being acquainted with these areas, you can provide input for your attorney in the contract drafting effort.

Accounts Receivable: If you, as the seller, retain the accounts receivable, a number of customer problems can develop. All customers have to be notified, and they frequently resent the inconvenience of making separate payments to the previous owner and to the new owner. One way to handle this is to have the buyer collect the bills and then pay you as the money is received. Any account over 90 days is given to you for collection. If the buyer purchases the accounts receivable, some provision must be made for discounting the face amount of doubtful accounts.

Method of Payment: The contract should include a detailed description of the terms, down payment, deposits, and guarantees. If you, as the seller, plan to carry back any loans, all of the documents and agreements, promissory notes, etc should be attached to the sales contract as exhibits.

Adjustments: There will be a number of adjustments at the time of closing. An actual inventory should be taken just prior (24-48 hours) to the transfer. Any increase or decrease in inventory over the estimated amount will be reflected in the sale price. Usually inventory adjustments as well as any other adjustments are added to the total price rather than the agreed-upon down payment. In this way, the buyer knows what cash requirements will be necessary. Other adjustments—insurance, rent, deposits, payroll taxes, license fees, etc.—are usually pro-rated based on the date the business actually transfers ownership.

Your Responsibilities: You will be responsible for assuring the buyer you have good title to all of the assets. You should determine whether there are any liens or claims and cure them prior to the sale. Additionally, most states require that you comply with the **Bulk Sales Law.** This law basically protects any of your creditors and assures that they are paid prior to or out of the proceeds of the sale. You are required, under oath, to provide the buyer with a list of creditors. Then the buyer is responsible for notifying them by registered mail ten days prior to closing. Failure to comply with the Bulk Sales Law can result in some serious legal problems.

Taxes: Many states provide that even a buyer of assets is liable for the state taxes owed by the former owner. So all tax claims should be settled out of the escrow account. (Directions for doing this are written into the contract and the escrow agent simply complies with the contract provision.)

Indemnification: Normally you will have to indemnify the buyer (agree to cure any problems or liabilities that you are responsible for that show up after the sale). This protects the buyer from any past problems or law suits. Frequently, the buyer will insist that part of the purchase price be placed in escrow for a period of time to ensure that money is available to cover any of these eventualities. Attempt to keep this indemnification fund to a minimum and for a limited period of time.

Non-Compete: Some buyers will insist on a non-compete agreement. If this is included in the sale, it should be part of the contract and carefully defined as to what can or cannot be done, the geographical limitations, and duration. Some businesses have a specific clientele (hair salons, professional practices, etc.) and should also include a section prohibiting the seller from contacting present customers.

Records of the Business: The buyer of a business should get all the necessary books and records. However, as the seller, you will also need these items to complete tax returns and wrap up the operation. The contract should provide for access to these documents, no matter who retains physical control.

Disputes: If the contract doesn't spell out sensible alternatives to settling disputes, then long and costly litigation may become the only way to solve future problems or disagreements between buyer and seller. There are two ways to help avoid unnecessary litigation. First, an arbitration provision may be included that forces the parties to solve disputes by using binding arbitration. Second, a section can be drafted that provides the winner of the dispute with attorneys fees. This has a way of keeping both parties away from any unnecessary litigation. Remember though that if either party violates the major provisions of the agreement, then the courts may be the only place the issue can be resolved.

Escrow and Closing: The seller should set up an account with an escrow agent (bank or attorney). An escrow officer with business transfer experience will "walk the deal through" various state and local requirements and actually set up a closing date. The day of closing should be convenient for both buyer and seller and is normally 30-45 days after the contract has been signed. this is a time of high tension. As a seller, you may have a small cash deposit in escrow (normally, approximately 10 percent of the purchase price) and a signed contract. However, you don't have the total proceeds from the sale, and furthermore, you must still run the business. As the closing date approaches, the buyer will frequently have second thoughts about the purchase. It's advantageous to keep the escrow time frame as short as possible. It is also important that both parties communicate. In this way, you can constantly reinforce the buyer's commitment. This is not the time to get involved in any conflicts!

If it appears to benefit both parties, consider a cooperative agreement. Outline a timetable and plan where the buyer can visit or even work in the business. Introduce the buyer to the suppliers. At the appropriate point, and with care, introduce the buyer to the staff. Attempt to make a smooth transition. Your objective is to leave the business with as few problems as possible. Your future peace of mind may depend upon it.

More About Leases

You will be extremely fortunate if you are able to transfer your lease without problems. Typically, a landlord seizes the opportunity to apply pressure in the form of a new lease, with increased rent and/or added conditions. Occasionally, a new lease that provides additional time can be a plus if the rent isn't increased substantially. Nevertheless, it is important to know your legal rights and to have a strategy for moving around this potential pitfall. A number of states have had precedent-setting lease transfer law suits in recent years. The courts have held in many cases that the landlord may not unreasonably refuse the transfer of a lease. This is an area of much change, so if your landlord is not cooperating, you may want to seek legal advice.

In terms of strategy, you will find that using an improvement plan outlined in Chapter 5 will be very effective in providing a positive reason for the landlord to accept a new owner. However, before you start negotiations with potential buyers, you should contact the property owners or their agents. If you receive a verbal approval for the lease transfer, send a registered letter confirming the conversation. You have now implemented what is legally called an *estoppel commitment*. This principle of law prevents the landlord from reneging on a verbal commitment. On the other hand, if you immediately run into resistance, contact an attorney. Take your lease, along with a written recap of your conversations, and any other pertinent data (rental receipts, list of other tenants that have successfully transferred leases, etc.). Ask the attorney to write a cordial letter, citing any legal precedence in your state covering tenant rights. This should be followed up as soon as possible to obtain a written approval of the transfer.

Without the landlord's approval of the lease transfer, negotiations and the ultimate sale will be problem oriented. Buyers will be very apprehensive about seriously discussing the business if they don't feel they can acquire a favorable lease.

Summary

All of this material must seem quite complicated—agreements, contracts, warranties, indemnification, liquidations, allocations. Unless you have bought or sold a business before, this surely is unfamiliar territory. Even if you have, unless you deal with these legal and tax matters frequently, there is no way you can be familiar enough to handle a "do-it-yourself" legal project.

Before you select an attorney or accountant, you may want to check the fees. First ask whether the individual is familiar with business sales, then explain the situation and ask what the charges will be.

When I sold one of my stores, I had an accountant prepare a financial package, an attorney draft the contract, and a bank escrow officer handle the closing and escrow proceedings. The total fees were less than $2,000. Since there were promissory notes, security agreements, and a lease transfer, I felt that was money well spent. When I sold other stores in a much more complicated transaction, the legal and accounting fees were close to $15,000. However, because the attorney participated in the negotiations and prepared and executed a complicated tax plan, I felt that these fees were also well spent. The point to remember: there are just too many legal and tax traps in the sale of a business to do it yourself or to hire someone incompetent or inexperienced. Retain expert professionals and sleep well at night.

FIGURE 18-2
WHAT AN ATTORNEY AND ACCOUNTANT SHOULD DO FOR YOU IN THE PURCHASE OR SALE OF A BUSINESS

1. Provide advice on the basic merits of the sale or purchase (outside objectivity and assistance in clarifying the situation).

2. Help in valuing the business.

3. Analysis of the pros and cons for the various alternatives available (e.g. stock versus assets sale, Section 337, Section 333, etc.).

4. Help in analyzing financial statements. If you are the seller, help in preparing those statements.

5. Preparation of asset allocation of the purchase price.

6. If necessary assisting in negotiations.

7. An attorney should prepare letters of intention, sales contracts, notes and other documents.

8. Analysis of the tax impact, both for the buyer and seller.

9. Arrangement for escrow, bulk sales and closing documentation.

All the above services can be expensive. Be prepared to discuss fees prior to requesting the work.

Chapter 19
How to Bail Out and Land Soft

You may wonder why I have left this chapter for last, considering the mortality rate of small businesses. As a typical new entrepreneur, you have a strong faith in your enterprise. You deserve all the encouragement possible. You'll need it to survive the real or even imaginary difficulties of starting and operating your own business. This book was written, for the most part, on an upbeat, positive, go-for-it basis. Yet, no matter how much faith, planning, or capital you put into a venture, there may come a time when you must realize it isn't working. As W.C. Fields once said, "If at first you don't succeed, try, try again . . . then give up. There's no use being a damn fool about it."

In fact, most ex-entrepreneurs feel very positive about their experience. They may not have liked the water, after taking the plunge, but most say they have learned valuable lessons about business in general and about themselves specifically. Most former entrepreneurs are even optimistic and feel they may try again if the conditions are right. Nevertheless, if you have exhausted all possibilities and it still isn't coming together, don't be heroic, strap on your parachute and get ready - there's always another opportunity on another day.

Actually the objectives of this chapter are three-fold. First, it will point out *early-warning signals* that tell you your business is in trouble. Second, it will outline a *survival strategy*. And third, if the problems are unsolvable, it will show you how to *bail out* and still have a soft landing.

Most businesses have problems from time to time. It really doesn't matter whether you are large or small. Consider the recent problems Chrysler has experienced, and before that Lockheed. Both were on the verge of bankruptcy. Both, of course, were bailed out by the government's loans, something you probably won't be lucky enough to enjoy. However, there are a number of ways a small business person can survive the trauma of a troubled business. First, you must be alert enough to recognize the problems before they become so serious that little can be done.

Figure 19-1 provides a list of reasons why people fail in business. It's extensive. Any of these business viruses can cause terminal illness; and certainly the combination of a number of them can intensify the malady very rapidly.

The S.B.A. states that of the new businesses that are started each year, 80% will fail within three years, with the greatest mortality being in the second year. The problem with these statistics is that every business that changes legal structure, alters its name, or moves from its start-up address, is included in the numbers. Their system cannot detect the variables, and therefore, it considers that all of these businesses are out of business.

FIGURE 19-1

The following list shows the factors which can contribute to the demise of a business:

Inadequate Financing
1. Improper use of capital.
2. Insufficient cash flow to restock the inventory.
3. Excessive payroll expenditures, e.g. salaries and personal draws.
4. Inadequate funds for initial promotion.
5. Miscalculation of overall expenses.

Personal Factors
1. Lack of specific skills necessary to accomplish the job.
2. Low stamina or burnout.
3. Unwillingness to work long hours in the business.
4. Inability to adjust to change.
5. Inability to handle all management roles.
6. Inability to work with people.
7. Inability to delegate responsibility.

Planning
1. Insufficient market analysis.
2. Incorrect estimate of the operation's potential.
3. Poor timing.
4. Lack of anticipated support from bank.
5. Lack of planning unforeseen circumstances (no margin for error).

Personnel
1. Poor caliber.
2. Poor training.
3. Poor motivation.

Competitive Factors
1. Aggressive reaction from your competitors (price war).
2. Competitor's advantage in pricing, promotion, etc.
3. Miscalculation of competitor's hold on the market.

Procedures and Controls
1. Lack of adequate control for inventory, administration, personnel and expenses.
2. External or internal theft or embezzlement.

Overall Industry
1. Decline in specific industry.
2. Decline in general sales (recession).

Location
1. Inadequate to attract sufficient customers.
2. Higher cost factors than affordable.
3. Change in customer's buying patterns.

At the other end of the spectrum, the Bank of America's Small Business Investment Subsidiary tells a very different story. Of those new companies they assist with financing, only 8% fail in five years. Most have growth rates averaging 10-30% annually. One factor worth mentioning - the bank will only invest in companies with a high potential for success. Their criteria include: a strong management team, a growth industry, well defined markets, and a carefully tested product or service. No wonder they are successful. Of course, your chance of success in a small business will be measured along the same criteria. Add in a sprinkle of adequate financing and a dash of experience, and your business will also flourish. You may even expand. On the other hand, if you make a few miscalculations - under capitalization, wrong market, bad timing - you will have a hard uphill battle.

Stay Alert

Even after you have been in business for a couple of years and you think the worst is over, a surprise is still likely to pop up. You must always stay alert for trouble. Small businesses are very temperamental, and can change rather quickly. There are a number of early warning signals that tell you that your operation needs attention. If you discover a problem soon enough, the task of correction is much easier. Don't wait until things have gotten out of control. Watch for these signs of deepening trouble:

1. Chronic cash flow problems.

2. Inability to pay bills, and particularly payroll taxes, on time.

3. Drop-off in sales below seasonal expectations.

4. Rise in percentage of expenses against sales, particularly fixed expenses like rent.

5. Major competition entering the marketplace.

6. Changes in buying patterns, or a fad phasing out.

7. Poor employee morale, or lack of interest in the operation.

8. Rising customer complaints.

9. Unexpected decrease in store traffic.

10. Change in your attitude to complacency or negativism.

Small businesses desperately need leadership. Once the owner neglects its care and maintenance, things start to come apart. Employees become lazy. Controls are abandoned and expenses skyrocket. If nobody is watching the business, then the business will eventually fall apart. Perhaps the first of the early warning signals is you. When you lose interest and enthusiasm, then it's not long before the business feels the vibrations.

Identify the Problem

What do you do if you become aware that your business has a serious problem? First, *don't panic.* Keeping an even keel can be the initial step in successfully turning things around.

Second, give yourself a positive psychological treatment. Your organization's problem is not the end of the world. Five years from now, virtually no one will ever remember that you had business troubles. Don't allow managerial paralysis to keep you from using your wits to figure out how you can regroup. Start by talking with someone that you trust and someone you value in terms of objective, sound thinking. An entrepreneur, like anyone else, often loses perspective in troubled times. You are so close to the trees, you fail to see the forest. The person should be someone who understands business, perhaps an accountant or fellow entrepreneur.

Then you have to explain the situation to your family. Your family must recognize the trouble and become supportive. You need a sanctuary for rest and recuperation, so that you can go back out and win the daily battles. Your home should become that place with family members providing the necessary support and encouragement. The alternative, hiding the situation, will only result in double trouble.

Strategy For Survival

This may be one of the most important entrepreneurial efforts you will ever undertake. Even if your ultimate plan is to sell the business, you must buy time. Business sales do not happen overnight and distressed businesses sometimes never sell.

The first task is to establish a *perspective* - a realistic appraisal of just how much trouble you're in. Carefully examine your financial records and objectively appraise the overall market. Try to determine precisely what has happened to cause the problem. Once you have identified the cause, it will be much easier to work on the solution. Don't expect to perform major corrective surgery the first week.

Immediately look for ways to stop cash drain:

1. Reduce or eliminate any nonessential business expenses (travel/ entertainment, memberships to clubs, etc.).

2. Review each expense for any waste (for example, non-productive advertising).

3. Don't purchase any questionable or extra inventory.

4. Review payroll and eliminate any over-staffing. Reduce hours. Assume more of the responsibility yourself or bring in family members.

5. Delay any major or even minor purchase (fix the cash register, instead of buying a new one).

Then look for ways to increase cash flow:

1. Promote aggressively. Have a sale. Turn that inventory into cash.

2. Set up bonus plans and incentives for your staff to perform at higher levels.

3. Sell off any asset that isn't making money.

4. Consolidate. Drop marginal lines. Return non-moving merchandise for credit.

While you're doing all of this, you need help from the people who control your future.

1. Landlords. Some are reasonable, most are not. Explain your situation and determine whether they will give you any slack. They have a powerful weapon—a three day notice. If you fail to pay rent, they can serve you with a "payment notice" giving you three days to bring your account current, or you're out. You want to avoid getting into that type of situation, and having a good relationship will often be the deciding factor.

2. Suppliers. Their objective is to see you maintain the business. Consequently they will be motivated to help you through the rough times. They recognize that if you go out of business, they will not only lose an outlet for their products, but probably the amounts you now owe them. They may be willing to go C.O.D. on future purchases and to offer a partial payment plan (e.g. $100 per shipment on back bills). They may also be willing to take back unsold merchandise for credit against new products. The suppliers will probably be the most flexible folks you will deal with.

3. Internal Revenue Service. These people are particularly tough. Typically business owners in trouble will begin filing payroll tax reports late and absorbing penalties. When cash flow is nonexistent, payroll taxes become low priority. You may get some official notices from the IRS in brown envelopes, but nobody calls. When they finally catch up with you, they normally have little patience. That's one of the major problems. It takes so long for them to surface. When they do, four to six months after the fact, you have a real crisis. A word of advice: try to keep your taxes current, and if you fall behind, go immediately and talk with them. Don't wait until they contact you. There are provisions in the tax code for payment plans. Don't expect them to be overly cooperative, but recent court rulings have forced the IRS to drop much of their heavy-handed tactics.

4. Bankers. If Argentina can restructure its debt, perhaps you will be able to do the same. If your business is being jeopardized by a bank loan, the banker may be receptive to reducing payments by stretching out the length of the commitment. The bank's alternative will be to accept cents on the dollar in a bankruptcy. Bankers are personally motivated to accept almost any restructuring plan, rather than seeing the loan go into default (that looks bad on their record).

5. Employees. They are frequently more aware of trouble than owners and probably already know the extent of the problem. They don't have a major personal stake in the operation, so they tend to be more objective and observant. Still, you should discuss the problems with them, particularly if things are critical. You must get them on your side. You may not be able to overcome the problem without their help. Begin by eliminating any of their fears. If you plan to cut staff, do it quickly and immediately talk to the survivors, reassuring them of their jobs. Lack of security is one of the greatest human fears, and demotivators. Explain the situation without going into great detail. Then provide positive scenarios. Show them your "turn around" plan. Ask for their help and offer some type of benefit (bonus plan, a party, merchandise certificates, etc.) if the objectives are met. Sometimes, crises can provide the rallying point for recovery. Everybody wants to root for the underdogs, some even like to play on their team. This will be the real test of your leadership skills.

Options

When your business is having difficulty, there are a number of less severe options other than closing the doors or declaring bankruptcy. Initially, you should examine each of the alternatives and then select the best course of action.

Find a buyer. Businesses in distress sell all of the time. One thing that is critical—operate fast. If the business is draining capital, you can last only so long. Consider listing the business with a good business broker, one who is familiar with selling problem operations. You may not get the price that you want, but you will be out. Be flexible and accommodating. But be sure to get guarantees from the buyer, in writing, that you are not liable for any problems, including a lease. If you neglect to obtain these conditions, you may find yourself returning to more significant problems when the new owner fails.

Don't give the broker too much time to find a buyer. Keep the contract short (under 60 days) and only sign an exclusive agency listing. That gives you the right to find a buyer on your own, without paying a broker's commission. Remember, value is in the eye of the beholder. There are people who will see value in your business if the price is right. Don't forget to get a down payment that will cover all of your debts.

Find a partner. If you believe in your business, but lack the financial ability to see it through a particularly difficult time, consider adding a partner. There are a number of individuals with money who would like to participate in a business but, for one reason or another, haven't taken the plunge.

Considerable care has to be taken here, since you are vulnerable. There are two basic rules: don't give away the business, and pick the right person. Incidentally, that person may be a relative, loyal employee, or even a competitor. As a variation of the old saying: If you can't fight 'em, merge with 'em.

Eliminate or Reduce Your Debt. Despite your best efforts, the business may be failing. The liabilities may exceed the assets. Perhaps it is the principle and interest payments from the debt load which make positive cash flow impossible. All is not lost. If the business has accumulated a large debt, creditors may be willing to settle those debts for a very large discount in return for cash *now*. Something certain today may be much more attractive to the creditor than the risk, delay, and expense that a creditor will experience in a liquidation or bankruptcy.

Do a little projecting. What happens to net asset value and cash flow if the debts are eliminated? What if you could find a buyer with cash who could pay off the debts, perhaps at a discount. Call a meeting of creditors. Explain to your creditors that they have a choice. They can risk a liquidation or accept, for example, 40 cents on the dollar in settlement of their debt. Be prepared to show them financial records and your plan. You then sell the "rehabilitated" business to the prospective buyer free of debt and you may even be able to structure it so you receive some cash on a note.

Additional investment. Perhaps, after you have objectively analyzed your present state of affairs, you see encouraging signs. The Christmas season is coming, the economy is improving, new stores are opening in the area, or the plant is rehiring laid off employees. If you are convinced that the business can revive itself with a small transfusion of cash, consider backing your educated instincts with a personal investment. The possibility does exist that you're putting good money after bad. On the other hand, it would be also tragic if you walked away prematurely from a good business. Nobody said your entrepreneurial decisions would be easy!

Closing the Doors

Surprisingly, a large number of small firms simply quit. They pay off debts (occasionally at a reduced or negotiated figure), liquidate assets, and walk away. This frequently occurs when a landlord wants to raise the rent at the end of a lease period, and the owners are not interested in paying the additional amount. Many entrepreneurs, however, will decide to call it quits part way through the lease. Problems will arise if the landlord insists that the lease obligations be met. A negotiated settlement usually works. For example, offer six months' rent for cancellation of the lease. Regardless, the landlord must make all reasonable efforts to re-lease the space and if successful, your future liability is eliminated. An attorney can give you a full explanation on the concept of mitigating damages.

Shutting the doors is a possibility when the business is operating at a substantial loss. You may also be considering this option if you are feeling totally burnt-out. The idea of no problems to worry about is particularly appealing. Freedom from a negative business may be well worth the price. But still, try to find a buyer.

Give it Away

Approximately 25% of all business transfers go to employees. That doesn't necessarily indicate the owners gave the businesses away or that they were all problem operations. However, it probably indicates that the business was sold for less than true value. I spoke to a number of entrepreneurs who either purchased or sold a business in this way. They all indicated the price was far below market. I discussed it with one individual who sold a "failing" fast-food franchise to his employees for $1.00. He protected himself with a contract, was up-front with full disclosure, and literally gave his chronic headache to his employees. They ran it for another year, before finally throwing in the towel. Be careful here, be sure you're not giving a business away and acquiring a future law suit.

Bankruptcy

There is a possibility that no matter what you do or how hard you work, the problems are too insurmountable. Perhaps you really don't have a viable business, or some external or internal factors make it impossible for you to continue. You are still able to bail out. The landing may not be quite as soft as some of the other alternatives, but you will survive.

Essentially, what you are doing is using the protection of the Federal government to ease out of your predicament. Today, filing bankruptcy does not carry the stigma it once did. Some famous people, as well as large companies, have lessened the negative image. There are 200,000 bankruptcies filed annually. Nevertheless you will want to delay this action as long as possible, since once you file, the business will undoubtedly go through some additional problems.

You will definitely need the help of a qualified attorney in this area. But, don't wait too long in seeking legal help. The effective strategies work best when there is a favorable time factor.

There are actually fourteen chapters in the bankruptcy code. As a business person you will probably be concerned with only two of them. *Chapter 7* provides for the complete liquidation of a debtor's assets and can be used for a sole proprietorship, partnership, or corporation. The action can be started either voluntarily or involuntarily.

Yes, your creditors can force you into bankruptcy. Although rare, with involuntary bankruptcies amounting to only 5% of the total number, it's still something you should consider. However, Chapter 7 is not a particularly attractive option, since it involves immediate liquidation of your business.

Chapter 11 provides a method for reorganizing your business affairs. It really buys you time in order to determine whether you can salvage the operation. When you seek protection under Chapter 11, your creditors are notified, and all collection proceedings are put on hold. You have 120 days to provide the court with a repayment plan that is acceptable to half of those to whom you owe money. In other words, after you have filed, you have four months to negotiate actual settlements or mutually agreed upon payment schedules. If you can convince 51% of your creditors to go along with the plan, the others automatically must agree. You won't get much consideration from the IRS, and some companies will insist on long term pay-outs. However you have bought valuable time and may immediately improve your cash flow. If it doesn't work, then you can move into total liquidation.

Once you have had your plan approved, you must stay current. Otherwise, the court's trustee will lift the protection, and the creditors will have at you.

Consider this little known strategy for improving your financial future considerably. Let's say you have ten unsecured creditors who have accepted a 50% settlement of debt over a five year period of time. If you acquire some cash, you might approach each creditor, explaining that you have someone who will lend you money on the condition that your creditors would be willing to accept perhaps 60% of the reduced debt in cash and to sign a settlement. Most creditors will go along with the offer, rationalizing that a dollar in hand is better than future dollars in a bankruptcy program. You must be extremely tactful in this effort, for obvious reasons. Yet, it is well within the law. If you obtain releases from each named creditor, your bankruptcy will be dismissed. Discharging all of the debts outside of the arranged bankruptcy plan will literally erase your bankruptcy. The golden advantage is that you can avoid the seven year waiting rule (you can only seek bankruptcy protection once in seven years).

Someone made a wry observation about bankruptcy . . . it is a legal proceeding that, if done right, allows you to put your money in your pocket while you give your shirt to the creditors.

How to Clean a Spot

When faced with progressively difficult alternatives in the process of surviving a failing business, I sometimes think of this analogy: If you notice a spot on your carpet, it makes sense to first try removing it with just water. If that doesn't work, add some mild soap. Then you may have to purchase carpet cleaner at the store. And if that fails, a commercial solvent may be your next alternative. Finally, your last option may be a sharp knife where you extract carpet along with the spot. The point here is never to be premature or overzealous in attempting to solve your business problems. Sometimes a less drastic step will be sufficient.

Most on-going small businesses can be salvaged, or at least temporarily patched together so that they can be sold. Often a new owner with capital and a positive attitude can breathe life back into a troubled operation. The trick is to turn the listing ship around and get it to port before it sinks.

On that note, I leave you, hoping you'll never have to implement the strategies in this last chapter.

Granted, the entrepreneurial road is difficult, but the benefits are great. It normally takes between 5 and 10 years to become an overnight success. But the time passes quickly and furthermore, it's a lot more fun working for yourself than for someone else. ***GOOD LUCK!***

APPENDIX

SELLING A BUSINESS

Appendix 1
Sources of Information

SBA Programs and Publications

The U.S. Small Business Administration is a federal agency, created to assist and counsel American small businesses. The Agency also provides prospective, new, and established persons in the small business community with financial assistance, management counseling, and training. SBA also helps obtain and direct government procurement contracts for small firms.

The Agency makes special efforts to women, minorities, the handicapped and veterans to get into business, and stay in business, because such persons long have faced unusual difficulties in the private marketplace. The Agency has about 4,000 permanent employees and more than 100 offices in all parts of the nation.

Financial Assistance

The SBA offers a variety of loan programs to eligible small business concerns which cannot borrow on reasonable terms from conventional lenders without government help.

Most of SBA's business loans are made by private lenders and then guaranteed by the Agency. Guaranteed loans carry a maximum of $500,000 and SBA guarantees of the loan run as high as 90 percent. Maturity may be up to 25 years. The average size of a guaranteed business loan is $155,000 and the average maturity is about eight years.

Early in 1983, SBA began a pilot "Preferred Lenders Program," under which selected banks handle all loan paperwork and loan processing. Banks in this program also service the loans. This program is in line with the Agency's overall efforts to obtain greater private-sector involvement in SBA activities. The program significantly trims loan paperwork and loan processing time.

Management Assistance

The Agency's Management Assistance program is extensive and diversified. It includes free individual counseling, courses, conferences, workshops, problem clinics, and a wide range of publications. Counseling is provided through programs established by SBA's Management Assistance staff; the Service Corps of Retired Executives (SCORE); its corollary organization of active business men and women, the Active Corps of Executives (ACE); and numerous professional associations. SBA tries to match the need of a specific business with the expertise available through its counseling programs.

Small Business Institutes

Small Business Institutes (SBI's) have been organized through SBA on almost 500 university and college campuses as another way to help small business. At each SBI, senior and graduate students at schools of business administration, and their faculty advisors, provide on-site management counseling. Students are guided by the faculty advisors and SBA management assistance experts and receive academic credit for their work.

Small Business Management Series

Management, marketing, and technical publications issued by SBA on hundreds of topics are available to established firms concerned about prospective managers of small firms concerned about specific management problems and various aspects of business operations. Most of these publications are available from SBA free of charge. Others can be obtained for a small fee from the U.S. Government Printing Office. In addition to management assistance publications, brochures describing the Agency's programs are available at all SBA offices.

Following is a brief list of publications available. For a complete list request forms SBA 115A and 115B.

The books in this series discuss specific management techniques or problems.

Handbook of Small Business Finance, $4.50

Management Audit for Small Manufacturers — A questionnaire for manufacturers, $4.50

Management Audit for Small Retailers, $4.50

Financial Recordkeeping for Small Stores, $5.50

Small Store Planning for Growth, $5.50

Management Audit for Small Service Firms, $4.50

Purchasing Management and Inventory Control for Small Business, $4.50

Managing the Small Service Firm for Growth and Profit, $4.25

To Order: Send with your check or money order to the Superintendent of Documents, Government Printing Office, Washington, D.C. 20402.

Management Aids (MA's): These pamphlets are free of charge.

MA 1.001 The ABC's of Borrowing
MA 1.007 Credit and Collections
MA 1.011 Analyze Your Records to Reduce Costs
MA 1.015 Budgeting in a Small Business Firm
MA 1.016 Sound Cash Management and Borrowing
MA 1.019 Simple Breakeven Analysis for Small Stores
MA 1.020 Profit Pricing and Costing for Services
MA 2.002 Locating or Relocating Your Business
MA 2.004 Problems in Managing a Family-Owned Business
MA 2.010 Planning and Goal Setting for Small Business
MA 2.016 Check List for Going into Business
MA 2.017 Factors in Considering a Shopping Center Location
MA 2.018 Insurance Checklist for Small Business
MA 2.020 Business Plan for Retailers
MA 2.025 Thinking About Going Into Business?
MA 3.004 Preventing Retail Theft
MA 4.002 Creative Selling: The Competitive Edge
MA 4.008 Tips on Getting More for Your Marketing Dollar
MA 4.012 Marketing Checklist for Small Retailers
MA 4.014 Improving Personal Selling in Small Retail Stores
MA 4.015 Advertising Guidelines for Small Retail Firms
MA 4.019 Learning About Your Market
MA 5.001 Checklist for Developing a Training Program

To Order: U.S. Small Business Administration
P.O. Box 15434
Ft. Worth, TX 76119

BANK OF AMERICA PUBLICATIONS

The Bank of America offers a number of excellent brochures on various topics for small business management. Their "Small Business Reporter" series provides straightforward, practical information owning and operating a small business. It is for all those who need information about small business—the business owner, of course, but also bankers, attorneys, accountants, consultants, industry and trade associations, schools and libraries.

To Order: Copies will be sent by mail. Send check or money order made payable to Bank of America. Mail to:

Small Business Reporter
Bank of America
Department 3401
P.O. Box 37000
San Francisco, CA 94137

Charges for mail orders:

Individual copies
Inside California	$2.00
Outside California	$3.00

Publications Available

Business Operations

How to Buy or Sell a Business, 1982
Financing Small Business, 1983
Management Succession, 1981
Understanding Financial Statements, 1980
Steps to Starting a Business, 1983
Cash Flow/Cash Management, 1982
Advertising Small Business, 1982
Personnel Guidelines, 1981
Crime Prevention for Small Business, 1982
Equipment Leasing, 1983
Avoiding Management Pitfalls, 1981

Business Profiles

Bars and Cocktail Lounges, 1981
The Handcrafts Business, 1980
Restaurants, 1983
Gift Stores, 1980
Bicycle Stores, 1981
General Job Printing, 1979
Apparel Stores, 1978
Property Management, 1977

Professional Management

Establishing an Accounting Practice, 1982
Establishing a Veterinary Practice, 1974
Establishing a Dental Practice, 1982
Establishing a Medical Practice, 1982

Books

How to Pick the Right Small Business Opportunity, Kenneth J. Albert, McGraw-Hill.

How to Organize and Operate a Small Business, Clifford M. Baumack, Prentice-Hall, Inc.

Run Your Own Store, Irving Burstiner, Ph.D., Prentice-Hall, Inc.

You Can Negotiate Anything, Herb Cohen, Lyle Stuart, Inc.

The Small Business Survival Guide, Bob Coleman, W.W. Norton.

Up Your Own Organization, Donald M. Dible, Prentice-Hall, Inc.

How to Profitably Sell or Buy a Company or Business, F. Gordon Douglas, Van Nostrand Reinhold.

How to Start and Manage Your Own Business, Gardiner G. Greene, Mentor.

Independent Retailing, Herbert Greenwald, Prentice-Hall, Inc.

Own Your Own: The No-Cash Down Business Guide, Arnold S. Goldstein, Prentice-Hall, Inc.

How to Run a Small Business, J.K. Lasser, McGraw-Hill.

How to Become Financially Successful by Owning Your Own Business, Albert J. Lowry, Ph.D., Simon and Schuster.

How to Make Money in Your Own Small Business, Wendell O. Metcalf, The Enterepreneur Press.

How to Start, Finance and Manage Your Own Small Business, Joseph R. Mancuso, Prentice-Hall, Inc.

Starting Right in Your New Business, Wilfred F. Tetreault, Robert Clements.

Managing Your Profits, Tate, Megginson, Dow Jones-Irwin.

Partners in Business, Dr. Melvin Wallace, Enterprise Publishing, Inc.

Appendix 2
Trade Associations and Journals

The following list of associations (A) and Trade Magazines (M) does not cover all the possibilities. There are other business segments and even additional associations and publications for the categories listed. If you are interested in additional sources, contact your local library. They have directories listing each publisher and group associated with various businesses. Also, ask suppliers and business owners to recommend trade journals and associations they belong to.

A phone call or short letter requesting information or back issues of a publication will provide a wealth of material. Some associations even provide courses and "How to do" manuals for opening businesses in their field.

ACCOUNTING

Robert L. Shultis, Exec. Dir.   (A)
National Assoc. of Accountants
919 Third Ave.
New York, N.Y. 10022

Diane Senese, Exec. Dir.   (A)
Amer. Society of Women Acc'ts.
35 E. Wacker Dr.
Chicago, IL 60601

Paul L. Gerhardt, Exec. Dir.   (A)
Amer. Accounting Association
5717 Bessie Dr.
Sarasota, FL 33581

Sidney Daniels, Exec. Dir.   (A)
Nat. Assoc. of Min. CPA Firms
1522 K St. N.W. Suite 1115
Washington, DC 20005

ANSWERING SERVICE

Monte Engler, Counsel   (A)
Assoc. of Tel. Answering Service
1345 Ave. of the Americas
New York, NY 10105

Joseph N. Laseau, Exec. V.P. (A)
Assoc. Tel. Answering Exchange
320 King St., Suite 500
Alexandria, VA 22314

Pat Itake, Pres.   (A)
Prof. Assoc. of Secretarial Serv.
2200 E. 104th Ave., No. 103
Denver, CO 80233

Frank Fox, Exec. Dir.   (A)
Nat. Assoc. of Secretarial Services
2093 Michigan Ave. N.E.
St. Petersburg, FL 33703

ANTIQUE STORES

Ms. Nancy Adams   (M)
Antiques Dealer
1115 Clifton Ave.
Clifton, NJ 07013

Shirley Knowning, Pres.
Nat. Assoc. of Dealers in Antiques
R.R. 6   5859 N. Main Rd.
Rockford, IL 61103

Cleo M. Foran, Pres.   (A)
Assoc. Antique Dealers of America
P. O. Box 296261
Cumberland, IN 46229

APPLIANCE DEALERS

Retailer News   (M)
Target Publishing, Inc.
1550 B. So. Anaheim Blvd.
Anaheim, CA 92805

Merchandising   (M)
Gralla Publications
1515 Broadway
New York, NY 10036

Mart Magazine   (M)
Gordon Publications, Inc.
Box 1952, Dover, NJ 07801

AUTO & TIRE

Mr. Berkley C. Sweet   (A)
Truck Body and Equip. Assoc.
P.O. Box 70409
Washington DC 20088

Mr. Philip P. Friedlander   (A)
Nat'l Tire Dealers & Retreaders
Association
1250 Eye St., N.W. Suite 4000
Washington, DC 20005

Mr. Jeffrey S. Davis
Brake & Front End
11 S. Forge St.
Akron, OH 44304

Stanley M. Schuer, Exec. Dir. (A)
Gasoline & Auto. Serv. Dealers
6338 Ave. N.
Brooklyn, NY 11234

Dan C. Ray, II, Exec. Dir.   (A)
National Independent Auto.
Dealers Association
3700 National Drive, Suite 208
Raleigh, NC 27612

Mr. John Rettie   (M)
Import Auto. Parts/Accessories
Import Automotive Publishers
7637 Fulton St.
North Hollywood, CA 91605

Mary N. Sweeney, Exec. Dir. (A)
American Car Rental Association
1750 Pennsyl. Ave. NW Suite 1303
Washington, DC 20006

Mr. Gary Gardner   (M)
Specialty & Custom Dealer
Babcox Publications
1 S. Forge T.
Akron, OH 44304

Ms. Sheryl Davis   (M)
RV Business
29901 Agoura Rd.
Aguor, CA 91301

AUTO & TIRE (continued)

Service Station Management   (M)
Hunter Publishing Co.
950 Lee St.
Des Plaines, IL 60016

R.R. Gus Trantham   (A)
CAE Exec. Dir.
Internat. Carwash Assoc.
4415 W. Harrison St., Suite 200
Hillside, IL 60162

Automotive Parts and   (A)
Accessories Association
1025 Connecticut Ave.
N.W. Suite 707
Washington, D.C. 20036

Modern Tire Dealer   (M)
Rubber & Automotive Group
Div. Bill Communications
P.O. Box 5417
110 N. Miller Rd.
Akron, OH 44313

Automotive Marketing   (M)
Chilton Co.
Chilton Way
Radnor, PA 19089

National Automobile Dealers   (M)
Association
8400 Westpark Dr.
McLean, VA 22102

BAKERIES

Robert N. Pyle, Pres.   (A)
Indep. Bakers Assoc.
P. O. Box 3731
Washington, DC 20007

Jill Goran, Editor   (A)
Specialty Bakery Owners of Amer.
299 Broadway
New York, NY 10007

Willis W. Alexander, Exec. V.P. (A)
American Bakers Association
1120 Connecticut Ave., N.W.
Washington, DC 20036

Retail Bakers of America
Presidential Bldg. Suite 250
6525 Belcrest Rd.
Hyattsville, MD 202782

Baking Industry   (M)
Putman Publishing Co.
301 E. Erie St.
Chicago, IL 60611

Bakery Production & Mktg.   (M)
Gorman Publishing Company
O'Hare Plaza
5725 E. River Rd.
Chicago, IL 60631

BICYCLE/MOTORCYCLE SHOPS

National Bicycle Dealers (A)
c/o Bostrom Management Corp.
Tribune Tower Suite 1717
435 N. Michigan Ave.
Chicago, IL 60611

Motorcycle Dealer News (M)
Hester Communications, Inc.
1700 E. Dyer Rd. Suite 250
Santa Ana, CA 92705

Quinn Publications (M)
1904 Wenneca, P. O. Box 1570
Fort Worth, TX 76101

Amer. Bicyclist/Motorcyclist
Cycling Press, Inc.
80 Eighth Ave.
New York, NY 10011

Bicycle Dealer Showcase (M)
Hester Communications, Inc.
P. O. Box 19531
Irvine, CA 92713

BOOKSTORES

Janice M. Farina, Adm. Asst. (A)
Antique Booksellers Assoc.
of America
50 Rockefeller Plaza
New York, NY 10020

Harold C. Mintle, Pres. (A)
Assoc. of Christian Publ. and
Booksellers
3360 N.W. 110th St.
Miami, FL 33167

Mr. Garis F. Distlehorst (A)
National Association of
College Stores
528 E. Lorain St.
Oberlin, OH 44074

American Booksellers Assoc. (A)
122 E. 42 St.
New York, NY 10017

Publishers Weekly (M)
1180 Ave. of the Americas
New York, NY 10036

Magazine & Bookseller (M)
North American Publ. Co
322 8th Ave.
New York, NY 10001

BRIDAL SHOPS

W.P. Gelinas, Exec. Sec. (A)
Amer. Assoc. Prof. Bridal Cons'ts.
42 Woodridge Circle
West Hartford, CT 06107

Nancy Dver, Pres. (A)
Bridal Industry Association
41 Madison Ave.
New York, NY 10010

BROKERS

Mark M. Singer, Pres. (A)
National Food Brokers Assoc.
1010 Massachusetts Ave. N.W.
Washington, DC 20001

Mr. Robert Kralicek (A)
Motel Brokers Assoc. of Amer.
10920 Ambassador Dr.
Kansas City, MO 64153

BROKERS (continued)

James J. Gibbons, Pres. (M)
Mfg. Agents National Assoc.
P. O. Box 16878
2021 Bus. Center Dr.
Irvine, CA 92713

BUILDING SUPPLIES

Bldg. Supply/Home Center (M)
Cahners Publishing Co.
Div. of Reed Holdings, Inc.
1350 Touhy Ave.
Des Plaines, IL 60018

Building Products Digest (M)
Cutler Publishing Co., Inc.
4500 Campus Dr., Suite 480
Newport Beach, CA 92660

CHILDREN'S WEAR

Ms. Mary Ann Wood (M)
Teens and Boys
71 W. 35th St.
New York, NY 10001

Mr. Dan DeWese (M)
Tack 'N Togs Merchandising
Box 67
Minneapolis, MN 55406

United Infants & Children's (A)
Wear Association
520 Eighth Ave.
New York, NY 10018

Juvenile Merchandising (M)
Columbia Communications, Inc.
370 Lexington
New York, NY 10017

Earnshaw's Infants, (M)
Girls and Boys Wear Review
Earnshaw Publications, Inc.
393 Seventh Ave.
New York, NY 10001

Teens & Boys Magazine (M)
Larkin Publications
210 Boylston St.
Chestnut Hill, MA 02167

CLOTHING (WESTERN)

Mr. Larry Bell (M)
Western & English Fashions
Bell Publishing
2403 Champa
Denver, CO 80205

Ms. Ann DeRuyter (M)
Western Outfitter
5314 Bingle Rd.
Houston, TX 77092

COMPUTER STORES

John Dinsmore, Exec. Dir. (A)
Assoc. of Better Computer Dealers
861 Corporate Dr.
Lexington, KY 40503

National Assoc. of Computer (A)
Stores
3255 South U.S.I.
Ft. Pierce, FL 33450

Computer Retailing (M)
W.R.C. 1760 Peachtree Rd. N.W.
Atlanta, GA 30357

COMPUTER STORES (continued)

Computer Merchandising (M)
Eastman Publishing Co.
Intern'l. Thomson Bus. Press, Inc.
15720 Ventura Blvd., Suite 222
Encino, CA 94136

Software Retailing (M)
Computer Dealer
Gordon Publications, Inc.
13 Emery Ave.
Randolph, NJ 07869

Computer Retail News (M)
CMP Publications, Inc.
111 East Shore Rd.
Manhasset, NY 11030

PC Retailing (M)
Dealerscope, Inc.
115 Second Ave.
Waltham, MA 02154

CONSTRUCTION BUSINESS

Charles B. Lavin Jr. (A)
CAE Exec. Director
Nat'l. Assoc. of Plumbing –
Heating and Cooling
1016 20th St. N.W.
Washington, DC 20036

Elaine Murray, Exec. Dir. (A)
Nat'l. Assoc. of Remodeling Ind.
11 E. 44th St.
New York, NY 10017

Fred Good, Exec. V.P. (A)
National Roofing Cont. Assoc.
8600 Bryn Mawr Ave.
Chicago, IL 60631

Association Builders (A)
and Contractors
44 N. Capital St. Suite 409
Washington, DC 20001

Building Design and Constr. (M)
Cahners Publishing Co.
270 St. Paul St.
Denver, CO 80206

Home Improvement Cont. (M)
Maclean Hunter Publication
300 W. Adams St.
Chicago, IL 60606

CONSULTING

John F. Harshorne, Exec. Dir. (A)
Institute of Mgmt. Consultants
19 W. 44th St., Suite 810-811
New York, NY 10036

Groceanne W. Morris, (A)
Administrative Director
Association of Mgmt. Consultants
500 N. Michigan Ave.
Chicago, IL 60611

Jan Shepherd, Exec. Dir. (A)
Prof. & Tech. Consult. Assoc.
1190 Lincoln Ave., Suite 3
San Jose, CA 95125

Joseph J. Brady, Pres. (A)
ACME Inc. The Association of
Management Consultants
230 Park Ave.
New York, NY 10169

DECOR & DESIGN

Marilyn J. Miller CAE (A)
Exec. Director – Nat'l Home
Fashion League
P. O. Box 58045
107 World Trade Center
Dallas, TX 75258

Edward U. Gips, Exec. Dir. (A)
American Society of Interior Des.
1430 Broadway; NY, NY 10018

Robert E. Petit Exec. V.P. (A)
Nat'l. Decorating Prod. Assoc.
1050 N. Lindbergh Blvd.
St. Louis, MO 63132

Gregory S. Harris, Exec. Dir. (A)
Interior Design Society
405 Merchandise Mart
Chicago, IL 60654

DISCOUNT STORES

Discount Store News (M)
Lebhar-Friedman, Inc.
425 Park Ave.; NY, NY 10022

Discount Merchandiser (M)
Schwartz Publications
MacFadden Holdings, Inc.
2 Park Ave.; NY, NY 10016

DRUG STORES

National Association (A)
of Retail Druggists
1750 K St. N.W. Suite 1200
Washington, D.C. 20006

Pharmacy West (M)
Western Communications, Ltd.
Suite 116 1741 Ivar Ave.
Los Angeles, CA 90028

American Druggist (M)
The Hearst Corp.
555 W. 57th St., NY, NY 10019

Drug Store News (M)
Lebhar—Friedman, Inc.
425 Park Ave.; NY, NY 10022

Drug Topics (M)
Medical Economics Co., Inc.
680 Kinderkamack Rd.
Oradell, NJ 07649

DRY CLEANERS

Mr. R. Daniel Harris (M)
Cleaning Management
17911-C Sky Park Blvd.
Irvine, CA 92714

Bernard H. Ehrlick Assn. (A)
Institute of Indus. Launderers
1730 M. St. N.W., Suite 613
Washington, DC 20036

International Fabricare Inst. (A)
12251 Tect Rd.
Silver Spring, MD 20904

American Drycleaner (M)
American Trade Magazines, Inc.
Div. of Crain Communications, Inc.
500 N. Dearborn St.
Chicago, IL 60610

FINANCIAL PLANNERS

O. Whitfield Broome, Jr. (A)
Exec. Dir. Inst. of Chartered
Financial Analysts
P. O. Box 3668, Univ. of Virginia
Charlottesville, VA 22903

Dianna Rampy, Exec. Dir. (A)
Inst. of Cert. Financial Planners
9725 E. Hampden Ave. Suite 33
Denver, CO 80231

Vernon D. Gwynne, Exec. Dir. (A)
Internt'l Assoc. of Finan. Planning
5775 Peachtree-Dunwoody Rd.
Suite 120C
Atlanta, GA 30342

FITNESS CENTERS

Mr. Michael J. Keighley (M)
Fitness Industry, Inc.
1545 NE 123rd St.
North Miami, FL 33161

Jimmy D. Johnson, PhD. (A)
Exec. Dir. Assoc. of Physical
Fitness Centers
5272 River Rd., Suite 500
Washington, DC 20016

John McCarthy, Exec. Dir. (A)
Intern. Racquet Sports Assoc.
Ten Concord Ave.
Cambridge, MA 02138

FLOOR COVERING

Mr. Edward S. Korczak (A)
Retail Floorcovering Institute
1889 Merchandise Mart
Chicago, IL 60654

Mr. Michael Korsonsky (M)
Flooring Magazine
757 3rd Ave.
New York, NY 10017

Wade Newman, Exec. Dir. (A)
National Association of Floor
Covering Distributors
13-186 Merchandise Mart
Chicago, IL 60654

AIDS International (A)
2009 14 St. Suite 203
Arlington, VA 22201

Floor Covering Weekly (M)
FCW Division of Hearst Business
Communications, Inc.
919 Third Ave.
New York, NY 10022

Flooring (M)
Harcourt Brace Jovanovich, Inc.
120 W. Second St.
Duluth, MN 55802

Modern Floor Coverings
U.S. Business Press
124 E. 40th St.
New York, NY 10016

Western Floors (M)
Specialist
17835 Ventura Blvd.
Suite 312
Encino, CA 91316

FLORISTS

Edward Smith, Exec. Officer (A)
Florists Association
3908 W. Warren
Detroit, MI 48208

Intern'l Florists Assoc. (A)
2117 Centre Ave.
Pittsburgh, PA 15219

The Florist (M)
Florists' Transwd Delivery Assoc.
P.O. Box 2227
29200 Northwestern Hwy
Southfield, MI 48037

Flower News (M)
Central Flower News
549 W. Randolph St.
Chicago, IL 60606

Flowers & Telefora Inc. (M)
Teleflora Plaza, Suite 260
12233 W. Olympic Blvd.
Los Angeles, CA 90064

GENERAL/SMALL BUS. ASSOC.

Alina Novak, Pres. (A)
Networks Unlimited Inc.
342 Madison Ave.
New York, NY 10017

Herbert Liebenson, Exec. Dir. (A)
Small Bus. Legislative Council
1604 K. St. N.W.
Washington, DC 20006

Nat'l Fed. of Independent Bus.
150 W. 20th Ave.
San Mateo, CA 94403

Dr. Thomas R. Horton (A)
American Management Assoc.
135 W. 50th St.
New York, NY 10020

James G. Black, Pres. (A)
Score and Ace
822 15th St. N.W.
Washington, DC 20416

Leslie Hitch, Exec. Dir. (A)
Small Bus. Found. of Amer.
69 Hickory Dr.
Waltham, MA 02154

Thomas Olson, Exec. Dir. (A)
Young Presidents' Organization
52 Vanderbilt Ave.
New York, NY 10017

Sally Livingston, Pres.
Women Entrepreneurs
3061 Fillmore St.
San Francisco, CA 94123

Robert R. Statham (A)
General Counsel – Nat'l Family
Business Council
1001 Connecticut Ave. N.W.
Suite 638
Washington, DC 20036

Theodore R. Hagans, Jr. Pres. (A)
Nat'l Business League
4324 Georgia Ave. N.W.
Washington, DC 20011

GENERAL/SMALL BUS. ASSOC. (continued)

Walter B. Stults, Pres.   (A)
Nat'l Assoc. –Women Bus. Owners
500 N. Michigan Ave.
Chicago, IL 60611

Robert H. Brockhaus, Pres.   (A)
Inter. Council for Small Business
3674 Lindell Blvd. St. Louis Univ.
St. Louis, MO 63108

Marilyn French-Hubbard   (A)
Pres./CEO Nat'l Assoc. of Black
Women Entrepr.
P. O. Box 1375
Detroit, MI 48231

Wendy Lazar, Pres.   (A)
Nat'l Alliance of Homebased
Business women
P.O. Box 95
Norwood, NJ 07648

Ira H. Latimer, Exec. V.P.
Amer. Federation of Small Bus.
407 S. Dearborn St.
Chicago, IL 60605

H. Patrick Parrish, Exec. Dir.   (A)
Chief Executives Organization
2000 Palm Beach Lakes Blvd.
Suite 777
West Palm Beach, FL 33409

Donald J. Jonovic, V.P.   (A)
Center for Family Business
P. O. Box 24268
Cleveland, OH 44124

Joseph R. Mancuso, Pres.   (A)
Center for Entrepren. Mgmt.
83 Spring St.; NY, NY 10012

Alexander B. Trowbridge   (A)
Nat'l. Assoc. of Manufacturers
1776 F St. N.W.
Washington, DC 20006

GENERAL BUSINESS MAG.

Mr. George Gendron   (M)
Inc.
38 Commercial Wharf
Boston, MA 02110

Mr. Stephen Wagner   (M)
Income Opportunities
380 Lexington Ave.
New York, NY 10017

Mr. Marshall Loeb   (M)
Money Magazine
Time & Life Bldg.
New York, NY 10020

Brian Wood, Publisher   (M)
American Entrepreneur Assoc.
2311 Pontius Ave.
Los Angeles, CA 90064

GIFTWARES

Scott Borowsky Pres.   (A)
Souvenir/Novelty Trade Assoc.
401 N. Broad St. Suite 904
Philadelphia, PA 19018

Gift/Decorative Access. Assoc. (A)
372 Park Ave. S.; NY, NY 10010

GIFTWARES (continued)

Giftware News   (M)
Talcott Communications Corp.
2700 River Rd., Suite 409
Des Plaines, IL 60018

Giftware Business   (M)
Gralla Publications, Inc.
1515 Midway
New York, NY 10036

GLASS STORES

Frank S. Child, Exec. Sec   (A)
Society of Glass Decorators
207 Grant St.
Port Jefferson, NY 11777

Glass Digest   (M)
Ashlee Publishing Co, Inc.
310 Madison Ave. Suite 1826
New York, NY 10017

The Glass Dealer   (M)
National Glass Dealers Assoc.
8200 Greensboro Drive
Suite 302
McLean, VA 22102

GOLF & FISHING STORES

National Golf Foundation   (A)
200 Castlewood Drive
North Palm Beach, FL 33408

Golf Shop Operations   (M)
Golf Digest/Tennis, Inc.
495 Westport Ave.
Norwalk, CT 06856

Fishing Tackle Trade   (M)
Fishing Tackle Trade News, Inc.
P. O. Box 70
Wilmette, IL 60091

GRAPHIC ARTS

Mr. Roger Ynostroza   (M)
Graphic Arts Monthly
875 Third Ave.
New York, NY 10022

Robert P. Starnes Exec. Dir.   (A)
IPMA-A Graphic Comm. Mgmt.
Association
2475 Canal St., Suite 300
New Orleans, LA 70119

Robert L. Fitzpatrick   (A)
Exec. V. P. Nat'l Graphic Arts
Dealers Assoc.
P. O. Box 1302
Boca Raton, FL 33429

Gilbert W. Bassett, Exec. Dir.   (A)
Graphic Arts Tech. Foundation
4615 Forbes Ave.
Pittsburgh, PA 15213

GROCERY STORES

Ms. Barbara J. Bagley   (M)
Convenience Store News
BMT Publications, Inc.
254 W. 31st St.; NY. NY. 10001

Mr. Michael Keighley   (M)
The Gourmet Retailer
1545 N.E. 123rd St.
North Miami, FL 33161

GROCERY STORES (continued)

Carol Christinson, Exec. Dir.   (A)
International Cheese and Deli
Association
P.O. Box 5528
Madison, WI 53705

National Assoc. of Retail   (A)
Grocers of the U.S.
Box 17208
Washington, DC 20041

Progressive Grocer   (M)
Maclean Hunter Media, Inc.
1351 Washington Blvd.
Stamford, CT 06902

Supermarket News   (M)
Fairchild Publications
7 East 12th St.
New York, NY 10003

Supermarket Business   (M)
Fieldmark Media, Inc.
25 W. 43rd St.
New York, NY 10036

HAIR SALON

National Hairdressers and   (A)
Cosmetologists, Assoc.
3510 Olive St.
St. Louis, MO 63103

American Hairdressers and   (M)
Salon Owners Service
Publications, Inc.
100 Park Ave.
New York, NY 10017

Modern Salon   (M)
Vance Publishing
300 W. Adams St.
Chicago, IL 60606

HARDWARE STORES

Mr. Ken Morrison   (M)
Chain Saw Age
3455 N.E. Broadway
Portland, OR 97232

Mr. Wyatt Kash   (M)
Nat'l Home Center News
Lebhar-Friedman, Inc.
425 Park Ave.
New York, NY 10022

Anthony A. Font, Exec. Dir.   (A)
Door & Oper. Dealers of America
14780 Pearl Rd.
Strongsville, OH 44136

Nat'l Retail Hardware Assoc.   (A)
770 N. High School Rd.
Indianapolis, IN 46224

Hardware Merchandiser   (M)
The Irving–Cloud Pub. Co.
7300 N. Cicero Ave.
Lincolnwood, IL 60646

Hardware Age   (M)
Chilton Co., Inc.
Chilton Way
Radnor, PA 19089

HEALTH FOODS

Syndicate Magazines (M)
Communication Channels, Inc.
390 Fifth Ave.
New York, NY 10018

Health Foods Business (M)
Howmrk Publishing Corp.
567 Morris Ave.
Elizabeth, NJ 07208

HOBBY & TOY STORES

Ronald L. Watkins Exec. Dir. (A)
Miniatures Industry Assoc. of Amer.
1130 15th St. N.W.
Washington, DC 20005

Hugh Stephens Exec. Sec. (A)
Model Railroad Industry Assoc.
P. O. Box 15th St. N.W.
Cedarburg, WI 53012

Hobby Indus. Assoc. of Amer. (A)
319 E. 54 St.
Elmwood Park, NJ 07407

Toy & Hobby World (M)
U.S. Business Press, Inc.
124 E. 40th St.
New York, NY 10016

Model Retailer (M)
Boynton & Assoc.
Clifton House
Clifton, VA 22024

Toy Trade News (M)
Harcourt Brace
Jovanovich, Inc.
120 W. Second St.
Duluth, MN 55802

Hobby Merchandiser (M)
Hobby Publications, Inc.
Box 420, 490 Route 9, Rd. 3
Englishtown, NJ 07726

Playthings (M)
Geyer-McAllister Publ.
51 Madison Ave.
New York, NY 10010

HOME FURNISHING

Ms. Lynda Utterback (M)
Unfinished Furniture Magazine
United States Exposition Corp.
1850 Oak St.
Northfield, IL 60093

Mr. Eliot Sefrin (M)
Kitchen & Bath Design News
K B C Publications
Box 1719
Fort Lee, NJ 07024

Mr. Kurt Indrik (M)
Flotation Sleep Industry
Hester Communications, Inc.
1700 E. Dyer Rd., Suite 250
Santa Ana, CA 92705

Ms. Barbara Hall (M)
Lighting Dimensions Magazine
1590 S. Coast Hwy., Suite 8
Laguna Beach, CA 92651

Michael S. Sherman, Exec. Dir. (A)
Summer Furn. Mfg. Assoc.
5515 Security Ln., Suite 530
Rockville, MD 20852

HOME FURNISHING (continued)

Michael S. Sherman, Exec. V. P. (A)
National Association of
Furniture Manufacturers
5515 Security Ln., Suite 530
Rockville, MD 20852

James R. Banister, Exec. Dir. (A)
Furniture Rental Assoc. of America
50 W. Broad St., Suite 1325
Columbus, OH 43215

Nat'l Home Furnishings Assoc. (A)
405 Merchandise Mart
Chicago, IL 60654

National Home Center News (M)
Lebhar-Friedman, Inc.
425 Park Ave.; NY, NY 10022

Furniture Today (M)
Communications/Today, Ltd.
200 S. Main St., P.O. Box 2754
High Point, NC 27261

Casual Living (M)
Columbia Communications
370 Lexington Ave.
New York, NY 10017

The Competitive Edge (MO
National Home Furnishings
405 The Merchandise Mart
Chicago, IL 60654

Furniture World (M)
Towse Publishing Co.
127 E. 31st
New York, NY 10016

Profess'l Furniture Merchant (M)
Vista Publications
9600 W. Sample Rd.
Coral Springs, FL 33065

HFD (M)
Fairchild Publications, Inc.
7 E. 12th St.
New York, NY 10003

HOUSEWARES

Ronald A. Flippinger, Mng. Dir. (A)
National Housewares Mfg. Assoc.
1324 Merchandise Mart
Chicago, IL 60654

Ms. Maddalena S. Vitriol (M)
Linens/Domestics & Bath Products
370 Lexington Ave.
New York, NY 10017

Ms. Susan Grisham (M)
China Glass & Tableware
Ebel-Doctorow Publications, Inc.
Box 2147
Clifton, NJ 07015

Mr. Michael Scott (M)
Ceramic Scope
3632 Ashworth N.
Seattle, WA

Totally Housewares (M)
Dinan Communications
134 Main St.
New Canaan, CT 06840

Housewares (M)
Harcourt Brace Jovanovich, Inc.
120 W. Second St.
Duluth, MN 55802

HOUSEWARES (continued)

Housewares Merchandising (M)
Dinan Communications, Inc.
134 Main St.
New Canaan, CT 06840

ICE CREAM

Craig E. Peterson, Exec. Dir. (A)
National Ice Cream Ret. Assoc.
1800 Pickwick Ave.
Glenview, IL 60025

Joe E. Maxwell, Exec. Officer (A)
Nat'l. Assoc. of Ice Cream Vendors
5600 Brookwood Terrace
Nashville, TN 37205

Al Heilman, Sec-Treasurer
Retail Confectioners Intern'l
1701 Lake Ave., Suite 250
Glenview, IL 60025

JEWELRY STORES

Ms. Jayne L. Barrick (M)
Watch & Clock Review
2403 Champa St.
Denver, CO 80205

Morton R. Sarrett, Pres.
Jewelry Industry Council
608 Fifth Ave.
New York, NY 10020

George R. Frankovich, V. P. (A)
Mfg. Jewelers & Silversmiths of Am.
The Bilt. Plaza Hotel; 3rd fl. Ken Pl.
Providence, RI 02903

Alfred L. Woodill Exec. Dir. (A)
American Gem Society
2960 Wilshire Blvd.
Los Angeles, CA 90010

Michael P. Danner Admn. Dir. (A)
American Watchmakers Institute
3700 Harrison Ave.
Cincinnati, OH 45211

Jewelers of America (A)
1271 Ave. of the Americas
New York, NY 10020

National Jeweler (M)
Gralla Publications
1515 Broadway
New York, NY 10036

Modern Jeweler (M)
Hurst House, Inc.
15 W. 10th St.
Kansas City, MO 64105

LADIES CLOTHING

Ms. Christina Holmes (M)
Sew Business
Box 1331
Ft. Lee, NJ 07024

Seth M. Bodner, Exec. Dir.
Nat'l. Knitwear & Sportswear Assoc.
51 Madison Ave.
New York, NY 10010

National Retail (A)
Merchants Association
100 W. 31st
New York, NY 10001

LADIES CLOTHING (continued)

Fashion Retailer   (M)
Larkin Publications
210 Boylston St.
Chestnut Hill, MA 02167

Fashion Showcase Retailer   (M)
Taylor Communications, Inc.
P. O. Box 586398
2300 Stemmons, Suite 6G82
Apparel Mart
Dallas, TX 75207

California Apparel News   (M)
California Fashion Publ., Inc.
945 S. Wall St.
Los Angeles, CA 90015

Women's Wear Daily
Fairchild Publications
7 E. 12th St.; NY, NY 10003

LANDSCAPERS

Robert F. Lederer, Exec. V.P.   (A)
National Landscape Association
230 Southern Bldg.
Washington, DC 20005

Glenn W. Bostrom Exec. Dir.   (A)
Profess. Lawn Care Assoc. of Amer.
435 N. Michigan Ave. Suite 1717
Chicago, IL 60611

Alan A. Smith, Exec. Dir.   (A)
Assoc. Landscape Cont. of Amer.
1750 Old Meadow Rd.
McLean, VA 22102

LIQUOR STORES

Douglas W. Metz, Exec. V.P.   (A)
Wine & Spirits Wholesalers of Amer.
2033 M. St. N.W. Suite 400
Washington, DC 20036

National Liquor Stores Assoc. (A)
1025 Vermont Ave.
N. W. Suite 1104
Washington, DC 20005

Liquor Store   (M)
Jobson Publishing Corp.
352 Park Ave. S.; NY, NY 10107

Beverage Retailer Weekly   (M)
250 W. 57th St.
New York, NY 10107

LUGGAGE STORES

Nat'l Luggage Dealers Assoc.   (A)
350 Fifth Ave.; NY, NY 10018

Luggage & Travelware   (M)
Business Journals
22 S. Smith St.
Norwalk, CT 06855

MAINTENANCE

Charles F. Wheeler, Jr. Sec.   (A)
American Institute of Maintenance
P.O. Box 2068
Glendale, CA 91209

Walter L. Cook   (A)
CAE Exec. V.P.
Bldg. Serv. Contractors Assoc. Int.
8315 Le Hwy Suite 301
Fairfax, VA 22031

MEN'S CLOTHING

Katherine Ogan, Dir.   (A)
Amer. Formalwear Assoc.
1290 Ave. of the Americas
New York, NY 10104

Mensware Retailers of America (A)
2011 Eye St. N.W. Suite 600
Washington, DC 20006

Men's Apparel News   (M)
California Fashion Publications
945 South Wall St.
Los Angeles, CA 90015

Men's Retailer   (M)
Taylor Communications
P. O. Box 586398
Suite 6G82
Apparel Mart
Dallas, TX 75207

MINORITY BUSINESSES

Mr. Jesus Chavarria   (M)
Hispanic Business
P. O. Box 6757
Santa Barbara, CA 93160

Mr. John F. Robinson   (M)
Better Business
National Minority
Business Council, Inc.
235 E. 42nd St.
New York, NY 10017

Mr. Earl G. Graves
Black Enterprise
130 Fifth Ave.
New York, NY 10011

MISCELLANEOUS

Mr. Arthur E. Yohalem   (M)
Vending Times
545 Eighth Ave.
New York, NY 10018

Mr. R. A. Lesmeister   (M)
American Firearms Industry
American Press
Media Association, Inc.
2801 E. Oakland Park Blvd.
Ft. Lauderdale, FL 33306

Mr. Malcolm L. Fleischer   (A)
Retail Tobacco Dealers of America
New York Statler Hilton Hotel
Seventh Ave. at 33rd St.
New York, NY 10001

Mr. Michael H. Goldstein   (A)
Nat'l Assoc. of Catalog Showroom
Merchandising
276 Fifth Ave. Suite 900
New York, NY 10001

Dr. Diane Rothberg, Pres.   (A)
Association of Part-time
Professionals
P. O. Box 3419
Alexandria, VA 22302

Joyce A. Laurie, Exec. Dir.   (A)
Assoc. Locksmiths of America
3003 Live Oak St.
Dallas, TX 75204

MUSIC STORES

Mr. Wilbur McCullar   (A)
National Association of School
Music Dealers
901 E. Fairfield Dr.
Pensacola, FL 32503

National Association of Music (A)
Merchants
500 N. Michigan Ave.
Chicago, IL 60611

Music Trades Magazine   (M)
Music Trades Corp.
80 Wet St. P. O. Box 432
Englewood, NJ 07631

Musical Merchandise Review   (M)
Larkin Publications
210 Bolyston St.
Chestnut Hill, MA 02167

OFFICE & ART SUPPLIES

Ms. Jo Yanow   (M)
Art Business News
2135 Summer St.
P. O. Box 3837
Stamford, CT 06905

Mr. Curt Kennington   (A)
Independent Cash Register
Dealers Association
701 E. Morehead St.
Charlotte, NC 28202

Mr. Tom McKnight   (A)
National Office Machine Dealer
Association
810 Lively Blvd.
Wood Dale, IL 60191

G. Stiebel, Pres.   (A)
International Confederation of
Art Dealers
32 E. 57th St.
New York, NY 10022

National Office   (A)
Products Association
301 N. Fairfax St.
Alexandria, VA 22314

Art Material Trade News   (M)
Communications Channels, Inc.
6255 Barfield Rd.
Atlanta, GA 30328

Western Office Dealer   (M)
Allen-Pacific Company
41 Sutter St.
San Francisco, CA 94104

Geyer's Dealer Topics   (M)
Geyer-McAllister Publications
51 Madison Ave.
New York, NY 10010

PAINT/WALLCOVERINGS LIGHTING STORES

International Association of (A)
Lighting Designers
40 E. 49th St.
New York, NY 10017

Intern'l Drapery Assoc. (A)
11555 Monarch St.
Garden Grove, CA 92645

Ms. Elizabeth G. Berglund (M)
American Painter
300 W. Adams St.
Chicago, IL 60606

Mr. Gerald L. Wykoff (M)
Painting/Decorating Contractors
7223 Lee Hwy.
Falls Church, VA 22046

Ms. Lynn Mohr (M)
Draperies and Window Coverings
P. O. Box 13079
North Palm Beach, FL 33408

American Painting Contractor (M)
2911 Washington Ave.
St. Louis, MO 63103

T. David McFarland Mng. Dir. (A)
American Home Lighting Institute
435 N. Michigan Ave. Suite 1717
Chicago, Il 60611

Wallcoverings (M)
Publishing Dynamics, Inc.
2 Selleck St.
Stamford, CT 06902

Home Lighting & Accessories (M)
Ebel-Doctorow Publ, Inc.
1115 Clifton Ave.
P.O. Box 2147
Clifton, NJ 07015

Decorating Retailer (M)
Nat'l Decorating Products Assoc.
1050 N. Lindbergh Blvd.
St. Louis, MO 63132

PET STORES

Mr. Robert D. Reynolds (A)
National Dog Groomers Assoc.
Clark, PA 16113

Mr. Bob Behme (M)
Pet Business
7330 N.W. 66th St.
Miami, FL 33166

Mr. Roy S. Bloss (A)
Nat'l Retail Pet Store and
Groomers Association
P.O. Box 265
Danville, CA 94526

Mr. Horst H. Backer (A)
Pet Industry Distributors Assoc.
P.O. Box 36956
Tucscon, AZ 85740

Mr. Alan Richman (M)
The Pet Dealer
Howmark Publishing Corp.
567 Morris Ave.
Elizabeth, NJ 07208

Pet Industry (A)
Joint Advisory Council
1050 17th St. N.W. 12th Floor
Washington, DC 20036

PET STORES (continued)

Pet Age (M)
H.H. Backer Assoc., Inc.
207 S. Wabash Ave.
Chicago, IL 60604

Pets/Supplies/Marketing (M)
Harcourt Brace Jovanovich Publ.
120 W. Second St.
Duluth, MN 55802

PHOTOGRAPHIC STUDIOS

Mr. Bert Eifer (A)
Assoc. Photographers Intern'l.
21822 Sherman Way
Canoga Park, CA 91303

Anthony Andriolli (A)
Exec. Officer of Society of
Photographers & Artists Rep.
P.O. Box 845 FDR Station
New York, NY 10022

Ms. Maureen V. Coyne
Photographic Society of Amer.
2005 Walnut St.
Philadelphia, PA 19103

Mr. H. Jeffrey Valentine
National Free Lance
Photographers Association
60 E. State St.
Doylestown, PA 18901

Professional Photographers (A)
of America
1090 Executive Way
Des Plaines, IL 60018

Studio Photography (M)
PTN Publishing Corp.
101 Crossways Park West
Woodbury, NY 11797

Photo Weekly (M)
Billboard Publications, Inc.
1515 Broadway
New York, NY 11036

Photo Marketing (M)
The Photo Marketing Assoc.
3000 Picture Place
Jackson, MI 49201

POOL SUPPLIES

Ms. Susan Kipoicki (M)
Spa & Sauna Trade Journal
Hester Communications, Inc.
1700 E. Dyer Rd. Suite 250
Santa Ana, CA 92705

Mr. J. Field (M)
Pool & Spa News
Leisure Publications
3923 W. 6th St.
Los Angeles, CA 90020

Mr. Bill Gregory (M)
Swimming Pool and Spa
Merchandiser
Communication Channels, Inc.
6255 Barfield Rd.
Atlanta, GA 30328

Jewel Moffat Bolton (A)
Exec. Dir. Intern'l Spa and Tub
Institute
240 S. Feldner Rd.
Orange, CA 92668

PRINTERS

Mr. Dan Witte (M)
Instant Printer
P.O. Box 368
Northbrook, IL 60062

James R. Nielsen, Exec. Dir. (A)
Binding Industries of America
200 E. Ontario St.
Chicago, IL 60611

Barbara Chalik, Exec. Dir. (A)
Nat'l Assoc. of Quick Printers
111 E. Wicker Dr. Suite 600
Chicago, IL 60601

Rodney L. Borum Pres. (A)
Printing Industry of America
1730 N. Lynn St.
Arlington, VA 22209

Don Piercy Exec. Dir. (A)
Amer. Quick Printing Assoc.
1324 N. Clay St.
Houston, TX 77019

John M. Crawford, CAE Pres. (A)
Screen Printing Assoc. Intern'l
10015 Main St.
Fairfax, VA 22031

PRINT & FRAME SHOPS

Professional Picture Framers (A)
Association
4305 Sarellen Rd.
Richmond, VA 23231

Decor (M)
Commerce Publ. Co.
408 Olive St.
St. Louis, MO 63102

REAL ESTATE

Dr. Jack Carlson (A)
Nat'l Assoc. of Realtors
430 N. Michigan Ave.
Chicago, IL 60611

Ms. Llani O'Conner
Realtors Nat'l Marketing Inst.
430 N. Michigan Ave.
Chicago, IL 60611

RESTAURANTS

Nat'l Restaurant Assoc. (A)
311 First St. N.W.
Washington, DC 20001

Independent Restaurants (M)
EIP Inc.
2132 Fordem Ave.
Madison, WI 53704

Restaurant Hospitality (M)
Penton/IPC
1111 Chester Ave.
Cleveland, OH 44114

Nation's Restaurant News (M)
Lebhar-Friedman, Inc.
425 Park Ave.
New York, NY 10022

SPORTING GOODS

Mr. Nick Romano   (M)
Golf Shop Operations
495 Westport Ave.
Norwalk, CT 06856

Mr. Clay Lloyd   (M)
Golf Course Management
Golf Course Superintendents
Association of America
1617 St. Andrews
Lawrence, KS 66044

Ms. Olga Badilo   (M)
Boating Industry
850 Third Ave., NY, NY 10022

Glen Helgeland, Exec. Sec.   (A)
Archery Range & Retailers Org.
Box 188 7626 W. Donges Bay Rd.
104N, Mequon, WI 53092

Howard J. Bruns, Pres.   (A)
Sporting Goods Mfg. Assoc.
200 Castlewood Dr.
North Palm Beach, FL 33408

James L. Faltinek, Pres.   (A)
Nat'l Sporting Goods Assoc.
Lake Ctr. Plaza Bldg.
1699 Wall St.
Mt. Prospect, IL 60056

B.J. Ferguson, Exec. Dir.   (A)
Marine Retailers Assoc. of Amer.
1124 Lovett Blvd.
Houston, TX 77006

Nat'l Sporting Goods Assoc.   (A)
717 N. Michigan Ave.
Chicago, IL 60611

Sports Merchandiser   (M)
W.R.C. Smith Publishing Co.
1760 Peachtree Rd. N.W.
Atlanta, GA 30357

Action Sports Retailer   (M)
Pacifica Publishing Co.
P. O. Box 348
South Laguna, CA 92677

The Sporting Goods Dealer   (M)
1212 N. Lindbergh
P. O. Box 56
St. Louis, MO 63166

Sporting Goods Business   (M)
Gralla Publications
1515 Broadway Ave.
New York, NY 10036

TRAVEL AGENTS

Mr. Eric Friedheim   (M)
The Travel Agent
2 W. 46th St., NY, NY 10036

Travel Trade   (M)
Travel Trade Publ., Inc.
6 E. 46th St., NY, NY 10017

RETAIL (GENERAL)

Mr. Michael J. Anderson   (M)
Retailer & Marketing News
Box 191105
Dallas, TX 75219-1105

Mr. Richard Hersh   (A)
Nat'l Mass Retailing Institute
570 Seventh Ave.
New York, NY 10018

RETAIL (GENERAL) – continued

Mr. James R. Williams   (A)
National Retail Mer. Assoc.
100 W. 31st St.
New York, NY 10001

Ms. Beatrice L. Cohen   (A)
American Retail Assoc. Exec.
c/o Nat'l Retail Mer. Assoc.
100 W. 31st St.
New York, NY 10001

Mr. Lloyd Hacker   (A)
American Retail Federation
1616 H. St. N.W.
Washington, DC 20006

Ms. Sandie Stambaugh   (M)
Jobber/Retailer
Bill Communications
Box 5417
Akron, OH 44313

Mr. Wayne DeWald   (M)
Business Today
Meridian Publishing
1720 Washington Blvd.
Ogden, UT 84404

SHOE STORES

Mr. Arthur W. Jacob   (A)
National Shoe Traveler's Assoc.
230 S. Bemiston
St. Louis, MO 63105

Nat'l Shoe Retailers Assoc.   (A)
200 Madison Ave.
New York, NY 10016

Footware Focus   (M)
National Shoe Retailer Assoc.
200 Madison Ave.
New York, NY 10016

Footware News   (M)
Fairchild Publications
7 E. 12 St.
New York, NY 10003

SKI SHOPS

David Ingemie, Exec. Dir.   (A)
Ski Industries America
83778 Greensboro Dr.
McLean, VA 22102

Ski Retailers Council   (A)
600 Madison Ave.
New York, NY 10022

Ski Business   (M)
Nick Hock Assoc., Inc.
975 Post Rd.
Darien, CT 06820

VIDEO STORES

Dan Davis, Exec. V. Pres.   (A)
Video Software Dealers Assoc.
1008-F Astoria Blvd.
Cherry Hill, NJ 08034

Mr. Frank Moldstad   (M)
Video Business
CES Publishing
135 W. 50th St.
New York, NY 10020

John Power, Exec. Dir.   (A)
American Video Association
2634 W. Baseline Rd.
Mesa, AZ 85202

GENERAL BUSINESS – MAG/ASSOC

Mr. Robert Gray, Ed.   (M)
Nation's Business
1615 H. St. NW
Washington, DC 20062

Editor, Small Business Report (M)
203 Calle del Oaks
Monterey, CA 93940

Mr. Christopher M. Lehman, Pres.
Venture
521 5th Ave., NY, NY 10175

Margaret E. Horan, Ed.   (M)
Women in Business
P. O. Box 8728
Kansas City, MO 64114

Mr. Jerome Goldstein, Publ. Ed. (M)
In Business
Box 35 Emmaus, PA 18049

Mr. George Gendron, Ed.   (M)
Inc. Magazine
38 Commercial Wharf
Boston, MA 02110

Mr. Douglas H. Thompson, Jr. (M)
Exec. Ed. The Indep. Professional
P. O. Box 13485
Gainsville, FL 32604

Mr. Thomas J. Martin, Ed.   (M)
The Business Owner
383 S. Broadway
Hicksville, NY 11801

Elaine Siposs   (M)
How to Start/Manage Own Bus.
International Bus Info. Ser.
P. O. Box 4082
Irvine, CA 92716

Mr. Mark Stevens   (M)
Small Business Stevens Features
P. O. Box 487
Chappaqua, NY 10514

Business to Business   (M)
3740 Campus Dr.
Newport Beach, CA 92660

Betty Burns, Ad. Dir.   (A)
Nat'l Assoc. of Women Bus. Owners
645 N. Michigan Ave. Suite 1058
Chicago, IL 60611

Mr. Stephen Wagner   (M)
Income Opportunities Magazine
380 Lexington Ave.
New York, NY 10017

Personal Finance Magazine
380 Lexington Ave.
New York, NY 10017

Business News   (M)
Mr. Jerry Buchanan, Ed./Publ.
Towers Club USA Newsletter
P. O. Box 2038
Vancouver, WA 98668-2038

Mr. Joe Glickman   (M)
So You Want to be in Business
Dickson-Bennett Int'l Features
1324 ½ N. Third St.
St. Joseph, MO 64501

Mr. Earl G. Graves, Publ/Ed.   (M)
Black Enterprise
130 Fifth Ave., NY, NY 10011

Appendix 3 Sample Business Purchase Agreement

Note: Certain sections have been removed that relate to the specifics of this particular sale. There are many ways to construct a purchase agreement, this is just one.

AGREEMENT FOR THE PURCHASE AND SALE OF ASSETS

THIS AGREEMENT is made to be effective as of the first day

of _____ by and between _____

a California Corporation (hereinafter called "Seller"), and

_____ Corporation (hereinafter called "Buyer").

RECITALS

WHEREAS, Seller is in the business of _____

and other related products under the name of _____

_____

WHEREAS, Buyer desires to purchase from Seller and Seller desires to sell to Buyer on the terms and conditions set forth herein, Seller's interest in certain leases, true copies of which leases are attached hereto as Exhibits "A" and "B" and incorporated herein by reference, together with all associated leaseheld improvements, fixtures and equipment on the leased premises, and certain other assets of Seller.

NOW, THEREFORE, for valuable consideration, the receipt of which is hereby acknowledged, and for the mutual covenants, representations and warranties contained herein, the parties agree as follows:

---

1. Subject to the terms and conditions set forth in this Agreement, Seller agrees to sell to Buyer and Buyer agrees to purchase from Seller, assets, properties, and business of Seller which pertain to or are held for use in connection with the Business, except for those items specifically excluded in Sub-paragraph 1 (c) as follows:

(a) All rights of Seller under the leases attached hereto as Exhibits "A" and "B," and all such rights in and to leasehold improvements and trade fixtures located on or attached to the premises subject to said leases.

(b) All included assets listed on the attached Exhibit "C," free and clear of any liens or encumbrances, on an "AS IS" basis; provided, however, that all inventory shall be in saleable condition.

(c) Expressly excluded from this purchase and sale agreement are all other assets of Seller, including, without limitation, cash, inventory in excess of that listed in Exhibit C, accounts receivable and equipment not listed on Exhibit "C."

2. It is expressly understood and agreed that Buyer shall not assume and shall in no event be deemed to have assumed or agreed to pay or to perform any debt, liability, obligation or commitment of Seller. Seller shall indemnify and hold Buyer harmless from and against any losses, costs and expenses resulting from any claims asserted against Buyer or paid by Buyer in connection with the transaction herein agreed to.

3. The total purchase price of the assets described in Paragraph

1 shall be _____

and shall be paid at the time and in the manner set forth in Paragraph 13 of this Agreement.

---

4. Seller and Buyer each hereby covenants and agrees to indemnify and hold harmless the other party and its successors and assigns against any and all claims, losses, expenses (including reasonable attorneys' fees), obligations, damages and liabilities suffered or incurred by the other party which arise out of, result from or are related to any breach or failure of the other party to perform or comply with any of its warranties, representations, commitments or other obligations hereunder.

(a) Without limiting the generality of this Paragraph 4, Seller agrees to defend, indemnify and hold Buyer harmless from and against and in respect of any and all claims, losses, expenses (including reasonable attorneys's fees), obligations, damages, taxes and liabilities which (i) may be asserted by third parties against Buyer as transferee of the included assets to be purchased hereunder including, without limitation, the rights of creditors of Seller under the Uniform Commercial Code Bulk Transfer Act or (ii) relate to or arise out of or in connection with any conduct or Seller prior to the Closing Date, whether or not ascertained or asserted prior to the Closing Date, including, with limitation,

_____

(b) Without limiting the generality of this Paragraph 4, and in addition to the rights and remedies of Buyer provided herein, Buyer shall have the right to settle any claim by customers of Seller based on (i) defective merchandise sold by Seller prior to the Closing Date or (ii) Seller's failure to deliver proper;

_____

(c) All statements contained in any instrument delivered by or on behalf of the parties in connection with the transactions contemplated hereby shall be deemed representations and warranties hereunder. All representations, warranties and agreements made by the parties shall survive the Closing Date and any investigations made by or on behalf of the parties. The parties shall be notified promptly in writing of any claims which may arise hereunder after the Closing Date.

(d) Seller agrees that Buyer may, at its option, set off against amounts then or thereafter due and owing to Seller under any Promissory Note to be delivered to Seller pursuant to this Agreement, any and all losses, expenses, damages or costs incurred by Buyer against which Seller has agreed to indemnify Buyer pursuant to this Paragraph 4. Any such set-off by Buyer shall be credited first against interest and then against principal then or thereafter due under such Promissory Note.

5. Buyer and Seller shall each pay 50 percent of all sales and use taxes arising out of the transfer of the assets hereunder. Buyer agrees to furnish any resale certificates or other documents reasonably requested by Seller in order to comply with the provisions of such sales and use tax laws.

6. Buyer shall have given notice, incompliance with Division 6 of the California Commercial Code, of the bulk transfer contemplated by this Agreement, and shall cause the notice described in Commercial Code Section 6107 to be recorded and published as further described in said section at least twelve (12) business days prior to the Closing Date. At least twenty (20) business days before the Closing Date, Seller shall furnish Buyer with the information necessary to prepare such notice.

7. Until the Closing Date, Seller shall carry on the Business in substantially the same manner as the Business has been carried on previously and shall use reasonable efforts to preserve Seller's present relationships with suppliers, customers, and employees.

8. Until the Closing Date, Seller shall continue to carry its existing insurance and, at Buyer's request, shall use reasonable efforts to arrange for transfer of such insurance to Buyer as of the Closing Date, except if Buyer elects on or before the Closing Date, not to continue any or all of such insurance in force after the Closing Date or if any or all of Seller's insurance is not transferable to Buyer.

9. Buyer's obligations hereunder are subject to the satisfaction, at or before the Closing Date, of the following condition:

(a) Seller shall have performed and complied with all covenants and agreements and satisfied all conditions required by this Agreement to be performed or complied with by them on or before the Closing Date.

(b) All representations made by Seller shall be true on the Closing Date as if made on that date and the Seller will certify to such and deliver such certificate at the closing;

(c) Any documents, instruments, or certificates to be delivered are reasonably satisfactory to Buyer.

(d) The premises and each of them shall be tenantable within seven (7) days after the closing date in the same condition they are in on the date hereof, broom clean; provided that if there has been damage or destruction to the premises or either of them, said premises shall be tenantable within thirty (30) days after the Closing Date. All repairs will be made at the expense of Seller, and in such case, payments on the Promissory Note issued in connection with this Agreement shall not first become due and payable until thirty (30) days following the first day upon which the premises are tenantable.

(h) Buyer is not obligated to hire Seller's employees, but Buyer shall have the right to do so without interference from Seller.

(i) Seller agrees that on the Closing Date, all rental, utilities and other costs of occupancy will be current and an adjustment will be made for these and other prepaid expenses, including utility deposits. In connection with the utilities, Seller agrees to notify the companies that supply these services so that the final readings can be made as of the Closing Date. Seller shall be obligated to pay these final statements upon receipt of same.

(j) Seller agrees that, on the Closing Date, the internal electrical, plumbing, heating, cooling, exhaust and filtration systems servicing each of the leased premises will be in good order and in the condition necessary to properly operate a

_____

(k) Seller shall do all acts and sign whatever documents are reasonably required by Buyer so as to make available for Buyer's use and control, on and after the Closing Date, the telephone number or numbers presently used by the Store.

(l) Seller agrees to indemnify and to hold Buyer harmless for any loss or expense incurred with regard to any actions, suits, claims (including, without limitation, claims on product warranties, such as dog warranties), arbitrations or proceedings (including without limitation such actions, etc., instituted by governmental or quasi-governmental bodies) against Seller or Buyer which result from products or animals sold or acts or omissions taken by Seller prior to the Closing Date, provided that Buyer gives Seller prompt notice of any such claim, action, suit, arbitrations, or proceedings, and provided further Buyer gives Seller the right to defend the same.

(m) Seller warrants that the leases (copies of which are attached hereto as Exhibits A and B) are presently in full force and effect, and neither Seller nor the Landlord are now nor as of the Closing Date will be in default thereunder, and Seller agrees that all obligations due such Landlord shall be paid currently as of the closing date.

11. Buyer hereby represents and warrants as follows:

(a) Buyer is a corporation duly organized and validly existing, or otherwise qualified to do business under the laws of the state in which the Store is located and has the corporate power to execute and perform this Agreement.

(b) The execution of this Agreement constitutes the valid and binding agreement of Buyer and no further corporate action is necessary to make this Agreement valid and binding upon Buyer. The execution, delivery and performance of this Agreement, and the consummation of the transactions contemplated hereby, do not violate any statute, indenture, mortgage, option, lease, Articles of Incorporation, bylaws or other agreement or instrument to which Purchaser is a party or is bound.

(c) Buyer agrees that it shall promptly do all such things as are necessary and incidental to the successful consummation of this Agreement, including the execution of all necessary documents whether prior to or after the Closing Date.

12. (a) The transfer of assets by Seller, partial payment of the purchase price by Buyer and Exchange of documents hereunder

(the "Closing") shall take place at the offices of _____

_____

10:00 a.m. Pacific Standard Time on _____
or at such other time or place as the parties may agree in writing (the "Closing Date").

(b) At the Closing, Seller shall deliver to Buyer a duly executed Bill of Sale, in form and substance satisfactory to Buyer and its counsel, against the delivery of items specified in Exhibit C.

(c) At any time on or after the Closing Date, the Seller shall execute and deliver any further documents or instruments of transfer as may be reasonable requested by Buyer for the purpose of assigning, transferring, conveying and confirming to Buyer, or reducing to possession any or all of the assets to be transferred hereunder.

13. (a) Upon of this Agreement, but in no case later than

_____, Buyer shall deliver (or cause to be mailed), as earnest money, a check to Seller in the amount of _____. Said amount shall be nonrefundable unless Seller fails to perform under this Agreement.

(b) At the Closing, Buyer shall deliver to Seller good funds payable to the order of Seller in the amount of _____ The balance of the purchase price shall be paid by a promissory note made by Buyer to Seller in the amount of _____ with interest at _____ percent per annum on the unpaid balance, said note to be substantially in the same form and on the same terms and conditions as the promissory note attached hereto as Exhibit "D."

(c) Notwithstanding the foregoing, the Buyer shall have the right to substitute at Buyer's sole discretion any parties as Payr(s) of the Promissory Note issued in accordance with this Agreement or any portion thereof, provided that Buyer has provided Seller with a guarantee of such substitute Payor's performance under said Promissory Note or the performance of any Payor under a substitute Promissory Note identical in every substantive way with this Promissory Note. Any such guarantee shall be accompanied with a certified copy of the resolutions of the Board of Directors of Buyer authorizing said guarantee.

14. The warranties and representations contained in this Agreement shall survive the Closing.

15. Each of the parties represents and warrants that it has dealt with no broker or finder in connection with any of the transactions contemplated by this Agreement, and so far as it knows, no broker or other person is entitled to any commission or finder's fee in connection with this transaction. If the acts or omissions of a party cause the other to suffer any losses, costs and expenses resulting from any commission or finder's fees claimed or paid in connection with the transaction herein agreed to, the party so causing said losses, costs or expenses shall indemnify and hold the other party harmless.

16. This Agreement, including Exhibits "A," "B," "C" and "D," contains the entire agreement between the parties hereto and supersedes any and all prior agreements, arrangements and understandings between the parties relating to the subject matter hereof. No oral understandings, statements, promises or inducements contrary to the terms of this Agreement exist. No supplement, modification or amendment of this Agreement shall be binding unless executed in writing by all of the parties hereto. No waiver of any of the provisions of this Agreement shall be deemed or shall constitute a continuing waiver. No waiver shall be binding unless executed in writing by the party making the waiver.

17. This contract shall be governed by the law of the State of California.

18. Any dispute that arises between Seller and Buyer with regard to this Agreement or with regard to the Promissory Note (or any substitute notes) given as partial consideration for the assets transferred under this Agreement shall be referred to a board of three arbitrators, one of whom shall be selected by Seller, another of whom shall be selected by Buyer, and the third of whom, who shall be the Chairman, shall be selected by the other two arbitrators. The three arbitrators so selected shall then hear and determine the controversy according to law and their decision shall be final and binding on Seller and Buyer. The

arbitration shall be held in _____
The cost of the arbitration shall be borne equally by Seller and Buyer.

Appendix 4   Sample of Financial Recap

This is a sample of a financial statement provided to a potential buyer by a seller.

Statement of Income and Retained Earnings
For the twelve months ended June 30, 1979

Sales		$ 304,480
Cost of sales		155,066
Gross Profit		149,414
Operating Expenses		
Salaries and wages	$ 74,363	
Payroll tax expense	6,519	
Rent	21,481	
Outside labor	1,723	
Telephone and utilities	5,224	
Legal and accounting	700	
Automobile expense	619	
Repairs and maintenance	2,585	
Advertising	1,982	
Taxes and license	675	
Travel and entertainment	3,056	
Dues and subscriptions	426	
Bank service charges	1,283	
Depreciation and amortization	5,168	
Storage expense	56	
Bonus	700	
Other expense	1,131	
Total operating expense		127,691
Income from operations		21,723
Other expense		
Management fee		15,000
Income before income taxes		6,723
Corporation income taxes		619
Net income		6,104
Retained earnings beginning of year		7,689
Retained earnings, June 30, 1979		$ 13,793

SEE ACCOUNTANT'S COMPILATION REPORT
SEE ACCOMPANYING NOTES

1

Balance Sheet
June 30, 1979

ASSETS

Current Assets		
Cash	$ 1,852	
Advances to employees	1,300	
Inventory – estimated	12,000	$ 15,152
Property and Equipment – at cost		
Furniture and fixtures	6,600	
Leasehold improvements	43,379	
	49,979	
Less accumulated depreciation	8,326	41,653
Other Assets		
Stockholders Loan	2,000	
Deposits	1,180	
Organization expense	510	3,690
		$ 60,495

LIABILITIES AND EQUITY

Current Liabilities		
Accounts payable trade	$ 16,836	
Due to parent company	24,270	
Payroll tax payable	2,146	
Sales tax payable	1,031	
Corporation income taxes payable	419	$ 44,702
Capital		
Common stock	2,000	
Retained earnings	13,793	15,793
		$ 60,495

SEE ACCOUNTANT'S COMPILATION REPORT
SEE ACCOMPANYING NOTES

2

Statement of Changes in Financial Position
Twelve months ended June 30, 1979

Source of Funds		
Income from operations		
Net income		$ 6,104
Items not requiring capital outlay		4,998
Working capital provided from operations		11,102
Decrease in other assets		170
Increase in working capital		$ 11,272
Increase in Working Capital By Element		
Current assets		
Cash		$ (7,094)
Stockholders loan		1,300
		(5,794)
Current liabilities		
Accounts payable		(10,421)
Notes payable		960
Payroll and sales tax pay		541
Income tax payable		123
Intra Company		25,863
		17,066
Increase in working capital		$ 11,272

SEE ACCOUNTANT'S COMPILATION REPORT
SEE ACCOMPANYING NOTES

3

Notes to Financial Statement
For the year ended June 30, 1979

A. **Summary of Significant Accounting Policies**

The company is on the accrual method of accounting.

Inventory is recorded at estimated value as the company does not take a physical inventory.

Depreciation is computed on the straight line basis over a ten year period.

The Concord store charged Vintage Faire Pet Center a $15,000 fee for management services and insurance provided for the year ended June 30, 1979.

B. **Lease Commitment**

The company is leasing real property at 443 Vintage Faire Mall, Modesto, California. Rent including common area maintenance is $1,530 per month. Rents are increased by 6% of sales in excess of annual sales of $336,000.

The lease expires in November 1991.

4

—INDEX—

ORDER FORM

QTY.	BOOK	PRICE EACH	TOTAL
	HOW TO START, EXPAND & SELL A BUSINESS The Complete Guide Book for Entrepreneurs *James C. Comiskey*	$17.95	
	NEGOTIATING THE PURCHASE OR SALE OF A BUSINESS This comprehensive book contains 40 worksheets that help a buyer or seller clarify their objectives and better understand the complex process of negotiating the purchase or sale of a business. A must for anyone considering buying or selling a business. (200 pages). *James C. Comiskey*	$32.95	
	If California resident, add 7% sales tax		
	Add $2 handling for single book orders or $1 for multiple book orders.		
	TOTAL		

☐ I have enclosed my check or money order

Please make checks payable to: **VENTURE PERSPECTIVES PRESS**
4300 Stevens Creek Blvd., Suite 155
SEND ORDER TO: *(Please Print)* San Jose, California 95129
(408) 247–1325

Name _____

Address _____

City _____ State _____ ZIP _____

Phone(s) _____

If you are not totally satisfied, you may return your order within 30 days for a full refund.

TAGS

reinvented

new approaches to creating scrapbook tags
by Erikia Ghumm

SUNSHINE

MEMORY
MAKERS
BOOKS

Executive Editor Kerry Arquette **Founder** Michele Gerbrandt

Author, Artist and Hand Model Erikia Ghumm

Associate Editor Emily Curry Hitchingham

Art Director Nick Nyffeler

Graphic Designers Robin Rozum, Andrea Zocchi

Art Aquisitions Editor Janetta Wieneke

Photographer Ken Trujillo

Contributing Photographers Lizzy Creazzo, Brenda Martinez, Jennifer Reeves

Editorial Support Jodi Amidei, Karen Cain, MaryJo Regier, Lydia Rueger, Dena Twinem

Contributing Artists Jodi Amidei, Kelly Angard, Kerry Arquette, Miki Benedict, Jennifer Bertsch, Emily Curry Hitchingham, Sarah Fishburn, Clara Fricke, Pamela Frye Hauer, Kari Hansen-Daffin, Marah Johnson, Trisha McCarty-Luedke, Torrey Miller, Nick Nyffeler, Jennifer Pollman, Tricia Rubens, Michelle Nicole Smith, Melissa Smith, Rhonda Solomon, Andrea Lyn Vetten-Marley, Cherie Ward, Janetta Wieneke, Holle Wiktorek, Andrea Zocchi, Terri Zwicker

Memory Makers® Tags Reinvented

Published by Memory Makers Books, an imprint of F+W Publications, Inc.

12365 Huron Street, Suite 500, Denver, CO 80234

Phone (800) 254-9124

First edition. Printed in the United States.

08 07 06 05 04 5 4 3 2 1

A catalog record for this book is available from the U.S. Library of Congress

Distributed to trade and art markets by

F+W Publications, Inc.

4700 East Galbraith Road, Cincinnati, OH 45236

Phone 1-800-289-0963

ISBN 1-892127-47-4

Memory Makers Books is the home of *Memory Makers,* the scrapbook magazine dedicated to educating and inspiring scrapbookers. To subscribe, or for more information, call (800) 366-6465.
Visit us on the Internet at www.memorymakersmagazine.com.